D0097729

Class and Ideology in
the Nineteenth Century

Class and Ideology in the Nineteenth Century

R S Neale

Associate Professor of Economic History
University of New England, Armidale

Routledge & Kegan Paul

London and Boston

First published 1972
by Routledge & Kegan Paul Ltd
Broadway House, 68–74 Carter Lane,
London EC4V 5EL and
9 Park Street,
Boston, Mass. 02108, U.S.A.
Printed in Great Britain by
Clarke, Doble & Brendon Ltd
Plymouth

ISBN 0 7100 7331 3

Contents

Tables

Acknowledgments

I would like to thank the editors of various journals for their permission to reprint the following articles: Victorian Studies for 'Class and Class Consciousness in Early Nineteenth-century England: Three Classes or Five?' (vol. 12, no. 1, September 1968); Our History for 'Class and Ideology in a Provincial City: Bath 1800–1850' (Pamphlet no. 42, summer 1966); Historical Studies, Australia and New Zealand for 'H. S. Chapman, Class Consciousness and the Victorian Ballot' (vol. 12, no. 48, April 1967); Labour History for 'Working-class Women and Women's Suffrage' (no. 12, May 1967).

I also acknowledge my debt to the following organizations for research grants which made much of the research possible: the University of New England; the Australian Research Grants Committee; the Australian Humanities Research Council.

I thank Mr Peter Pagan, Mr John Kite and the staff of Bath Reference Library, and the library staffs at the Alexander Turnbull Library, Wellington, the Mitchell Library, Sydney, and the University of New England. I am especially grateful to Ann and Wolf Rosenberg of Christchurch, New Zealand, who gave me great and friendly assistance by allowing me free access to the papers of H. S. Chapman and their home to work in. I thank, too, Dr Miriam Dixson, who criticized and encouraged me in the preparation of the central thesis, and the following for the benefit of discussions with them: Dr E. J. Tapp, Alex Tyrrell, H. M. Boot, Fritz Diehl and Professor J. P. Belshaw. I also acknowledge my debt to my research assistant Neil Keft who is joint author with me of chapter 5. Finally, my thanks to my wife, who corrected the manuscript and did all she could to get me to write clearly. The remaining faults are all my own.

Abbreviations

The abbreviations in the chapter notes refer to the following journals:

CHJ	*Cambridge Historical Journal*
EHR	*Economic History Review*
HRA	*Historical Records of Australia*
HSANZ	*Historical Studies, Australia and New Zealand*
JRAHS	*Journal of the Royal Australian Historical Society*
LWR	*London and Westminster Review*
MQ	*Marxist Quarterly*
NZJ	*New Zealand Journal*
PP	*Past and Present*
PS	*Population Studies*
SEJ	*Southern Economic Journal*
SR	*Sociological Review*
THR	*Tasmanian Historical Research Association, Papers and Proceedings*
VFW	*Votes for Women*
VHM	*Victorian Historical Magazine*
VS	*Victorian Studies*

RC indicates that the documents are in the Rosenberg Collection, Christchurch, New Zealand.

Introduction

The theme of these essays is class: class, class consciousness and ideology in England between 1800 and 1850, some aspects of class in early Australia between 1788 and 1860, and class and relationships between social strata in the women's movements of the late nineteenth and early twentieth centuries. In bringing these essays together I hope to persuade students of history to think critically about the terminology of class and to consider the heuristic value of conflict models of social change in historical study. They may also help students to develop an awareness of the ways in which accepted opinions and beliefs work to influence the outcome of their own studies. It is not my wish to try to replace old or newer orthodoxies by another, but that more students of history will recognize, and accept, the importance of explicitly clarifying assumptions about the structure of society and the mechanisms of social change which influence their choice of problems to study, their procedures and interpretations.

My general recommendation is that historians and history would profit if historians were to become more sociologically minded in their approach to the study and teaching of history.[1] My specific proposal is that conflict models of social change, other than a three- or two-class one, can be of considerable assistance in understanding and interpreting the first half of the nineteenth century in England. In making this suggestion I use a simplified version of Dahrendorf's conflict model for marshalling and interpreting data. This device or explanatory apparatus I call the five-class model. All the essays, except the final one, are presented here within the framework of that model.

One consequence of this use of models is that most of the questions and criticisms which have already arisen have been about

1

methodology. Therefore, I intend now to discuss some of these criticisms.

It is probably true to say that most historians are especially interested in particular events, or in unique series of events, which most easily lend themselves to the narrative form. Their generalizations are frequently, although not always, of the 'instance' kind based on a selection of examples or instances believed to be typical or common; and are often made within loosely conceived and mostly implicit conceptual frameworks. Accordingly, the most general criticism of my approach is expressed in the question, 'Why have a model at all? Why not let the facts burgeon forth, value, classification and model free?'

My short answer to this question reflects my own shortcomings as a historian. Without some kind of framework as an aid to selecting and ordering the complex mass of data and artefacts left over from the past, I find the past incomprehensible. Without a device for concentrating my attention, I find that going to the past is very like doing a tourist visit of the National Gallery—after an hour or so every picture merges into every other picture, into one overflowing mélange of light, colour and form. The traditional ways in which historians concentrate their attention are rarely appropriate for the sort of problems I am interested in. Historians generally succeed in focusing attention by concentrating on chronology, topic and text. They move, as it were, on a railway track with only rare diversions along little-known loop lines and only occasional stops for excursions into the surrounding countryside. This approach—which is itself model-building of a sort—has produced excellent historical writing. I do not find it a particularly fruitful method when my purpose is to move on a broad front, keeping in mind as many facets of the total inter-relationships of the social situation as possible, with the object not only of describing but also of explaining the shifting relationships between large aggregates of people.

There are other less personal considerations that lead me to advocate the use of explicit, rather than implicit, models or conceptual frameworks in the study of history. The first is that historians use terms like 'feudalism', 'capitalism', 'middle class', 'democracy', and 'nation'. They also use words like 'most', 'many', 'majority', 'typical', 'representative' and so on, all of which imply classification and involve value-loaded quantitative judgments. In fact they cannot avoid using a multitude of broad general concepts, classifications and abstractions. The problem is that many of these terms are loosely and privately defined. Second, few historians succeed in writing history without the use of an implicit interpretative framework or some broad explanatory system such as those discussed in the following essays. When historians and their students do not explicitly define the frontiers of their classifications, or the process of interaction and cause and effect in the explanatory systems they use, they can easily make *ad hoc* changes in terminology and concepts. For example, the shift from three to four classes, or the possibility of one social class being able to produce two types of social class consciousness, noted in chapter 1. Such shifting of terminology, loosely articulated explanatory systems and implicit assumptions and definitions frequently make it difficult, if not impossible, to follow the main thrust of an argument and permit contradictory positions to be upheld with equal conviction.

What a model should do is to compel us to make explicit our concepts and explanatory apparatus. The five-class model I offer is a very simple one. It includes the following : a definition of social class not generally used by historians; a notion about human motivation which is only just beginning to creep into historical discussion; a concept of social class consciousness distinguishing between proletarian, privatized and deferential images of social class consciousness; and a classifying concept, 'the middling class', which as an unstable volatile class must be comprehended as being different from the homogeneous entities of Marxist sociology. In this model, the middling class has no historical mission and the model is not teleological. In bringing these notions to a level of consciousness in the form of a model, and in employing that model in analysing a number of historical questions in the nineteenth century, it has been possible to throw fresh light on them. If, as I hope, teachers and students of history confronted by my use of the model become dissatisfied with it and seek to clarify their own terminologies and conceptual frameworks, so much the better.

An important criticism of the five-class model and of the categories of social strata and social classes employed throughout these essays, is that the classifications are arbitrary. This I admit. What this criticism frequently means and frequently goes on to say, however, is that there are some other unspecified classifications which, being less arbitrary or not arbitrary at all, are somehow more 'real'. This I dispute.

It has been said, for example, that the classification of the political élite in chapter 5 is too formal, and that I ought to have included individuals who exerted great influence without formal position. This would be a valid comment except that the object of the definition by formal position was to exclude as much subjective evaluation about the exercise of power as possible, and to define the authority position of the ruling élite as objectively as possible. Not to define the élite objectively, is to raise the problem of how to assess the exercise of great influence without formal position—the problem of who to include in the sample. However, even if this problem could be resolved to the satisfaction of all, it seems to me that those with and those without formal position would usefully make two categories rather than one. Surely it is no more arbitrary to try to discover some of the characteristics of the Australian administrative/ political élite, than it is to isolate and study characteristics of eighteenth-century industrial entrepreneurs, members of nineteenth-century cabinets, or Meiji bureaucrats! The advantage of the classification actually used is that it is clear who is included and why. That it does not include everyone who ever made or influenced a political decision is an argument for devising additional categories—which I hope to do—and not for deliberately introducing a subjective element into something which can be treated objectively.

Those critics of the general structure of the five-class model who have also criticized the classifications used, have a valid point. It is true that the criteria used to classify people into classes are central to the whole model. A different classification would give a different result. This was my point and purpose in trying to free myself from the three-class model. But, since none of the specific objections to my decision has convinced me that I ought to abandon my classification, or that the five-class model is a useless heuristic device for analysing developments in the period 1800 to 1850, I prefer to keep to it.

The first of three objections to the five-class model is that there were in fact only three social classes—at least by the end of the period. According to this view, the Ricardian abstractions—landowner, capitalist and labourer—postulated as ideal types in the agricultural sector are held to remain the same ideal types over time, although what developed during the period of the Industrial Revolution was a more diversified economy in which all factors of production were increasingly differentiated. However, there were no categories in Ricardo's model for self-employed shopkeepers and artisans, peasant farmers, industrial labour, the expanding professions, or for women except as adjuncts to husbands and fathers in one of the three classes. And while a three- or even a two-class model seems a good fit for Oldham in the 1830s, one must question whether anything less than the five-class model can accommodate the 'real' social structure of towns like South Shields, Northampton, Birmingham, Bath, Rochdale, Exeter or Leicester.[2] The fact is that the Ricardian model was not intended to describe the 'real' world in the first decades of the nineteenth century. Neither was the model which Marx erected upon it intended to describe the 'real' world at mid-century. In his treatment of class, Marx was very conscious of the existence and importance of the intermediate classes, but was more concerned to forecast the future division and conflict between two great classes. As far as Marx was concerned, the intermediate classes in the transitional stage were unstable classes which 'do not matter for our investigation'.[3] They had but one historical function : to break up and disappear into the ranks of the bourgeoisie and the proletariat. For other purposes, such as comprehending the political and social movements in the seventy years before 1850, some other model seems preferable. Such a model ought to have more than three classes. It ought also to recognize that a working-class social class consciousness, which does not incorporate a notion about the historical role of the working class, is not necessarily 'false'.

For some time now it has seemed to me that part of the appeal of the Ricardian–Marxist model in the Victorian period was that it sustained that epoch's sense of impending doom. Both Ricardo and Marx put the bourgeoisie into models of economic development which doomed their world to stagnation or destruction. The categories in their models were simply defined and homogeneous. Relationships between groups were inflexible. There was, let it be said, an attractive puritan simplicity and certainty about both models. In the five-class model, however, categories, which are not objectively homogeneous, are defined in a rather more complex fashion and attempts are made to incorporate instability. Movement, seen as the ebbing and flowing rather than the polarization of social classes, is an important characteristic of the five-class model. Thus the model is both more complicated and less certain than the conventional one, and has no teleological undertones. If 'reality' is to be the test of the usefulness of a conceptual framework, it certainly comes closer to 'reality' than any other currently in use.

The second objection to my classification is that since men I categorize as middling class frequently thought of themselves as 'middle class', they must only be thought of by historians as 'middle class'. This objection involves the notion that we ought only to categorize, rank or grade men according to their own self-evaluation. In reply to this I can only observe that in other social sciences men can be and are categorized in countless ways, and that while it is legitimate to rank them according to self-evaluation, such a ranking may tell us more about what people imagined or hoped they were than about what they actually were. I suspect that many who defined themselves as 'middle class' were more sure about what they were not than what they were. Obsessed by fear of the seething animal-like masses beneath them, and ever fearful of their own fall from respectability, they clutched at straws. They defined themselves negatively. To be 'middle class' meant not being a labouring man, a rag-picker or a street woman, not living in a courtyard of back-to-backs foetid with the smell of waste and people, not depending on charity. It was fear of the glottal stop and the dropped 'h'. In this connection it is worth noting that the term 'middle class' is neither a synonym for the Marxist 'bourgeoisie' nor for the term 'capitalist'. Moreover, there were elements in the social class consciousness of the middling class, many of whom were no doubt prepared to rank themselves as 'middle class', which led them to distinguish themselves from the 'middle class' even though they did not use the term middling class. Thus Wakefield identified a social stratum he called the 'uneasy class',[4] and J. S. Mill distinguished between the 'privileged' or 'satisfied classes' and the 'disqualified'. Within the ranks of the 'privileged' he included 'the whole class of very rich men' and senior members of the professions as well as the great landowners. The main strength of the politically Radical among the 'disqualified' he found among the 'ten pound electors', who were 'the greatest sufferers of all by low profits and an overcrowded field of employment. They belong almost universally to the "uneasy class", and amongst all those in skilled employments'.[5] As will be shown, J. A. Roebuck, H. S. Chapman and others had interests and attitudes which repeatedly brought them into conflict with men of the 'middle class', and led them to define themselves as representatives of 'the people'. Thus it is difficult to see that the term 'middle class' can be very helpful when applied by historians to all who applied it to themselves.

The third and most important point of criticism turns on my political definition of social class. Most recent historians who still employ a terminology of class use an economic definition of one kind or another. Take two examples. John Foster in the discussion of his provocative essay, 'Nineteenth-Century Towns—a Class Dimension', emphasizes that class formation meant for him 'the formation of a mass group orientated to conflict in a system of inequality'.[6] His text makes it clear that this inequality referred to 'unfairness in the way opportunities of social success were distributed', and that there could be no class formation where 'there was no critique of capital'.[7] Professor Perkin, in denying there was a class society in late eighteenth-century England, wrote: 'Nor was it, like the Victorian, a class society, divided into mutually hostile layers each united by a common source of income'.[8] He also said: 'A class society is characterized by class feeling, that is, by the existence of vertical antagonism between a small number of horizontal groups, each based on a common source of income.'[9] The essence of both definitions is that social class and social class conflict are products of property relations and income distribution. Thus conflict in society in the first half of the nineteenth century is still examined within the framework of the conventional model. My interpretation, which seeks to offer an alternative framework as a basis for examining events in this period, has still to contend with these deep-seated convictions about class, and with fixed notions about the vantage point from which conflict in society should be subjected to scrutiny. Thus F. M. L. Thompson, in a comment in the *Economic History Review* on the five-class model, wrote: 'His [Neale's] alternative, though it is set out initially in terms of economic and social categories . . . tends increasingly to revert to political attitudes as its definitional touchstone. He has opened, but not settled, an issue.'[10]

The traditional position in regard to class which is the basis of this criticism of the political definition has two aspects. First, social class must always be defined according to some objective criterion like income, source of income, occupation, wealth or education. Second, social class conflict is the product of antagonisms generated by differences, generally extreme differences, in income and/or property relationships. Thus, by definition, conflict generated by other polarities or complex inter-relationships is not class conflict.

The point that Dahrendorf has made, which I have attempted to incorporate into my model, is that there is a difference between sorting people into groups according to some objective criterion like income, and identifying the nature of conflict groups in society. Therefore it is methodologically important to keep the two notions distinct, and to call the first sorting according to objective criteria, social stratification, and to reserve the terminology of social class for identifiable conflict groups. Then, if it can be shown that intra-societal conflict always arises from stratification polarities like rich v. poor, property-owning v. property-less, most educated v. least educated and top v. bottom, then social strata can be regarded as social classes. If, as is usually the case, conflict does not occur between the extremes, and if the rankings of people involved in conflict do not have a high correlation with rankings according to stratification, then a methodological device is necessary to link social strata with social classes. Dahrendorf makes a link by recognizing and identifying the authority/subordination sources of conflict which overlay those generated by social stratification, and provide the basis for the generation of a social class consciousness more likely to be explicitly conflict orientated.[11]

> I have introduced, as a structural determinant of conflict groups, the category of authority as exercised in imperatively co-ordinated associations. While agreeing with Marx that source and level of income—even socio-economic status—cannot usefully be conceived as determinants of conflict groups, I have added to this list of erroneous approaches Marx's own in terms of property in the means of production. *Authority is both a more general and a more significant social relation.*

My own detailed empirical studies of social stratification and social class, originally carried out on a regional basis within the framework of the conventional Marxist model, also convinced me that social strata are not social classes, and that the conventional terminology could not handle the problem. It seemed to me that Dahrendorf's definition of social classes as conflict groups arising out of the authority structure of imperatively co-ordinated associations, provided the best insight into what had happened in Bath politics from about 1810 to the mid-nineteenth century.

Since many people have been uncertain about what constitutes an imperatively co-ordinated association, this seems a good point to say a little about it. An imperatively co-ordinated association is an association of men held together by an authority structure resting ultimately on the force of law. Thus a nation is an imperatively co-ordinated association, as is a closed corporation, a parish, an industrial enterprise, a landed estate, a farm, an established church, a trade union, a military organization, a university, a school, a family and so on. Each of these associations has an authority structure in which some exercise authority and give orders, and the rest are subordinate. Although, in the last resort this authority is legitimized by the force of law, authority for as long as it works or appears to work in the interests of all, is also legitimized by convention and deference. However, men are also aggressive and covet power—power over themselves as well as over others—and there is a good deal of latent conflict as well as overt hostility and aggression in all imperatively co-ordinated associations.[12]

Conflict is likely to be most intense when all the authority/ subordinate positions of most men point in the same direction, i.e. are superimposed. In my version of the model the intensity of conflict was heightened in the early nineteenth century by the existence of upwardly mobile men with high need for achievement but with subordinate positions. By the end of the eighteenth century, Britain had begun to experience rapid economic change. At the same time the boundaries of social strata began to break down and traditional authority was subjected to greater stress. Thus a young journeyman shoemaker with ambitions to set up on his own, who was also a Baptist or a Primitive Methodist, living in a low rental house in a parish administered by a Church of England controlled vestry, in a city ruled by a closed corporation, legislated against by the combination laws and other government decrees, in conflict with his employer over piece-rates, and looked down upon by his neighbours as well as by his employer's customers, was likely to be seething with barely suppressed hostility to all authority. He was more likely to be non-deferential than deferential. Whether or not this potential hostility could be harnessed for political action directed at changing the social order depended on other influences, such as: the similarity of his experience with that of his immediate associates, his level of achievement motivation, his exposure to articulate spokesmen of protest movements, the degree to which he sensed the possibility of changing conditions and so on. Whether or not his social class consciousness would be predominantly proletarian or privatized again depended on a variety of factors, most important of which were his work situation and his relationship to the means of production, the ideology already

B

prevailing in his immediate neighbourhood and the availability of groups he could join. In any case the key factor in shaping his social class consciousness was not social stratification *per se*, but his experience as a subordinate in a variety of conflict situations increased by the degree to which he felt unable to shape the course of his own life. Thus, in Bath in 1847, shoemakers with the franchise voted in a ratio of 2 : 1 (5 : 2 in St James parish) to support J. A. Roebuck—among those who barely qualified to vote the ratio was more than 6 : 1 ! Since, according to the conventional model, these shoemakers were working class, one might have expected them to generate a proletarian social class consciousness. It is interesting to note, however, that the man they openly supported was an advocate of an extremely privatized ideology, and that they were still supporting him as late as 1847. But I anticipate too much the discussion in the first three chapters.

It appears to me that social class seen merely as social strata is a dead thing, useful as a background for description but lacking that element of movement over time which is the essence of history. Social classes comprehended as conflict groups generated by shifting relationships of authority and subordination, rather than exclusively by property relationships, become immediately alive and suggestive of unintended outcomes. It is just this fluidity of social classes that critics find objectionable in the five-class model. Confusing social strata with social classes, they claim that my classes cannot be classes, since not being firmly anchored in objectively defined strata they are not objectively homogeneous. I admit this. My classes are not objectively homogeneous in the conventional sense. They do not need to be. Indeed, one of the weaknesses of my attempt to represent the five-class model in a two-dimensional diagram is that it suggests that social classes defined as conflict groups are also collections of objectively defined social strata. In some measure, they are, because relationships of authority and subordination are frequently partly matched by polarities in property, wealth, education, income and so on. But they do not have to be. Hence the Philosophic Radicals as the political activists of the middling class were drawn from a very wide spectrum of income groups, and in his constituency Roebuck had the support of a handful of the wealthiest men and property-owners in Bath, as well as that of a Roman Catholic bishop and of all leading ministers of the Dissenting Churches. Nevertheless, there is an objective basis for, and a sense in which the quasi-groups which produce social classes as conflict groups are objectively homogeneous. It is that they contain people ranked according to their positions of authority or subordination. However, although some groups can be objectively defined and ranked, for example the colonial *élite* in chapter 5, or members of closed corporations and cabinets, ranking according to this criterion is not easy for large or more heterogeneous aggregates of people in regions or nations. The evidence is scrappy and interpretation is necessarily subjective. Moreover, social class formation is also a function of social class consciousness, and this can only be inferred from expressions of social class consciousness and from the existence of continuous political organization with aims expressed in terms of conflict with, or opposition to, other social classes.

I hope that this discussion, in addition to that in the following chapters, will have clarified at least some of the points I seek to make; principally that historians would do well to consider the appropriateness of always distinguishing between social strata and social classes, and realize that in the five-class model the objective bases for the formation of social classes are positions of authority and subordination, plus social class consciousness. I realize that nothing I have said settles any issue in the sense of settling what is right or correct in regard to social class in history. This was never intended. Sociological models employed as heuristic devices in historical study should not be regarded as either right or wrong; they should be assessed for their fruitfulness in raising new questions, in clarifying or discarding unsatisfactory terminology, and in assisting in the marshalling, explanation and interpretation of data. The usefulness of the five-class model in all these respects may be seen in the essays included in the collection.

One final point. F. M. L. Thompson has also noted that the five-class model 'lacks a catchy terminology'.[18] It does. And deliberately so. Catchy terminologies usually become clichés in the manner of the conventional class terminology. But a value-free terminology which grates on ears accustomed to value-loaded ones is more likely to compel critical appraisal. Indeed I would prefer to regard all those groups called social classes as quasi-groups at different levels of social class consciousness, and therefore at different levels of political activity such that in the early 1820s only the upper class and the middling class were political classes. I would also be content to label these quasi-groups A, B, C, D and E!

In spite of all that has already been said about the importance of terminology, methodology and so on, there is also a good deal of what many would regard as real or quite ordinary history in these essays.

The narrative begins in Bath round about 1800. It focuses on the careers of two men: one, J. A. Roebuck, whose later career is already well known through Asa Briggs's *Victorian People*; the other, H. S. Chapman, scarcely known at all even in Australia where he made his greatest mark. Although the story has its roots firmly in Roebuck's constituency at Bath it does move rapidly through a series of complex relationships between Bath Radicals and other urban Radical groups in Birmingham, Bristol and London. Roebuck and the social class he represented are seen to be important in the national movement against the taxes on knowledge, and important to the political arm of the Philosophic Radicals. They also played a vital part in the formulation of the Charter and were instrumental in linking English Radicals with their Canadian counterparts. Chapman, who based much of his optimistically Radical interpretation of the development of English politics in the 1830s on events at Bath, urged the Canadians to rebellion. In fact he has to bear some of the responsibility for that rebellion. When the rebellion failed and the Canadians got Lord Durham instead of responsible government, the Radicals, with Roebuck foremost among them and with Chapman working in the background, attacked him for his banishment ordinance and secured his recall. An unintended result of Durham's recall was to speed up the compiling and publication of the Durham Report. But the part of the story which centres on the issue of responsible government and highlights the conflict between middling class and authoritarian approaches to the governing of Canada and deals with Roebuck's part in it is not included here because the method employed in my essay on this question is mainly that of textual analysis.[14]

Thus the focus of the story shifts from England's domestic affairs to the growth of ideas about Empire. Systematic colonization, much propagandized for by Chapman, is here viewed as an ideological development meeting and easing the needs of the middling class. Empire is also seen as creating an environment favourable for the formation of a new *élite* out of otherwise subordinate groups in Britain. Some of this *élite* are introduced anonymously in chapter 5 and one of them, H. S. Chapman, is described more fully in chapter 4.

Chapman's life is also used to show something of the way in which a middling-class ideology was carried to the Australian colonies. A Radical in England, almost a rebel in Canada, he was a ruler in Australia. After almost a century of agitation for the ballot —the central symbol of protest against arbitrary authority—Chapman was enabled to act as midwife to the ballot in Victoria. He attempted other Benthamite tasks as well. Through his contact with the thought of J. S. Mill there is a link with the women's suffrage issue discussed in chapter 7. Chapman departs from the story with Mill telling him that the Radical purpose in overthrowing established arbitrary authority can never be more than half completed in Australia so long as there remains the 'Toryism of sex'.

The chapter on 'middle-class' morality mainly questions the proposition that the 'Toryism of sex' and its accompanying sexual mores was functionally related to the economic system in the manner argued by Steven Marcus and Peter Cominos. It argues that beliefs about the need to accumulate profit for its own sake were not the notions which most influenced actions, nor, as far as one can guess, dominated the unconscious of all strata in the 'middle classes'. It suggests an alternative explanatory concept in the form of the notion of achievement motivation or the performance principle, and tries to indicate the importance in 'middle-class' morality of the beliefs of minorities such as the neo-Malthusians, the social scientists and the consumption orientated systematic colonizers.

Chapter 7 is also concerned with the 'Toryism of sex'. Votes for women was a logical extension of manhood suffrage and the suffragists were the last of the Philosophic Radicals. Suffragists were also mainly women from the lower middle strata of society organized into a women's middling class. However, the suffragists and then the Suffragettes were torn by divisions within their ranks. Partly because working-class women's proletarian social class consciousness was more developed in the period 1900 to 1914 than that of their menfolk had been from 1820 to 1830, women were not considered as a class and did not present a united front in their claim for the suffrage. Proletarian initiatives in the women's movement were few, and Annie Kenney was more a symbol of working-class women's deference towards women with higher status than she is a shining example to present-day women's liberation movements which claim to represent women as a class.

The historical theme running through these essays is authority, and aspects of the response and challenge to it made by men and women throughout the nineteenth century. Consequently they are essays on minorities, minority movements and deviations from 'middle-class' ideology, and therefore are important as aids to understanding the nineteenth century in all its variety.

Class and class consciousness
in early nineteenth-century England:
three classes or five?

The three-class model of social structure in the early nineteenth century is that in which, for the sake of convenience, individuals are
placed into one of three categories: aristocracy, middle class, working class. The boundaries of the classes, particularly of the two lower
ones, are rarely clearly or explicitly explained, and there is little
general agreement among writers about the bases of classification.
Nevertheless this model and these categories are regularly used in
analysing the interplay of economic, social, political and cultural forces.

It is my contention that both model and categories have outlived
their usefulness for any rigorous analysis of the relationship between
class, class consciousness, and political ideology in the early nineteenth century.

Of course, it may be that historians and others only use the three-
class model of Victorian society as a convenient shorthand form of
expression for something which, implicitly, they recognize to be more
complex. If this is so, then in order to communicate with each other,
we need to be sure of two things. First, we need to be sure that each
of us uses the same shorthand symbol for the same idea, that is, we
need a key to the shorthand. Second, we need to be sure that our
system of shorthand has as many symbols as we have ideas worth
expressing. It is in connection with this second observation that I
wish to press my point.

Generations of students brought up on the conventional shorthand
are too frequently hamstrung by it. Either they find difficulty in
comprehending that the social structure is indeed more complex than
the conventional shorthand indicates, and cling desperately to the
signs they know, however unhelpful they are in pointing the way,
or, when they find that the shorthand does not describe the real
world, they reject altogether the possibility of handling history
through the medium of aggregative concepts like class.

Some students grow up to be historians. If they do, unless they clearly and explicitly add new symbols to the shorthand and continually refine their concepts they will find difficulty in advancing the frontiers of their discipline. They will become Schoolmen.

Take as an example the continuing debate on the standard of living between 1780 and 1850. By the early 1960s it had reached a stalemate because both optimists and pessimists seemed increasingly happy to regard labour as a homogeneous class experiencing and participating in the process of industrialization as a whole, and both sides were content to use one or more global indicators like mortality rates, consumption indices and figures of national income *per capita*. Such an approach has its uses. For the purpose of amassing evidence about broad shifts in the rate of economic development, the growth rates of income *per capita* have a place. But the same approach immediately becomes useless if the problem is to say something about the welfare of specific groups of short-lived workers and to relate changes in the welfare of these groups to other phenomena. This was the reason for suggesting that historians should and could move away from the position of stalemate simply by employing a more fruitful disaggregative, regional and multi-class approach to the problem.[1]

Recent discussion on the relationship between various social classes, class consciousness and ideology during the early nineteenth century seems to point to a similar stalemate. It is my purpose in this chapter, therefore, to take a close look at the usefulness of the conventional three-class apparatus. My schema is: (1) Show something of the limitations of the three-class model by commenting on two recent contributions to the problem of class and ideology in the early nineteenth century. These initial comments should also show that in taking to task those historians who use the three-class model as an analytical tool I choose real historians and not straw men; (2) Suggest the need for a clarification of the terminology of class; (3) Using this improved terminology and empirical data, discuss the relationship of Philosophic Radicalism to English society with the purpose of showing that this relationship can be fully comprehended only if the three-class model is explicitly rejected; (4) Suggest that we would do well to try to increase the number of concepts we can handle by abandoning the three-class model. The five-class model to replace it is described. Its purpose is to focus attention on the crucial role of a dynamic, achievement-motivated middling class which, as a political class throughout the 1820s and 1830s, was neither middle nor working class; (5) Finally, use the concept of the middling class to throw some light upon the problem of the Charter and its relationship to class consciousness.

The first contribution which shows the limitation of the three-class model is that by D. J. Rowe on the 'Peoples' Charter'.[2] Rowe begins by positing the existence of *a* middle-class consciousness *vis-à-vis* the aristocracy and the labouring classes. He contrasts this with the absence of *a* working-class consciousness. That is, he adopts the conventional three-class descriptive model into which he incorporates the new orthodoxy about middle-class and working-class consciousness. Rowe then attempts to show that the Charter was not a political manifestation of working-class consciousness because the Charter, and the forerunner of the London Working Men's Association— the Association of Working Men to Procure a Cheap and Honest Press—were themselves the product of a *Radical middle-class initiative.*

In arguing thus the author introduces another concept, 'a Radical middle class', and makes the next analytical step, using what is in fact a four-class model. This is a useful advance. But it is so only if its main implication is made explicit. It is that the author sees the possibility of two images of social class consciousness developing in one social class, i.e. that the one middle class in the descriptive model can generate a *Radical* middle-class consciousness as well as one which is, presumably, purely *a* middle-class consciousness. The recognition of the possibility of such a phenomenon is itself a denial of the initial assumption about the existence of *a* middle-class consciousness. It could be that a more rigorous attempt to delineate the various social strata and social classes in the omnibus term 'middle class' might help to account for the dualism in middle-class social class consciousness which changes Rowe's model from a three-class to a four-class one.

In this same article, there is an implicit identification of *a* working-class consciousness with a 'proletarian' social consciousness. But, to approach the problem of the connection between class consciousness and the Charter with the preconception that what one is looking for is a 'proletarian' social class consciousness means that the historian is constrained within a mental strait jacket as soon as he attempts to show of which social class consciousness the London Working

Men's Association and the Charter were organizational and political manifestations. Again it could be that discussion of the existence of working-class consciousness would be improved given a more rigorous attempt to differentiate workers according to social stratum and social class.

Another historian, Joseph Hamburger, in attempting to identify the Philosophic Radicals, correctly concluded that their political philosophy was not an expression of middle-class aspirations.[3] But, because he began his analysis within the framework of the three-class model and because, as it were, he never went into a constituency, he also concluded that it was a political philosophy devoid of all class interest or connection. The essence of his position seems to be something like this. The Philosophic Radicals were hostile to the aristocracy. Yet they were not representative of the middle class and clearly not associated with the working class. If this was the case, where did they come from and how did they develop as a political faction? The answer given is that Philosophic Radicalism was a mental construct in the minds of its adherents owing nothing to the existence of social classes or class consciousness, except, perhaps, that it did have a distant connection with the Philosophic Radicals' own concept of 'the people'.

In this manner, the answer narrows the range of concepts available to us. It offers the two-class model employed by the Philosophic Radicals themselves and requires us to admit their claims that they represented no class except the people in their struggle against the aristocracy. We are asked to comprehend these historical figures according to their own self-evaluation though we know, on general grounds, that it is not uncommon for leaders of political parties to set out programmes and contribute to ideologies which they claim to be above class and other factional interests, but which, nevertheless, attract class or factional support.

An answer to the question, 'Was there any class content in the doctrines and policies of the Philosophic Radicals?' cannot be resolved simply by asking the Philosophic Radicals what they thought about the matter, or by using a three- or two-class model to find it. It can only be found by approaching the problem of class and class consciousness in the manner already suggested and through detailed local studies of constituency politics. Furthermore, a clarification of the class content in Philosophic Radicalism might throw additional light on the problem of class consciousness and the Charter.

Historians who may be concerned with identifying the derivation and nature of class consciousness and of political class in the early nineteenth century face problems similar to those faced by sociologists concerned with the same question in the mid-twentieth century. These problems fall into two categories: conceptual and methodological, and empirical. Most probably the empirical problems in each period will have to be resolved in different ways. But with regard to the shared conceptual and methodological problems, the concerns and methods of attack of historians and sociologists should be the same.

Four principal concepts will need to be distinguished.[4] They are social stratification, social class, class consciousness and political class.

Social stratification will probably be determined by some objective, measurable and largely economic criteria such as source and size of income, occupation, years of education or size of assets. Some aspects of stratification, however, are more likely to be identified by other less easily quantifiable criteria, i.e. by things like values, social custom and language. Many of these criteria will be particularly difficult to identify since, in addition to the problem of measurement, they may exist in the minds of members of a social stratum only as norms which are not always matched by behaviour.

Social classes, however, are really conflict groups arising out of the authority structure of imperatively co-ordinated associations.[5] Social class defined in this way can be objectively identified, at least in part, by setting out the authority structure of associations. But this in itself is not enough for the identification of social class as a conflict group. At best it will produce a sorting out of people with similar authority or subjection positions into what Ginsberg and Dahrendorf have called quasi-groups. Quasi-groups, however, function as recruiting fields for classes.[6]

Whether a quasi-group produces or becomes a social class will depend upon the technical, political and social conditions of organization and the generation of class consciousness within it. These, in turn, will depend on the specific historical conditions. Nevertheless, the formation of a social class as a conflict group will always have much to do with the growth of sensations of collective identity of interest among individuals in a quasi-group vis-à-vis other groups or social classes, and much to do with relationships of authority and subjection as felt and experienced in a quasi-group. The crucial notion to grasp is that there is a distinction between social stratification and social class, and that social classes are conflict groups based on relationships of authority and subjection.

The existence of social class as a political class will be most easily inferred from the existence of continuously organized political and/ or industrial action.

It is at the point of determination of the existence of class consciousness that the investigator should be especially careful to make explicit his preconceptions about class consciousness. It is all too easy, as the example of Rowe shows, to slip into assuming that a working-class consciousness must be a 'proletarian' one. Historians who do assume this will, of course, look for what they assume. Consequently it will be what they find or do not find. The same will be true of the search for a middle-class consciousness. In connection with this problem Lockwood has recently reminded us that in the twentieth century there is at least a trinity of working-class social consciousness: 'proletarian', 'deferential' and 'privatized'.[7] The first two terms are readily understood, but the 'privatized' worker is one whose work situation is socially isolating and whose social consciousness will approximate most nearly to a pecuniary model of society in which the cash nexus is the dominant relationship between individuals. It is important that, with some modification, we carry this reminder with us into the study of the early nineteenth century.

Any attempt to describe social stratification and social class for the early nineteenth century must incorporate at least two broad groups of factors if it is to bear any relation to the world as contemporaries saw it. These are: for social stratification, things like occupation, income, wealth and manners; and, for social class, authority positions derived from ascribed status as conferred according to the consensus of opinion and convention about rank, pedigree and authority. In contemporary opinion, authority positions derived from ascribed status generally outweighed income, wealth and occupation while the latter, by themselves, rarely granted status and authority. Because of the difficulty in weighing these opposing elements in some rational balance, much of early nineteenth-century literature centred on the problem of social identity. This problem of social identity was further complicated as the traditional status of high-ranking social classes was eroded through the increase in geographic and social mobility associated with rapid economic growth. Nevertheless, for a large part of the nineteenth century an important

determinant of social class, and a very important element in relationships of authority and subjection, was derived from ascribed status
and authority.[8]

In these circumstances it is unlikely that any social class consciousness, other than a deferential one, will be found at the lower
end of the social stratification and social class spectrums. Likewise,
where the barriers to higher status for the most economically successful of the aspirants for higher status are surmountable at some level
of achievement, the social class consciousness of new members of the
highest social strata is likely to be deferential vis-à-vis those with
high ascribed status, and they are likely to be more willing than
unwilling to conform to the mores of those already strong in an
authority derived from it. In practice they are likely to be desperate
for approval. Therefore, one should look elsewhere for situations
more likely to be productive of conflict between those with and
without authority, hence more likely to be productive of a social
class consciousness resulting in the formation of a political
class.

Such a situation is one in which there appears to be an unresolv-
able incongruity between the positions men have according to social
stratification and ascribed status. Where men possessed of a high
need for achievement[9] move from lower to higher social strata while
retaining low ascribed status and are geographically concentrated in
regions in which insistence on the observance of traditional relationships remains strong, a quasi-group generating a social class consciousness which is highly privatized or individuated and non-
deferential is likely to emerge. Furthermore, because of the geographical concentration and strength of traditional relationships,
this social class consciousness is likely to lead to attempts by individuals in the quasi-group to overcome their isolation and produce
a political class hostile to traditional authority.[10] The point is that
men come to recognize a personal conflict and begin to identify their
own dilemma with those conflict situations in society at large which
may be formulated in general or philosophic terms. In these circumstances class conflict is likely to be intense. This, in short, was the
basis of class conflict and of the emergence of a middling class with
a social class-consciousness making them receptive to the ideas of the
Philosophic Radicals throughout the 1820s and 1830s. It came about
as follows.

In the course of the eighteenth century there was an acceleration

in the rate of industrial growth and change. Consequently there
were more opportunities for advancement. At the same time population grew and there were many more applicants for both old and
new opportunities. This increase of applicants was the result of the
increase in family size and the uncertainties of economic life which
repeatedly reduced erstwhile economically successful families to
indigence. Probably the number of respectable places for the increasing number of sons grew less than the number of applicants.[11]
On the other hand many of the places that were created were still
allocated through nepotism, influence and graft.[12] Even where opportunities for economic advancement existed, traditional restraints
associated with status continued to bear heavily. Furthermore the
growth of urban communities created large pockets of these aspiring
and marginally disaffected men.

In more concrete terms, the early stages of industrialization in
Britain brought about a proliferation of petty producers, retailers
and tradesmen—collectively the petit bourgeois—and a class of
professional men, as well as bringing into existence the big industrial,
commercial, and professional capitalist—the big bourgeois. The children of the petit bourgeois and of the professionals flooded the grammar and private school systems only to be turned out half-educated,
half-gentlemen unfitted for industrial employment.[13] Accustomed to
living standards something above subsistence, they feared a decline to
some lower social strata. Many of them also lacked the capital and
connections as well as the education which might have brought them
the rewards they had come to feel were properly theirs. As this
group of what I call 'literates' came to maturity they added to the
competition for the limited number of respectable places.

In this manner the middle classes came to include at least two
sub-groups or social strata whose economic experience and status
relationships with other groups created conditions favourable to the
development of a social class consciousness which was especially
highly individuated and non-deferential. These were the petit
bourgeois and the professionals, and the literates. Many of the latter
might well be described as under-employed intellectuals. Such was
James Mill. Such, too, were the ninety-seven barristers contending
for eighty-nine briefs at the York Assizes in 1840.[14] Members of the
literate and professional social strata possessed of few liquid assets
and having no property or connections were particularly inclined
to assert the rights of man as against the rights of property, status

and traditional authority. Prominent among them were doctors as well as lawyers.

By the 1820s, individuals in these social strata were also members of a social class in the sense that enough of them were sufficiently class conscious to co-operate with each other in organized political activity, particularly at local level. They were becoming a political class to be reckoned with. Sometimes, as in their opposition to aristocratic privilege, they appear to be submerged in the omnibus 'middle class'. Indeed in the 'middle-class' agitation for reform the men who did the work in the constituencies and the political unions were often men from these two social strata.[15] Nevertheless a distinctive element in their social class consciousness was a sense of difference from other sections of the 'middle class'.[16] Their social class consciousness was not always at one with that of the more cautious, propertied and outstandingly successful members of the commercial and industrial bourgeoisie, the older gentry, senior military and naval men, successful professional men or those on fixed incomes.

Edward Gibbon Wakefield, who had squandered a small fortune and slipped a few rungs on the social ladder as a result, had a collective name for both the petit bourgeois and the under-employed literates. It was the 'uneasy class',[17]

> Distress [he wrote] is not confined to those small capitalists who employ a material capital. The learning, skill and reputation, united, of a professional man may be called his capital. Great professional capitalists, those who possess all at once great skill, great learning and a high reputation still make large incomes: but none of those, whose learning or skill or reputation is small, make enough to live upon. . . . Two thirds, therefore, at the very least, of professional men may be reckoned amongst the uneasy class. . . . The general rule with daughters of men of small income, whether fixed or not is a choice between celibacy and marriage with one of the uneasy class. Now, a great proportion of young men in the uneasy class dread marriage, unless there be a fortune in the case, as the surest means of increasing their embarrassment. This is one of the most important features in the social state of England.

The point to be noted is the belief that the 'uneasy class' existed as a class which included lesser professional men who had interests different from those of the successful professional men just as the interests of the petit bourgeois were different from those of the big bourgeois. Distressed they may have been, aspiring they certainly were. In this they were like the petit bourgeois. Whatever the real reasons for the frustration of the ambitions of these people, they came to believe that a very important one was the weight of ancient restriction and aristocratic and oligarchic privilege. What was additionally galling were the attitudes of superiority adopted by people who were regarded by the petit bourgeois and the literates as inferior to themselves, at least in terms of usefulness and intellect.

The most successful and systematic political ideology to which the class conscious in the two social strata most readily subscribed was Philosophic Radicalism. But even the Philosophic Radicals were not always unanimous or united.[18] Like other political groupings they spread over a spectrum, which in their case is best expressed in terms not of left and right, but of ultra and whiggish. By the mid-1830s the ultra wing circulated loosely around the waspish and doctrinaire J. A. Roebuck who, according to J. S. Mill, was that unique figure in English politics, a Napoleon-Ideologue.[19] Perhaps, since Mill was himself atypical, his comment about the political uniqueness of Roebuck should act as a warning against any easy acceptance of the proposition that the political ideology of Roebuck and his associates was a manifestation of something called a middle-class consciousness.[20] There is also reason to doubt whether the phrase 'Radical middle class' is an adequate shorthand term for them. It is vague and can easily be used in a way which makes it only a little less inclusive than the parent term, 'middle class'. Leading Philosophic Radicals were themselves aware of this danger. Consequently they attempted to dissociate themselves from other forms of Radicalism and to identify themselves with the dynamic elements in society by referring to themselves either as Philosophic Radicals or as exponents of 'movement' Radicalism.[21] Like Marxist socialists they turned their backs on Utopian forms of their basic ideology and claimed to be rigorously scientific. A further qualitative difference between the Philosophic Radicals and those often described as the 'Radical middle class' is best comprehended by those who have grasped something of the qualitative difference between the Bolsheviks and the Mensheviks.

It is, indeed, difficult to place the leaders of the Philosophic Radicals into any one social stratum or social class. As an income group they were spread wide, from Sir William Molesworth, who paid £4,000 out of income to support the *London Review*, through J. S. Mill on £1,200 a year to H. S. Chapman struggling in the best years on a mere £260.[22] They ranged in social status from Charles Buller, Esquire, who was a darling man and of Cornwall's best, to Mr Francis Place, a successful breeches-maker, or to Roebuck himself, the barrister stepson of a Canadian farmer. On occasion they touched shoulders with deviant aristocrats who were among the leading men in the country, like Lords Durham and Brougham. In terms of education, although not of intellect, the range was equally great.

Nevertheless, neither the diversity of origin of the intellectual and Parliamentary leaders, nor the doctrinal nature of their political beliefs, nor yet their claim to represent the whole of 'the people' should divert attention away from the fact that Philosophic Radicalism was an ideology with appeal to a clearly differentiated class in the constituencies. Philosophic Radicals who were also members of Parliament, like Roebuck, Hume, Grote and Charles Buller, rested solidly on the electoral support of tradesmen, artisans, petty producers and a few military and professional men. Roebuck, for example, had the active support of both Napiers, and of a great many shopkeepers and producers; and his right-hand man in many a national issue was H. S. Chapman, an ex-bank clerk and unsuccessful commission agent turned political journalist and agitator. That contemporaries recognized the class nature of this movement is suggested by the fact that, in the Tory and Whig press, these supporters of the Philosophic Radicals were execrated by, and on behalf of, the gentry and the middle class. In Bath, for example, the opponents of Roebuck frightened the respectable middle classes, as well as the aristocracy, with images of blood, the French Revolution, republicanism, and American democracy.[23]

Roebuck and the ultras constituted the group which, above all others, attempted to translate intellectual Philosophic Radicalism into a political programme at constituency level. After the demise of the *Poor Man's Guardian* in 1835 they were also the main agents disseminating Radical propaganda to lower social strata. It is true that they included members of the 'middle class' among their converts and adherents. Indeed some Philosophic Radicals believed that they ought to confine their educational activities to the 'middle class'. J. S. Mill, for example, advised the Saint Simonian Missionaries to this effect.[24] Roebuck on the other hand believed in trying to get through

C

to those social strata whose literate members did not normally read the literary reviews and political quarterlies. To achieve this object Roebuck, assisted by Chapman and others, produced a series of *Pamphlets for the People* which retailed at 1½d. and reached a circulation of 10,000 in 1835 and the early part of 1836. These pamphlets represented a sustained attempt to present a systematic political doctrine based on Philosophic Radicalism to a section of the reading public much wider than anything one could call 'middle class' or even 'Radical middle class'. They were also part of the campaign against the Newspaper Stamp at the head of which was a committee on which Dr J. R. Black and Francis Place (allegedly representative of middle-class consciousness) worked with Chapman, Thomas Falconer (another ultra), and others, to promote 300 petitions to Parliament on the subject.[25]

At the heart of these pamphlets and of Roebuck's programme was a seven-point Radical Charter. This Charter, written by H. S. Chapman and published in 1835, demanded an occupier suffrage, abolition of the property qualification, the ballot, abolition of the existing method of registration, equal electoral districts, shorter parliaments and abolition of the Newspaper Stamp.[26] Elsewhere the ultras emphasized the importance of the ballot, the case for single-chamber government, a wholesale reform of the law, national education, the abolition of all monopolies and privilege, municipal reform, and, through a reduction in government expenditure, a reduction in taxation. They also gave their support to the Canadian Radicals through two rebellions, and opposed Durham's ordinance and the Durham Report.

The social class to which these views appealed was made up of those who were low in the traditional scale of status and privilege, i.e. towards the bottom in relationships of authority and subjection, and those in this position who aspired to rise and could only do so through their own unaided efforts, whether efforts of mind and skill in trade and manufacture or in the professions. It was, therefore, and whatever its theoretical or philosophical origin, a political philosophy well suited to a society of petty producers and petit bourgeois. It mirrored that individuated, privatized, and non-deferential social class consciousness which grew among a middling set of people in a rapidly expanding and changing society, but which in no modern or late nineteenth-century sense was 'middle class'. This set of people or quasi-group included compositors as well as doctors, artisans as well as small producers, self-employed shopkeepers as well as bigger and more successful retailers. In Bath, where these groups were physically concentrated, despised by their customers, untouched by large-scale industry and technological innovation, and unacquainted with the phenomenon of an urban proletariat as distinct from the traditional urban poor and unskilled, their consciousness of themselves as a co-operating political class became particularly strong. There was less distinction in social stratification, status and social class consciousness between employers and employed, between skilled and professional workers, than there was between producers (of all kinds) and aristocratic consumers, and between regularly employed artisans and the mass of the poor. There was also little point of contact between the 'factoryized' proletariat of the northern regions and the local artisans.[27]

This class of petit bourgeois and literates to which we have added the artisans, was the vanguard of 'the people' so much admired by leading Philosophic Radicals. And 'the people' was really a middling class which was still neither middle class nor working class. Indeed because of the insistence of Philosophic Radicals on the need for education and enlightenment it seems very likely that their image of 'the people' was dominated by their own self-image and by their image of the industrious and literate workman and shopkeeper : by their image of a middling class. Certainly 'the people' addressed by Roebuck and others in the *Pamphlets for the People* were deemed to be rational, literate and respectable, even though they ranked low in the order of social stratification and social class. And, although the concept of 'the people' was meant to include everyone outside the ranks of the aristocracy, it was never intended to be used as a concept including the mob or the masses. Indeed James Mill expressly excluded half the population from his image of 'the people' since for him women were not people. The idea the concept was meant to convey was that of the mob or the masses after having been provided with the means of economic independence and after their transformation into respectable and responsible members of the middling set of people through a universal education based on associationist psychology.[28] Roebuck made no bones about it :[29]

My object has been through life to make the working man as exalted and civilized a creature as I could make him. I wanted to place before his mind a picture of civilized life such as I see in my own life ... my household has been a civilized household. It has been a household in which thought, high and elevated ideas of literature, and grace and beauty, have always found everything that could recommend them ... I wanted to make the working man like me.

The print by Henry Harris of 'The Gathering of the Unions in Birmingham in 1832'[30] is a pictorial representation of this image. Harris created the impression of numbers through dots signifying countless thousands of bodiless heads, and he emphasized the significance of individuals through the detail of the figures in the foreground. The women, a minority among them, are properly shawled and bonneted. The men are toppered and best-suited. Everywhere there is earnest conversation and attention. There is only one beer or mineral water drinker with his back to the procession, but he is dressed in a smock. The slogan most clearly readable is 'An honest man is the noblest work of God'.

As for the general question of the apparent separation of Philosophic Radicalism from social class, it was Marx who, in another context, suggested an answer. Writing of the coalition between the petit bourgeois and the workers in 1848, and of the content of French social democracy, he said:[31]

This content is the transformation of society in a democratic way, but a transformation within the bounds of the petty bourgeoisie. Only one must not form the narrow-minded notion that the petty bourgeoisie, on principle, wishes to enforce an egoistic class interest. Rather, it believes that the *special* conditions of its emancipation are the general conditions within the frame of which alone modern society can be saved and the class struggle avoided. Just as little must one imagine that the democratic representatives are indeed all shopkeepers or enthusiastic champions of shopkeepers. According to their education and their individual position they may be as far apart as heaven from earth. What makes them representatives of the petty bourgeoisie is the fact that in their minds they do not go beyond the limits which the latter do not go beyond in life, that they are consequently driven, theoretically, to the same problems and solutions to which material interest and social position drive the latter practically. This is, in general, the relationship between the *political* and *literary* representatives of a class and the class they represent.

It certainly seems to have been part of the relationship between the ultra wing of the Philosophic Radicals and their constituency workers and supporters.

The general point which I would like to make in connection with this brief survey is that we should not engage in an endless round of argument, based on limited alternatives, as to whether this or that political phenomenon was or was not the manifestation of *a* middle- or working-class consciousness. A more fruitful approach would be to discard the three-class model altogether and open up a greater range of possibilities by using a basic model containing a minimum of five classes and employing the category of a middling class.

Before the five-class model is introduced it is worth observing that although early Victorians often talked collectively of the 'middle class', the 'labouring classes', 'the people', and even the 'working class', they behaved as if there was a multiplicity of classes, the nuances of which were comprehensible to the population at large. Anyone accustomed to reading early nineteenth-century directories and local newspapers will be well acquainted with the usage, whereby a man with the name John Smith would be placed in any one of a number of categories: John Smith Esq.; Mr John Smith; John Smith carpenter or butcher; John Smith labourer; or just John Smith. At the bottom, of course, was John Smith's wife. Formal lists, like the lists of arrivals in the city of Bath,[32] would begin higher up with Lord John Smith, and work down through Sir John Smith, Col. John Smith, Rev. or Dr John Smith, to John Smith Esq. The result, a division into ten degrees or orders. Yet other works like Webster's *Encyclopaedia of Domestic Economy*[33] divided the five orders, ranging from Lord John Smith to John Smith Esq., into nine divisions according to income and number of servants. They ranged from 'An establishment of the first rate fit for a nobleman with an income of over £5,000 per annum employing twenty to twenty-four domestics' to one of the ninth rate with an income of £150 to £200 per annum employing a maid of all work. In addition, servants were carefully ranked in twenty-two categories.

A society as status conscious as this will appear to be cramped even within a five-class model. If, however, it is borne in mind that this approach to the ranking of people is concerned not with social classes as defined above but simply with social stratification, and if it is realized that each of the five social classes can embrace more than one social stratum however delineated, and if women are recognized as a sub-group in each social class, then the model could be made complex enough even for those historians who deny the usefulness of the concept of class.[34] Nevertheless, for the purpose of understanding the nature and existence of social and political class, five classes make better sense than many even if many could be shown to exist.

The basic five-class model is made up as follows:

(1) *Upper class*, aristocratic, landholding, authoritarian, exclusive.

(2) *Middle class*, industrial and commercial property-owners, senior military and professional men, aspiring to acceptance by the upper class. Deferential towards the upper class because of this and because of concern for property and achieved position, but individuated or privatized.

(3) *Middling class*,[35] petit bourgeois, aspiring professional men, other literates and artisans. Individuated or privatized like the middle class but collectively less deferential and more concerned to remove the privileges and authority of the upper class in which, without radical changes, they cannot realistically hope to share.

(4) *Working class A*, industrial proletariat in factory areas, workers in domestic industries, collectivist and non-deferential and wanting government intervention to protect rather than liberate them.

(5) *Working class B*, agricultural labourers, other low-paid non-factory urban labourers, domestic servants, urban poor, most working-class women whether from working-class A or B households, deferential and dependent.

This model is a static one. Yet one thing certain about early Victorian England is that it was changing. How then to incorporate a dynamic element?

The first thing to do is to cease visualizing or conceptualizing social strata or social classes as separate boxes, whether arranged vertically as in the traditional and United Nations models, or horizontally as in the San Gimignano model.[36] Instead, think of the five classes, each embracing a number of social strata, as separate pools of water linked together by streams of water and located on a convex but asymmetrical hill with the middling class on the summit exposed to all the elements. The upper- and middle-class pools lie on the sheltered sunny side of the hill and both working-class pools lie on the

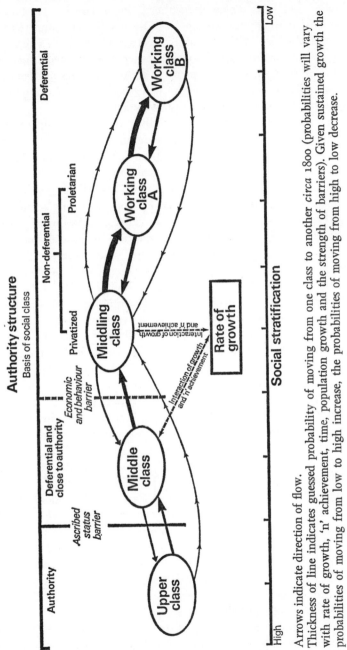

Diagram of the five-class model

Arrows indicate direction of flow.
Thickness of line indicates guessed probability of moving from one class to another *circa* 1800 (probabilities will vary with rate of growth, 'n' achievement, time, population growth and the strength of barriers). Given sustained growth the probabilities of moving from low to high increase, the probabilities of moving from high to low decrease.

higher and more exposed northern slope. The stream linking the summit or middling-class pool to the middle- and upper-class pools is controlled by traditional sluices between each pool. The two working-class pools are linked to each other and the middling-class pool by more sluggish streams but there are no obstacles to the downward flow of water although eddies will result in water moving backwards and forwards between any two pools.

Visualized in this way the middling class will begin to appear as the central and most unstable class. It undergoes continuous replacement from a variety of sources: from successful occupants of upper social strata in working class A, although very rarely from working class B, from less successful occupants, and their children, of the upper and middle classes, as well as from its own natural increase. It also loses population to all other classes. Consequently the middling class itself displays divergent political and social tendencies. In times of rapid economic growth and when traditional ascriptive relationships of authority and subjection are weak or absent there is likely to be a shift of many people to higher social strata and social classes. Where, however, traditional relationships of authority and subjection remain strong men may move from low to higher social strata without any effect on their authority positions. In this circumstance there will develop a strong middling-class consciousness, the essence of which is that it is individuated and non-deferential. The political class engendered by this class consciousness will contend for power against established authority. At other times the political way in which the disparate, because individuated or privatized, elements of the middling class will jump, will depend on specific historical conditions.[37]

By the 1820s enough people in the social strata covered by the middling class had generated sufficient similar social class consciousness to develop as a political class at least in some regions. The upper and middle classes were also class conscious and productive of political classes. Working class A was beginning to develop a distinctive proletarian social class consciousness, again in some regions, and was beginning to emerge as a political class. Working class B, however, was a long way from developing a social class consciousness that was anything other than deferential, and a long way from appearing as a distinctive political class.

The essential purpose of the model, in contrast with the three-class one, is that it represents an attempt to formulate a conceptual apparatus which focuses attention on a number of crucial aspects of early nineteenth-century England. These are : the existence of a middling class, the dynamic political and economic roles of this class, the difference between social stratification and social class, movement between social strata, and the rise and fall of political classes associated with economic growth.

As a theory of social change which seeks to link conflict-induced social and political change to economic change, the model is only set out in outline. Of course it might be helpful to write it down in precisely formulated mathematical functions. Nevertheless, what it would gain in mathematical precision could be offset by too great an abstraction from reality. My guess is that the most fruitful method would be to use a probability model based on a Markov-chain analysis. In such a model the probability of moving from one stratum to any other could be expressed as a function of (a) the rate of economic growth, (b) the level of achievement motivation, (c) population growth, (d) time. But even these would not express all the determinants of such probabilities. However, it should be possible to calculate something close to the real probabilities from existing data and to see how they are influenced, if at all, by the four factors (a), (b), (c) and (d) above. Even so, this exercise would tell us nothing mathematically about the probability of the emergence of social class consciousness or of the formation of political class.

The point is that in all historical studies we should distinguish between the usefulness of a model as a cognitive and explanatory apparatus and as a predictive one. I do not wish to claim any kind of predictive power for the five-class model other than that, just like any other aid to understanding in history, it might be an aid to thinking about the present.

With regard to the early nineteenth century the concept of a middling class within a five-class model is a useful device for clarifying real historical problems. Its usefulness in connection with the problem of Philosophic Radicalism and class consciousness has already been shown. I now propose to use it once more to continue with the story of Radicalism with the purpose of showing how the middling class, always unstable, was torn in two directions in the 1830s, yet was still sufficiently class conscious to produce the Charter and oppose the coercion of Canada.

One important social change in the last hundred and thirty years has been the growth and embourgeoisement of the professional classes. A change in the opposite direction has been the proletarianization of the artisan and the independent craftsman-producer, marked, for example, in my own family, by a three-generational shift from petit bourgeois coach-maker to artisan cabinet-maker to working-class carpenter and joiner. It seems to me that this proletarianization of the artisan began at about the same time as the embourgeoisement of the professional and petit bourgeois classes. In the 1830s, however, it had scarcely begun. What we seem to be witnessing in the mid-twentieth century is a political realignment resulting from a tendency towards the embourgeoisement of some social strata in Working Class A accompanied by a tendency towards a proletarianization of some professional or sub-professional groups. What the political consequences of such a coming together may be we can leave to the sociologist and the political scientist. The political consequence of a similar togetherness at a different stage of economic development was active support at constituency level for Philosophic Radicalism.

Philosophic Radicalism was the political ideology of the middling class. The Philosophic Radicals and the class they represented were also the immediate parents of the Charter. But they and it were not imbued with, nor the result of, a middle-class, Radical middle-class or working-class consciousness.

If a historian, equipped with a set of concepts suggested by the five-class model, looks at men close to the Charter, men like Dr Black, Francis Place, William Lovett, Henry Hetherington, J. A. Roebuck, H. S. Chapman, he will see, as in the conventional model, that they might be differentiated according to income and occupation in ways indicative of a stratification between working men and non-working men or between rich and poor. But he will also see, according to the authority/subjection aspect of social class, that they cannot be so easily divided, and that in terms of social class consciousness they were more alike than unlike. They were neither middle class nor working class but members of an unstable middling class outstandingly individuated and non-deferential. He might also see that the concept 'Radical middle class' is not the same as middling class. The former concept has connotations which imply that Black and Place were always and largely at home with the middle class but that on occasions they jumped over the back wall separating them from their lower-class neighbours in order to jog them into action, and that after doing this they jumped back again. The fact is that Place, like Roebuck and those who co-operated closely with him in the campaign against the Newspaper Stamp and over Canada, was a regular outsider. Since Dr Black, along with Chapman, Falconer and Place, was a member of a very active society founded in connection with the Roebuck *Pamphlets* in 1835, the chances are that he too was a regular outsider. As a regular outsider and a regular member of the middling class Dr Black was different from those members of the middle class who were sometimes Radical. He was different from Burdett and Durham, and unlike those who, outside the hard core of Philosophic Radicals, were really liberal Whigs—more middle class than Radical.

That professional men should take the initiative in writing, speaking and organizing on behalf of the class conscious among the middling class is scarcely surprising. They had more leisure and greater experience. That this kind of initiative should be interpreted to mean that other sections of the middling class lacked social class consciousness is, to say the least, questionable. As already suggested it is questionable because it is a view which implicitly assumes that what is looked for is either a middle-class or a proletarian social class consciousness. But it is also questionable, in Rowe's version, because it focuses attention on the formation of one organization and the drafting of the Bill embodying the Charter, while ignoring the complex inter-relationships between ideology, social classes, social strata, constituency workers, propaganda and people which made the LWMA and the Charter possible.

Before saying more about these inter-relationships let me deal with the proposition that the Charter was the result of a Radical middle-class initiative *because* Place drafted it on Lovett's request. The observation I wish to make hinges on a point of emphasis and interpretation. Which is the significant fact in connection with social class consciousness? Place's drafting or Lovett's request? For my part I opt for the request, otherwise, by analogy, constitutions drafted for new African and Asian nations by white lawyers from the late imperial powers must be interpreted as indicators of white imperial initiative rather than coloured nationalism. The two occurrences, Lovett's request and Place's drafting, reflect Lovett's initiative and Place's acquiescence and participation as an expert much more than they reflect Place's initiative and Lovett's lack of social class consciousness. Although, as I have argued, the important thing to grasp is that Place and Lovett had a very similar social class consciousness, hence Lovett's approach to Place in the first instance.

Now we can examine the complex inter-relationships between members of the middling class, their political representatives, their ideology, and the preparation of the Charter.

With regard to proximate political causes of the Charter the story began with James Mill's theory of revolution and the middle, middling and working classes of the Birmingham Political Union and the rash of similar bodies elsewhere in the country. Among these was the militant Bristol Union whose delegates fostered the establishment of an artisan-dominated Political Union in the city of Bath on 7 November 1831.[38] The movement, which was to culminate in the Charter, gathered momentum with the Reform Bill of 1832 and the effects of this on the electorate of Bath. The Reform Bill increased this electorate from thirty to 2,835, i.e. to nearly one-third of the adult male population. A political fraction, consisting of a few professional men and tradesmen, broke with the liberal middle classes and formed the Independent Association, a middling-class organization, in order to request Joseph Hume to suggest a suitable Radical candidate. The Chairman of the Association was a law student, Thomas Falconer. At about the same time as this Association made overtures to Hume, members of the Bath Political Union did the same. The upshot was that the Independent Association, much influenced by Falconer, chose J. A. Roebuck as their candidate.[39] Roebuck and Falconer were friends, soon to be brothers-in-law, both were lawyers and both were Philosophic Radicals.

At the election, Roebuck, the Philosophic Radical nominee of the Independent Association and the London Political Union, was returned with over 1,000 votes, 500 of which were from plumpers, mostly tradesmen and artisans. His election was made possible by strong ward organization which was dependent on the active and financial backing of his electoral supporters, i.e. it sprang directly from their social class consciousness. For the artisans who supported him this was not a proletarian class consciousness. For the shop-keepers and tradesmen this was not a middle-class consciousness. For both it was still a middling-class consciousness.

From this position of electoral strength, re-affirmed in 1835, Roebuck assailed London and its artisans and others of the middling class. The biggest thing in Philosophic Radical middling-class politics in these years, in spite of Grote inside the House and Mill outside it, was Roebuck's campaign, through the *Pamphlets for the People*, to frustrate the intentions of the Newspaper Stamp. Through the *Pamphlets* Roebuck was the prime mover in the establishment of the society previously mentioned, the society promoting petitions on the Newspaper Stamp. He was also a leading advocate for the creation of a separate working-class party. Dr Black was a member of the society originally moved for by Roebuck. Even though Black's membership may not have been the result of a direct response to Roebuck's initiative, Black himself certainly did not make the first move. Nevertheless, in all probability, as Rowe has argued, he did make the next. This was to encourage some London artisans to form the Association of Working Men to Procure a Cheap and Honest Press, the body which, with Black's assistance, became the LWMA and the immediate parent of the Charter (see Rowe).

But Black was not working in a political vacuum. The *Pamphlets*, as already mentioned, with a circulation of 10,000 were a recent and regular stimulus to political action, while Chapman's Charter, in *Pamphlet* no. 22, anticipated most of what was in the Charter and much that was not but which was incorporated into Chartist ideology. The writings of Roebuck, Place, Falconer, Chapman and others also played an important part as catalysts of middling- and working-class consciousness. Indeed Roebuck was so admired by Bath Chartists that they hung his portrait over the mantelpiece in their Trim Street Meeting House.

The question is, therefore, whose is the significant initiative and whose and what the social class consciousness? Is it that of the Birmingham, Bristol or Bath Political Union? Of the artisans and petit bourgeois of Bath? Of Thomas Falconer? Of the London Political Union? Of Roebuck? Of the ward committees and constituency workers? Of Dr Black? Of H. S. Chapman? Certainly Dr Black played a part. The question is, is it a part which can be used as evidence signifying the absence of social class consciousness on the part of followers? (If it is held to be so then Black as a follower himself must have lacked social class consciousness.) The point is, I think, that we must try to grasp the sorry scheme of things entire and to doubt whether any one man can work a change where conditions favourable to that change do not exist.

But there is more to it than this. The LWMA was founded in 1836. The proposal for the Charter, only slightly different from Chapman's Charter, was first made at a meeting in the Crown and

Anchor in February 1837. It was not formally published in the way Place drafted it, at Lovett's request, until May 1838. It is worth noting that during this fifteen-month period Roebuck was himself very close to drafting the Charter. In 1837 only the dissolution of Parliament and Roebuck's loss of his seat for Bath prevented him from presenting to Parliament a petition embodying the points first mooted at the Crown and Anchor meeting. And in 1838 it was his involvement with Canada, illness and the demands on his time of his work on circuit which prevented him giving more of his time to assisting Lovett and Place with the Charter.[40] During this same period, however, exponents of a new, different and more 'proletarian' class consciousness had begun to turn what was essentially a mid-dling-class Charter into their own rallying cry. This new 'proletarian' class consciousness had varied origins and an existence which cannot be ascertained merely by reference to developments in London and within the LWMA. The fact is, as regional evidence suggests, that by 1837 some members of 'working class A' were a political class in every sense of the word. Even in Bath, where middling-class politics were exceptionally strong, drawing nourishment from the aggressive tactics of Roebuck, a distinctive 'proletarian' consciousness was clearly at work producing self-conscious 'proletarian' political activity.[41]

The beginnings of such activity, in Bath, can be found at the time of the Bristol Riots, when local action effectively prevented the Bath Troop of Yeomanry from leaving to relieve Bristol. Subsequently, in November 1831, the instability of the middling-class consensus was emphasized by the formation of a Political Union with a council including a majority of mechanics. Six years later Roebuck's own artisan supporters refused him a hearing on the Poor Law question and in March 1837 a new Radical society was inaugurated with a majority of artisans on its management committee because, it was said, it 'should be a democracy in which the productive classes should have a preponderating influence'.[42] As the various elements in the middling class pulled in different directions a 'proletarian' class-conscious movement attracted some artisans and a few professionals towards it. Local leaders of this new movement were shoemakers rather than engineers, and itinerant petty traders rather than shop-keepers. By the time the basic points of the Charter were presented to the citizens of Bath, in October 1837, only two years after Chapman's Charter, all the leading professional and petit bourgeois members of the middling class were hesitant about supporting it. Both

Roebuck and Napier were aware of the existence of a separatist working-class movement and of the extent to which it signified the existence of a distinctive 'proletarian' class consciousness strong enough to bring together working-class representatives from London and Bristol as well as from Bath.

What Roebuck thought about this political phenomenon is made clear in the letter he wrote explaining his absence from this inaugural meeting :[43]

> The working men do wisely in their associating together for they have hitherto been excluded from all participation in Municipal Rights because disunion has rendered them weak and induced their enemies to condemn their demands. I would say to you, be united, be firm, learn distinctly what rights you ought to have, and steadily and earnestly demand them. While you do this, however, I would entreat you not to mix up social with political reforms. Social reforms can come only as the consequence of political ones—A good government, if attained, would conduce to all good social reforms, and it is not for us to decide beforehand what these last should be. I give you this warning, because I have been so long in the habit of advising the people of Bath; and also because I know that the weakness and disunion of the working classes have arisen mainly from their unwisely confounding these two essentially different classes of reforms.

It was clear to Roebuck that the middling-class consensus on which he depended was breaking up if not already broken. Individuated and non-deferential artisans had to decide, just like the literates, the petit bourgeois and the professionals, which way to go. By the time Henry Vincent arrived at Bath and there established the *Western Vindicator* as the organ of Chartism in the West Country in 1839, the majority of politically conscious literates, petit bourgeois and professionals were still a distinctly middling-class-conscious group feared by the middle and upper classes. Artisans, however, were divided and uncertain. Nevertheless all the elements in the middling class, including the artisans, did work together as a political class to return Roebuck to Parliament in 1841. But seven years later, in the face of a political alliance between representatives of the upper and middle classes in local and national politics, a similar but less cohesive movement including working-class Chartists was unsuccessful. Thereafter the local middling class lost its spokesman and its vitality.[44]

It has already been observed that in London in 1838 the artisans of the LWMA were still middling class conscious enough to approach other members of the middling class like Roebuck and Place, who remained favourable to their political aspirations, to ask for assistance in drafting the Charter. There is also evidence, for 1838, that London artisans felt able to identify themselves with the men of Lower and Upper Canada who they felt were in circumstances similar to their own.[45] In supporting the extreme demands of the Canadians the LWMA derived nothing from the support or initiative of the generality of the Radical middle classes. They did, however, share the sentiments and probably followed the lead of the ultra wing of the Philosophic Radicals of whom Roebuck, Chapman and Falconer were particularly active.[46] Even so these artisans were beginning to act on their own initiative in a self-consciously class-conscious manner although it was not yet wholly a proletarian one. That they were still in alliance with the ultras in 1838 is not evidence of a lack of social class consciousness, it is merely further evidence that the social class consciousness of both artisans and the middling-class ultras was similar.

Class and class consciousness are difficult concepts for the historian to handle. All the more reason, therefore, why he should employ a conceptual apparatus which does not force him to make judgments about the class origin of political phenomena within a very narrow range of choices, or which confines his view of working-class consciousness to a proletarian one. Hence the importance of the five-class model and the emphasis this gives to the role of an unstable middling class during the early stages of industrialization in early nineteenth-century England.[47]

2

Class and ideology in a provincial city: Bath 1800-50

Our conception of history [wrote Marx[1]] depends on our ability to expound the real process of production, starting out from the simple material production of life, and to comprehend the form of intercourse connected with this and created by this, as the basis of all history; further, to show it in its action as State; and so, from this starting point, to explain the whole mass of different theoretical products and forms of consciousness, religion, philosophy, ethics, etc., and trace their origins and growth, by which means, of course, the whole thing can be shown in its totality (and therefore, too, the reciprocal action of these various sides on one another).

It is only in recent years that important advances have been made in using sophisticated versions of this, or even other sociological approaches, in discussions of the development of progressive and working-class movements: trade unions, Radicalism, Chartism and women's suffrage.[2] And although the complexity of the inter-relationships between production, men and ideology, recognized by Marx, is increasingly recognized today the tendency to observe monistic causes of phenomena persists.

Recent work on Chartism and working-class movements, however, has focused attention on the need to (a) establish the exact nature of the ideology under discussion, (b) delineate the class structure in regions in which the ideology took root, (c) explore the relationships between sub-classes within the working class, as well as between the working class and other classes. It was with some of these pointers in mind that a number of detailed regional studies on Chartism were written. It is contended here that one of these pioneering studies, 'Chartism in Somerset and Wiltshire'[3] fails to offer a satisfying explanation of the relationship between the city of Bath and the surrounding industrial centres, and between the middle classes, Radicalism and Chartism. That it does fail is because the author

makes unwarranted assumptions about stratification in the city of
Bath, postulates an ideology, 'Radicalism', without describing it,
relates this ideology to economic developments by assertion rather
than analysis and brings forward an inadequate body of data to
support his claim. Consequently any full narrative history of
Chartism and working-class movements drawing upon it, is, in this
respect, likely to be defective.

The social stratification assumed by R. B. Pugh reflects the opinions
expressed by those local antiquarians and literary dilettantes who
have made the study of Bath their special preserve and perpetuates
the idea, set out by the Rev. Richard Warner in 1801, that, 'Bath
has little trade, and no manufactures, the higher classes of people
and their dependants constitute the chief part of the population; and
the number of the lower classes is small'.[4] The assumption is that
in the early nineteenth century, as in the eighteenth, Bath was
largely populated by the aristocracy and the very wealthy 'middle
classes' or the gentry. As a corollary it is also assumed that the city
had its beggars but no working or intermediate classes. In the past
this has meant that any evidence suggestive of a working class or
of distinctive proletarian political movements was either ignored,
denied or interpreted in such a way as to fit this accepted view. Cole
and Postgate maintained that the major activity absorbing the
energies of the citizens of Bath was match-making.[5] Writing of
Henry Vincent, they made no reference to Bath although Vincent
made the city his headquarters and published the *Western Vindicator* there.[6] G. D. H. Cole also considered that the young Roebuck
was not a Radical and thereby avoided the need to explain the support he received from the Bath electorate.[7] More recently A. R.
Schoyen, although aware of the Chartist/Repealer *détente* of 1841,
and the brief demonstration of 1848, instanced Bath as a city un-
affected by Chartist activity in 1839 and 1842.[8] R. B. Pugh, accepts
this view and endeavours to explain the place and role of Bath
Chartism by reference to it. His argument proceeds thus:[9]

[Bath] was a town in decay for its tourist industry had already
waned, and it had no other source of wealth. No doubt its half
derelict economy, its mounting population, and the beggars who
had infested it since the days of fashion helped to endow it with
Radical sentiments, and to make it, as it was said, 'the most
vigorous reforming City of the Empire'. Roebuck represented it in

the parliaments of 1832 and 1841; one of its Aldermen, James
Crisp, had been a Radical since the days of Hunt and often chaired
Chartist meetings; and two of the Napiers, also Radicals, lived in
or near it.

   Lying close to Bath on the east and south was a cluster of much
smaller towns . . . whose economy was being dislocated by technological changes in the manufacture of cloth. In this good ground
Chartism could easily take root. Bath, therefore, with its denser
population and pool of Radical gentry, furnished the little towns
with leadership, and received in return the adherence of a
proletariat largely dependent upon the declining cloth trade.

The essence of the argument is that the 'gentry' of Bath reacted to
an economic collapse—made worse by the growing pressure of
population—first by adopting Radical sentiments and then by
accepting more extremist political doctrines. These they were able to
keep alive, in the absence of an indigenous proletariat, by proselytizing the surrounding industrial areas. The implicit assumptions are
two : (*a*) Radicalism was 'middle class' and the product of economic
decline, and (*b*) a politically class-conscious working class cannot
exist apart from the nourishing background of factory employment.[10]
Whether these assumptions are valid, and whether this naïve view
of the social strata and classes of Bath in which the chief element is
a 'gentry' rendered dissident by a declining economy provides an
adequate explanation of the political affiliations of the different social
strata in the city, and of the relationship between Radicals and
Chartists, remains to be established.

   Before attempting what seems to me to be a more satisfying
although more complex explanation, it will be as well to say something about the contention that the economy of Bath was 'half
derelict' in the 1830s and to state clearly what is known about the
course of development in the city. It is true to say that by 1830
the seasonal tourist industry had waned. Yet it is equally true to say
that the city was adapting itself to its new function as a place of
permanent residence for retired clergymen, admirals, generals and
the like. Consequently, during the first four decades of the nineteenth
century, demand for the services that Bath could offer to residents
and visitors alike remained buoyant enough to induce Bath Corporation, ever a conservative body in economic matters, to raise substantial loans in order to undertake extensive rebuilding on two

separate occasions. In the period 1807–8 to 1814–15 the corporation's net borrowing totalled £14,450 and in the period 1829–30 to 1834–5 it totalled £25,800. Moreover, no other index indicates anything approaching a 50 per cent collapse in the economy. Rateable values remained at the high level reached in 1810 until 1830, and only then began a slow decline over the next twenty years. The number of houses unoccupied in the central parishes in 1830 was a mere 5 per cent of the total. It is true that by 1841 this proportion had risen to 12 per cent but in the still expanding suburban parishes the rise was an imperceptible one, from 8 to 9·5 per cent. It is also true that labourers' wages were lower in 1816 and 1832 than in 1809 but they were no lower throughout the rest of the 1830s than in 1832. Indeed, in May 1839 the average earnings of highway labourers rose 20 per cent and at the end of the year there was virtually full employment as work on the Great Western Railway was in full swing. By 1843 labourers' earnings were 30 to 40 per cent higher than for the early 1830s. It is also likely that real wages of artisans in full work rose in the same period. On the other hand there is evidence of high unemployment, particularly during the years 1830 to 1832, but also throughout the remainder of the 1830s. Overall, while there is every indication that living conditions for many people in the city were no better in the early 1830s than in 1800, there is also some to suggest that by 1839–40 they were no worse.[11]

Mr Pugh's suggestion that a mounting population contributed to the growth of Radicalism also appears improbable. The most Radical parish, St James, had an almost stationary, not a mounting, population between 1821 and 1851. Lyncombe and Widcombe, the second most Radical parish, did, it is true, increase its population by 60 per cent between 1821 and 1841 but the evidence suggests that it remained a thriving industrial suburb throughout this period of population growth.[12]

Thus there is no known economic indicator which can justify the description 'a half derelict economy' as applied to Bath in the 1830s. Some of the indices, however, do show that the economy of the central parishes was stagnating; idling as it shifted to a lower gear more suitable to the city's new role as a place of residence. Consequently it may still be argued that this condition of stagnation provided fertile ground for an out-growth of militant Radicalism among a discontented 'gentry'. Such an argument, however, still seems to rest on the assumption that Radicalism was the product of relative decline and was the ideology of the 'gentry'.

I have shown elsewhere that although in some ways Bath was outside the mainstream of eighteenth-century economic development, it was in others very much a product of that development and that incipient industrialization had occurred in the first decades of the nineteenth century.[13] Therefore, it will suffice to show, from Table 1, that the belief in the existence of only two principal strata, and in the absence of an indigenous working population from the city's social class structure, is nonsense.

The census for 1831 shows that out of a total population of over 50,000, 21,000 were males of whom 8,556 were over the age of twenty. They were classified according to occupation in the following way :

TABLE 1   *Occupations of men over twenty in Bath in 1831*

Capitalists, bankers and other educated men	1,196
Retail (mostly) and miscellaneous crafts	2,797
Building trades	1,074
Domestic service	670
Shoemaking	529
Furniture and coach-making	351
Tailoring	349
Labouring (non agricultural)	1,480
Labouring (agricultural)	110
Total	8,556

Source : *Census of Population 1831*

Thus, although 24 per cent of the men in the over-twenty age groups were unskilled labourers, most were either artisans, master craftsmen in a small way of business, shop assistants or retailers in business on their own account. That this should be so is hardly surprising, since from the early eighteenth century Bath had been pre-eminently a city attracting to it men of energy, industry, thrift and foresight. It was a city where some skill and a little capital offered attractive opportunities of independence to many, and where a multitude of skills were in high demand to build, maintain, furnish, feed, clothe and entertain its wealthy residents and visitors. The city was a paradise for the consumer industries, providing for men at all levels of society from ingenious beggar to successful builder for, as long as large incomes were spent there, wealth flowed inwards, transport was slow, and factory products non-existent or inferior.

In 1831 the measure of its attraction for these trades and industries was that, although its adult males were one-twelfth of the total for the county of Somerset, the city provided employment for one-half the county total of painters, one-third of pastry cooks, one-quarter of hatters, two-fifths of coach-makers, and one-sixth of shoe-makers. Indeed the degree of concentration of craftsmen within the city itself was even greater. The parish of St James contained 12 per cent of the total adult male population of the six parishes but was the home of 28 per cent of tailors, 24 per cent of bootmakers and shoemakers, 19 per cent of carpenters; and the proportion of men employed in building, furniture manufacture and coach-making, shoe-making and tailoring in the parish was twice that for the city as a whole. On the other hand the parish was lived in by only 5 per cent of the city's male servants and by only 293 out of more than 4,000 female servants.[14] It was, incidentally, the most Radical of the six parishes.

The city also attracted men in the professions such as architects, doctors, surgeons, lawyers and bankers. It provided opportunities for builders and other craftsmen to make their own successful way in the world, and offered many outlets for the investment of loanable funds in small amounts, and created numerous opportunities for successful innovational activities in building, transport, entertainment and industrial organization.[15]

The ideology which took root in this socio-economic environment was, as Pugh says, Radicalism. It was not, however, a philosophy of depression or decline. It was the philosophy of its leading local advocate, J. A. Roebuck. It was Philosophic Radicalism, and as such it reflected the rational anarchism of a community of small producers rejecting a socially and politically oppressive structure of society. It was, as it were, the philosophy of men on the frontier of industrialization. It is worth a closer look.

Roebuck's programme, which in 1832 won him one of the two Parliamentary seats with the support of 1,136 voters out of an electorate of 2,835, and gave him the undivided support of 507 plumpers, advocated the following: the repeal of the Septennial Act, the extension of the suffrage to all tax-payers, the ballot, the destruction of monopolies, the break-up of closed corporations, the removal of the monopoly of the Bank of England and of the China trade, the abolition of the Corn Laws, the assessed taxes and slavery, a reduction in expenditure on the armed forces, cheap justice, a scheme of national education, the repeal of the Six Acts and the extension of civil and religious liberty.[16] During the next five years Roebuck kept the support of the bulk of Radicals when he added to this list proposals for a reform of the House of Lords, opposition to the rate-paying clause in the Municipal Reform Bill, to Lord's Day observance and to the Irish Poor Law; and gave his support to the Poor Law Amendment Act and secular education. He kept their support, too, when in his *Pamphlets for the People* he went beyond these proposals for piecemeal opposition and reform. In *Pamphlet* no. 7 he urged the working classes, organized in trade unions, to extend their activities and establish election committees, 'To conduct the whole election, and, in most instances, determine the result.' This, he claimed, would be 'the true and most effective mode for the Working Men to attain the due protection of their interests by the legislative. A dozen men in the House of Commons, really and completely representing the Working Men, would be of more service than petitions signed by ten thousand persons.'[17]

In November 1835 Roebuck's good friend and colleague H. S. Chapman summarized the arguments put forward in Roebuck's pamphlets in the following seven-point Radical Charter.[18]

(1) An extension of the suffrage to all occupants.
(2) An abolition of the property qualification.
(3) Secrecy of suffrage, by means of the ballot.
(4) The abolition of the present complicated system of registration, and the reduction of the expenses of elections.
(5) A more equal distribution of members, according to population and territory.
(6) That the duration of Parliament be shortened.
(7) That the tax on knowledge be abolished.

I have little doubt that in mid-September 1835, when this programme was being hawked in the streets in its thousands for 1½d. a copy, it was a manifesto reflecting and representing the social resentment and political ambition of every Radical in Bath and at least a dozen other constituencies.

A list of leading Bath supporters of this Radical programme must include the names of men like Thomas Falconer, James Crisp, George

Cox, William and Charles Napier, John Allen, Robert Uphill and
Henry Stothert, as well as scores of others, all identifiable, all know-
ing what they wanted, all prepared to work and pay for it by
serving on Roebuck's election committees and returning him free of
all expense. And there is no reason—other than an unsubstantiated
a priori one—to link the Radicalism of any one of them with the
phenomenon of a stagnating, let alone a half derelict economy. In
fact both Napiers are representative of the class of retired military
men for whom Bath, in its new role, was well suited. Charles lived
in the city for a mere three years, after 1836, and was known to
have expressed Radical sentiments as early as 1817. William, who
played a more active part in local politics between 1831 and 1842,
actually lived at Freshford some six miles from the city. He also
developed Radical feelings early in his career, and attributed them to
his experiences in Ireland, and in the Peninsular Campaigns as a
commander of loyal and courageous Englishmen. Thomas Falconer
developed his Radical views in London as a law student, John Allen
was active in the Radical interest in 1812, Crisp was a Radical of
long standing and George Cox derived his Radicalism from his beliefs
as an active and leading Baptist and from his experiences as a self-
made master hatter. Indeed, the only known addition to the ranks
of the Radicals from the 'gentry' during the 1830s was W. P. Roberts
(later known as the Miner's Advocate) who made his first political
appearance as a Tory attacking J. A. Roebuck, and became, several
years later, a militant Chartist serving a two-year prison sentence
for conspiracy.[19]

Nor is there good reason to attribute the Radicalism of the 'five
hundred' who plumped for Roebuck in 1832 to an economic decline.
There is, however, an accumulation of evidence pointing to the
growth of strong Radical feelings, increasingly translated into action,
at least since 1812. In this year John Allen challenged the monopoly
of the closed corporation of thirty-three by standing as a freemen's
candidate for Parliament, and a liberal newspaper, which was to give
its full support to J. A. Roebuck in 1832, The *Bath and Cheltenham
Gazette*, was founded.[20] Then, in July, when Henry Hunt contested
Bristol as a Radical he got 235 votes including those of four Bath
men who, as freemen of Bristol, were entitled to vote. All four were
craftsmen : a cork-cutter, a tailor, a saddler and a wheelwright.

Four years later a series of meetings took place at Spa Fields at
which Hunt declared for universal suffrage, the ballot and annual

Parliaments. (Subsequently Watson, Thistlewood and other Spen-
ceans were charged with high treason.) The London meetings were
followed in December 1816 and January 1817 by meetings in Bristol
and Bath, organized by Hunt, to petition for the same three points.
The Bristol and Bath petitions contained 25,000 and 20,000 signatures
respectively. Hunt, as representative for Bristol and Bath, supported
by John Allen, also for Bath, took these petitions to the third Spa
Fields meeting on 24 January 1817. They had specific instructions
to support demands for universal suffrage. At the venue, the Crown
and Anchor, Cobbett and Cartwright, feeling that Sir Francis Burdett would not present a petition for universal suffrage, moved to
substitute household and direct tax-payer suffrage. Allen, the Bath
representative, without consulting Hunt supported the proposal.
However, Hunt's own move to press for universal suffrage was
carried. Both petitions were presented and Lord Camden, the Recorder
of Bath, attacked in the Bath petition as a holder of sinecures worth
£37,500 per annum, resigned from one of the posts, Teller of the
Exchequer (worth £35,500 per annum). Hunt's assessment of these
meetings[21] points to the significance and strength of Radical feeling
in the city of Bath at the time.

> I wish [he wrote] I had a copy of the resolutions and petition
> by me, that I might insert them here, as I conceive this [the
> Bath petition] to have been the most momentous petition that
> was ever presented to the House of Commons; and the effect
> which it produced was more important than that of any other
> petition that was ever passed at any public meeting, not excepting
> that which was passed at Spa Fields.

There is evidence too of organizational ability and Radical sentiments among trade unionists before 1831, from the efficient activity
of the shoemakers in 1802 to the formation of a Political Union
dominated by representatives of the working classes in 1831, such
that the *Gazette* declared, 'These classes [artisans and trade
unionists] in the city of Bath are in a perfect state of fitness to be
trusted with the elective franchise'.[22] Then there is ample evidence
of lively political activity by tradesmen and Dissenters in vestries
throughout the 1820s when population growth, construction and
investment activity were all high.

It is this growing, although largely latent, Radicalism of the years
before 1830, on which Roebuck was able to draw for support, which

has to be explained. If this can be done then the Radical upsurge of the 1830s becomes explicable in terms of the reform of Parliament in 1832 whereby the electorate in Bath was increased from 30 to 2,835.

In 1831 and 1832 the political climate in Bath was exhilarating. The agitation for the Reform Bill had worked as a catalyst in local politics and the Bill itself had given the franchise to one-third of the city's adult male population. So strong was the anti-Tory and anti-aristocratic mood in the city that no Tory was nominated for the traditional Tory share of the two-member representation. Instead, there were nominated Major-General Palmer, a city member since 1808 and an old liberal and, latterly, reforming Whig, and W. H. Hobhouse, a Whig banker of the Burdett School who regarded the passing of the Reform Bill as the consummation of reform politics. But there were two groups, for which the Reform Bill was the beginning and not the end of reform, which felt it right to ask of any candidate, 'Is he one at whose feet we should with such breathless haste, throw our virgin franchise, as if it were a bauble to be sported with?'[23] These were the working-class dominated Political Union and a Radical Independent Association representing the interests of a fraction of the middling class consisting of tradesmen, shopkeepers, petty producers and professional men. Both groups anticipated a political upheaval in the city, which, with similar upheavals elsewhere, would mark the overthrow of the old order and the real beginning of representative and responsible government in England. On the initiative of Thomas Falconer, a Bath man who was a member of a group of Radical lawyers and law students active in London, Roebuck was nominated with the clear purpose of opposing Hobhouse and the finality view of reform he represented. Roebuck's nomination was supported in Bath by the Independent Association and the Political Union, and in London by Joseph Hume, Francis Place and J. S. Mill.

The election campaign got under way in September. There had never been anything like it before in the constituency; four local newspapers argued about it, processions thundered in support of it, dinners were given in honour of it and jingles were sung about it. Everywhere election posters implied a parallel between Paris in 1788 and Bath in 1832; and for people to whom the bloody Bristol riots were only one year and twelve miles away it was a parallel not without meaning. These same posters frightened the citizens by demanding: Did they wish to be dominated by a political caucus in London? Did they wish to be represented by a man of no character and no property? Did they wish to be represented by a Republican and a Democrat? Did they wish to see their churches turned into barracks? Did they wish to see the barricades go up? If they did then they were advised to vote for Roebuck, who was not only a Democrat and a Republican but an atheist to boot.

When the results of the poll were declared Palmer and Roebuck were elected. It was a triumph for the Radical cause.

Tables 2 and 3 show the result of an attempt to analyse voting behaviour in 1832 according to parish and social stratum.[24] They make it clear that the bulk of strong Radical supporters were artisans—many perhaps in a small way of business—and tradesmen, and that Roebuck had least support in the wealthy suburban parishes of Bathwick and Walcot (the home of the gentry) and in the central parish of St Michael, which embraced many of the better-class shopping and trading areas. It is also clear that he had most support in the suburban industrial parish of Lyncombe and Widcombe, in the central parish of St Peter and Paul, but above all in the central artisan populated parish of St James, where he gained 45 per cent of all votes cast, coming top of the poll with the support of 203 out of 302 voters.

This numerical approach, which could be extended to show a breakdown of voting in all six parishes and for all three candidates, and to demonstrate how the election of councillors in 1835 reflected the distribution of Radical votes as in the general election, does not mean that the men who voted were faceless. This much has already been demonstrated.

Yet the problem remains, why did they vote the way they did? My answer—ignoring aspects of personal psychology which can never be known for more than a handful of men—is that Roebuck offered something to everyone outside the established ruling classes who possessed a measure of independence, integrity, ability and self-esteem and who felt his identity as a man denied by the city's social and political exclusiveness.

To the Political Union, the artisans and the Liberal press he offered short Parliaments, an extended suffrage and the ballot. To Dissenters he held out the promise of the abolition of slavery, and religious liberty. To the mass of enfranchised parishioners he offered the

TABLE 2   *Percentage of voters on the roll, according to parish, voting for J. A. Roebuck in 1832*

Parish	Bathwick	St Michael	Walcot	St Peter & St Paul	Lyncombe & Widcombe	St James
%	30	31	37	51	51	67

Source: *Poll Book 1832*

TABLE 3   *Number of plumpers in the parishes of Bathwick and St James in 1832 according to social stratum*

Parish	Artisans	Trades-men	Publicans and lodging-house keepers	Middle stratum	No title	Not recorded (possibly journey-men)
Bathwick (plumping Roebuck)	7	7	5	3	2	14
(plumping Hobhouse)	0	1	0	30	0	5
St James (plumping Roebuck)	19	17	10	3	4	32
(plumping Hobhouse)	0	2	0	1	2	0

Source: *Poll Book 1832*

repeal of the assessed taxes; and to all tax-payers a reduction in government expenditure. To the small trader and enterprising businessman he promised to restrict the power of monopolies. To frustrated freemen he offered a share in the offices and spoils of local government.

Everything Roebuck proposed was designed to further the cause of the individual against the authority of the state and the presumptuous power of persons, and to remove all vestiges of privilege and corruption. An extended suffrage and the ballot would emphasize the worth of individuals and protect them from intimidation. Cheap justice would ensure equality before the law. A system of national and secular education would produce a discerning and sceptical public, eliminate privilege and reduce the power of established religion. All his other proposals were attacks on existing positions and interests. Presented, as his programme was, in a city whose social strata included large and permanent bodies of artisans and petit bourgeois, both vitally important for the functioning of its economy yet denied political and social equality with their aristocratic and wealthy patrons, it gained a ready acceptance. Never was a candidate more suited to the economic and social structure of his electoral district than Roebuck was to Bath. He was its very mirror. These petty producers, active in vestries and ward committees, and these property-owning artisans, effectively organized in politically conscious unions, gave Roebuck and the Radical cause massive support. In October 1831 the grand demonstration of 22,000 vigorous pleaders for reform was attended by contingents from nine trades unions headed by the printers distributing pamphlets, straight from the press, declaring: [25]

> Hail to the Press ! to thee we Britons owe
> All we believe, and almost all we know;
> Resistless pleader of the People's Cause,
> Strong Guardian of our liberty and laws !
> Knowledge and truth by thee the Million gain,
> And Lords shall strive to make thee slaves in vain.

Later, in the election of 1841, the Engineers' and Ironfounders' Union, representing some of the several hundred men employed in these industries, displayed its banner and its loyalties. In the centre of the banner was a roe-buck between a railway engine and a tender with the inscription 'Stop it who can'.[26] For as long as the city's economy was able to provide opportunities for petty producers to become small capitalists, and to provide employment for hundreds of artisans, Roebuck was to remain one of the Parliamentary representatives for the city and Radicalism remained strong. Thus Roebuck's adaptation of Philosophic Radicalism to practical politics at constituency level resulted in a set of proposals for reform which appealed above all to the dynamic and progressive sections of local society—the middling class. On the other hand those members of the 'gentry' living in genteel poverty in the city centre were more inclined to tremble behind locked doors and to fear Roebuck and his fellow Jacobins,[27] while the 'gentry' of the wealthy suburban parishes, whether Tory or Whig, preferred a mixture of Hobhouse and Palmer with their emphasis on restraint and inaction. As one of Roebuck's supporters put it in 1837, 'Poor Bruges [the Tory candidate] and his friends must cry their eyes out at the reception that Mr. Roebuck meets with in the House of Commons. *The judgment of the people respecting him has turned out to be much more correct than that formed by the gentry.*'[28]

The rest of this paper traces the relationship between local Radicals and Chartists, in an attempt to comprehend the clash of ideology and the growth and role of an indigenous working class.

When the People's Charter was first presented to the citizens of Bath in October 1837 the city's Radicals had accumulated twenty-five years of political experience. This had been gained in political demonstration in support of reform, in activity in parish vestries and in ward organization. Their leading members had experience in intricate dealings with the Liberals, the Political Union, the trades unions; and they had built up an organization with sufficient popular support to win two general elections since 1832, and to gain control of the city council since 1835. They had also built up a network of connections with Radical groups in the surrounding counties and with the London Political Union. Through the pen of H. S. Chapman and the person of J. A. Roebuck they were known for their Radicalism throughout the Radical world, in England and Canada. It is true that these same Radicals had lost the recent 'Drunken Election', and failed to control the breakaway Working Men's Association. Even so they had a range of political experience and expertise beyond anything that the Chartists could have achieved in the first few months of their life as an independent political movement. And the main concern of the Radicals in the autumn of 1837 was to use this experience to heal the breach between themselves and the Liberals which had let in the Tories earlier in the year. Consequently the only Radicals who took time to concern themselves with the Chartists were James Crisp and Prowting Roberts. Roebuck, Napier and the rest held aloof, wary lest the Radical cause lose its clarity of purpose—to wrest power from the privileged and to establish a democratic government representative of the petit bourgeois and artisans—by becoming confused with a variety of programmes of social reform which, it was anticipated, would be implemented by violent means.[29]

On 18 December 1837, Radicals and Liberals, accompanied by

some Chartists, met to settle their differences.[30] Resolutions asking for the ballot and shorter Parliaments were passed without opposition, but a previously agreed compromise resolution, calling for an 'extension of the suffrage' instead of for the 'universal suffrage', which the Radicals wanted but had been prepared to forego in order to hold the meeting, was altered by a Radical amendment to 'universal suffrage'. The amended resolution was then passed with only token opposition. Leading Liberals, however, incensed at being outwitted by the Radicals, were afterwards reported to have declined to sign the joint petition.[31] As for the Chartists, with the exception of the old Radical Crisp and Bolwell, who spoke on a matter of procedure, none spoke at this meeting, and it is clear that the initiative still rested with the Radicals.

In succeeding months, as nationally the mood of sections of the working classes moved in support of the Charter, this local initiative too began to pass to the Chartists. As it did so, leaders of the movement spoke long and eloquently in their endeavours to stir the unenfranchised poor of the city to action. Vincent appealed for 'every village to send forth its Wat Tyler and every city its William Tell', and Roberts advocated the use of physical force.[32] Subsequently, during the next few months, there were sporadic outbreaks of violence. In March and April 1839, violence broke out in Devizes; in February, Trowbridge Chartists were armed with pikes; in March, there was serious rioting in Radstock; in April, an armed mob prevented the recapture of women escaped from Avoncliffe workhouse; and, in April and May, armed Chartists from Twerton and Bath paraded through Weston village until dispersed by the military.[33] But all this was a mere overture to the outbreak that was anticipated on Whit Monday in Bath when the Radical power of the West of England was expected to assemble so that, 'The whole country for 20 miles round the place will teem with myriads of ardent souls determined to strike a last blow for home, for freedom and for happiness.'[34]

As the heady excitement of this infant political movement grew, Radicals became increasingly cautious. The *Bath and Cheltenham Gazette* withdrew its support for universal suffrage; Napier repeated Roebuck's advice to the Chartists not to mix up social with political reforms; Kissock, an active Chartist, was decisively beaten in a contest for an aldermanic seat in the Radical parish of St James; the Radical council refused to hire a room in the Guildhall to the WMA,

and the only Bath Chartists proselytizing the surrounding industrial areas, with the exception of Roberts, were members of the
working classes.

After the final fiasco of the expected grand demonstration on Whit
Monday and subsequent arrests had revealed the strength of reaction
as well as the Chartist failure to mobilize support, the Chartists
found themselves entirely deserted by the middle classes and by
Radicals.[35] 'Has the spirit of Radicalism departed from the middle
classes [of Bath]?' demanded the *Western Vindicator*. 'Where are
those reformers among them, that at one time agitated this city
with Mr. Roebuck? Have they abandoned their long cherished principles, and gone over to the enemy? Or are they ashamed to mingle
with those who are now local agitators?'[36] Roebuck's own answer
to these rhetorical questions is expressed in a letter to Crisp. 'The
Chartists have as usual wanted prudence,' he said. But he hoped
that the arrests of Vincent and Roberts 'will frighten them, and
perhaps render them a little more prudent. If our plans here succeed
all prosecution of them will I hope cease. But they must not talk
nonsense.'[37] Thus it would seem that in spite of all their errors, Roebuck was still prepared to act with and for the Chartists—but not
on any terms.

For the moment, however, the Chartists were more confused than
ever. The loss of leaders through imprisonment, coupled with confusion about method and organization, reduced the Chartists to a
body without a head. The *Western Vindicator* urged the need to
organize but failed to make clear how and for what purpose. The
rank and file, meeting at the end of 1839 to decide what action to
take after the failure of the attack on Newport, still seemed to favour
militant action. This, their arrested spokesmen said, they had tried
to hold in check. The *Western Vindicator* and the organized trades
unions, too, argued against physical force and in favour of co-operation with the middle classes. Vincent confused matters still more by
appearing to speak with two voices. With the voice of a Dissenting
minister he offered his listeners their rewards in the Kingdom of
Heaven, with the voice of an imprisoned conspirator he seemed to
suggest that the road to salvation lay through a reign of terror.[38]
But to all except the most militant and the rank and file it grew
increasingly clear that physical force had failed locally and that the
real choice, throughout 1840 and 1841, had to be made from other
policies.

The choice was threefold. First, the Chartists could remain a separate and exclusive working-class organization using constitutional means to gain the points in the Charter. This was the position eventually adopted by George Bartlett and Thomas Bolwell. Second, they could attempt a *rapprochement* with the Radicals and through them with some of the more liberal members of the middle classes. This was the position accepted by Vincent when he left the city in 1841 to contest Banbury in the general election, and later when he hived off to form the Bath branch of the Complete Suffrage Association with the Rev. Thomas Spencer in 1842. It was the view of Roberts and Philp also. Third, they could eschew political action in favour of something like the socialism and direct action which had been advocated by Owenite Missionaries throughout 1839. The realistic choice in Bath with its literate, Radical artisans and its socially and politically frustrated petit bourgeois organized in support of the Radicalism of J. A. Roebuck, was a temporary alliance with the Radicals.

Eventually the Chartists led by Vincent chose realism. In June 1841, they responded to Roebuck's appeal 'to know nothing of one party or the other; Whigs, or Liberals, or Radicals, or Chartists. Union must be the watchword, or we shall never succeed.'[39] Known Chartists voted for Roebuck while Vincent left the city to contest Banbury. Throughout the country the swing of votes favoured the Tories who were returned with a majority of eighty. In Bath, however, as a result of the union of Liberals, Radicals and Chartists, the two sitting Tories were defeated by Duncan and Roebuck. In fact, Roebuck received the biggest vote he ever gained in the city and his poll of 1,151 votes gave him a majority of 227 over his nearest Tory rival.

Inspired by the election success, a series of meetings was begun in a determined attempt to consolidate Chartist, Radical and Liberal co-operation. The series culminated in the joint Chartist and Anti-Corn Law League demonstration of December 1841 at which old Radicals, new Repealers and Chartists appealed for the repeal of the Corn Laws and a full and fair representation of the people.

The Chartists, however, created uncertainty about the extent of their commitment to the alliance. Roberts attacked the liberal middle classes, and Vincent declared, 'If Sir Robert Peel refused to give the people their rights, the axe of democratic freedom would be laid at the root of the tree, and it would be dashed into a thousand atoms.'[40]

E

Confusion grew after O'Connor—who first welcomed the joint demonstration and petition to the extent of designating Vincent the Benjamin Franklin of the cause for having brought it about— attacked the desirability of Chartist co-operation with Radicals and Liberals.[41] So when the Sturge Declaration came to Bath, the Chartist leadership split into a Sturgeite majority and an O'Connorite minority.[42] Finally, in 1842 Vincent left the movement to join Thomas Spencer and to transfer his energies to the Temperance Movement. Thus the Chartists were reduced to an O'Connorite core, withdrawn from active politics and from co-operation with the Radical movement until 1847.

During the decade of the demise of Chartism, from 1841 to 1851, the city's economy, now more geared to the needs of residents than to those of visitors, continued to stagnate. There was some new building in the city but none of the quality and scale which had been the mark of building in Bath for the previous hundred years. There was, however, an increase in the proportion of women to men, particularly in the twenty to thirty age group, and, as the economic conditions, which had produced the artisans and a dynamic and enterprising petit bourgeoisie, began to disappear, the number of women increased by 1,600 and the number of adult males declined by 588.[43]

At the general election in 1847, a revived Tory organization, encouraged by growing success in local elections, by the movement of leading Whigs into the Tory fold, and by the growing opposition of Dissenters to Roebuck, sought a suitable candidate to put up against him. The man they chose was Lord Ashley. He was to be presented to the population, by working men from the north, as a practical reformer and generous worker on behalf of the working class—a kind of benevolent despot who placed welfare and a religious education above the specious claims of those 'who have everlastingly the expressions of political liberty on their lips'.[44] To make their claim to working-class support authentic the Tories approached Thomas Bolwell, as the leading Chartist, and requested him to chair the inaugural meeting of Ashley's campaign.

Bolwell saw the danger of Ashleyism—the danger of concessionary reforms without any change in the distribution of power—and called the Chartists together. At their meeting the Chartists agreed with Bolwell that 'Mr. Roebuck had gone beyond Lord Ashley in what he had done, for he had laid the foundation of a system which would give the franchise to all mankind; and placed in comparison with Mr. Roebuck, Lord Ashley sank into comparative nothingness'.[45] Consequently they agreed to form a committee of active working men to secure Roebuck's election, and once more gave their full support for a Radical transfer of power. They did so to no avail, for by now Roebuck was decidedly unpopular with middle-class Liberals and with Dissenters; Whigs were discovering that they were really Tories, Roebuck wanted justice in place of coercion for Ireland, and the social and economic structure of Bath was changing. Moreover, Chartist militancy had confirmed middle-class suspicions of and doubts about Radicalism. Thus merely liberal Radicals wavered in their support to the extent that an effective electoral alliance between artisans, petit bourgeois and the liberal middle classes became politically unreal. Even so the election was close run. Although Roebuck retained the support of 1,093 of the electorate he was defeated by 185 votes and he left Bath a very bitter and disappointed man. Subsequently the Tory/Whig alliance, which returned Ashley to the House of Commons, produced an agreement not to contest local elections and to share the offices of local government as if the events of 1832 and 1835 had never taken place.[46]

Thus Radicals, secure in artisan and petit bourgeois support, dominated local political life from 1830 to 1847. Their strength was such that the Tories could have hoped for political power only if they were supported by, or themselves supported, the moderate Whigs who, although resentful of the privileges enjoyed by the aristocracy and the city oligarchy, feared the levelling tendencies of the city's middling class and of the working classes even more. This had meant that for over fifteen years the Tories could have achieved electoral victory only if some marginal supporters of Roebuck could have been split from the Radicals. It was this that happened in 1847.

Chartism, too, which made an early appearance in the city, was itself attracted by the possibility of attaching many Radicals to the Chartist movement. An alliance of this kind could only have been temporary—as a means to achieve power—since, however confused the Chartists were, many of them were beginning to realize that political power of itself was not enough and that it must be aimed at achieving some centrally controlled policies serving working-class interests, whereas Roebuck's Radicalism was essentially anarchic. Consequently the alliance, as many Radicals feared, was the worst that could have happened to them for within five years the Radical

Charter became the People's Charter advocated by young working-class men, who, although politically inexperienced and inclined, in the first instance, to substitute words for organization, were justly incensed about social and economic degradation and advocated practical policies which caused mere Liberals to withdraw their support from the Radicals. As opinion polarized, the Radicals found themselves increasingly isolated from the left and the right. From the right because of the threat they represented to established social and political authority; from the left because of their emphasis on an anarchic individualism which was more suitable to the interests of tradesmen and petty producers than to the mass of journeymen and factory operatives. However, for as long as the Charter could be seen as a programme of action for those who were 'against' established authority and in favour of freedom and a share in authority for all, then a middling class, drawn from the middle range of social strata and united by the opposition of its members to authority, was a real force in Bath politics.

Thus Radicalism and, to a lesser extent, its Chartist derivative, was not necessarily or exclusively the result of changes associated with factoryization, the business depression of the late 1830s or economic collapse. The reverse is more nearly the case. Radicalism of the Roebuck kind was the ideology of the buoyant expectancy and individualism associated with a diversified economy of small producers. These men, their economic and social mobility and political aspirations curtailed by aristocratic privilege, appealed to the progressive ideologies of reason and utility to advance their cause. In Bath they made good their claim: 'If only fifty cities and boroughs in the Empire', wrote H. S. Chapman, had 'exhibited the same wholesome state of opinion as the City of Bath, the People of England would no longer have [had] to complain of bad government. The result would [have been]—not a feeble, but a strong minority representing the people.'[47]

Yet the problem was that by the late 1830s there were not fifty cities in the Empire with a socio-economic structure similar to that of Bath. Economic development was already moving towards concentration and centralization, and the conditions giving rise to the growth of independent artisans and petty producers declined. In their stead appeared a factory proletariat whose problems were not those of independent artisans and producers struggling for recognition. In this lay the dilemma of the Bath Chartists and an explanation of the extinction of the old Radicals, for, while the problems of an industrial society, which increasingly necessitated state interference and regulation, might have been more rapidly and effectively resolved by a democratic and Radically reformed system of government, there was, within Radicalism, that strain of social anarchism which acted against the formulation of policies of positive intervention. Thus, while Chartist co-operation with Radicals for the purpose of achieving power was probably tactically correct in the local situation, it is more difficult to decide, without the aid of hindsight, whether they were wise to refrain from total commitment to middling-class politics or, indeed, whether it was ever possible for them to have acted in any other way than they did. One thing, however, is certain. After 1847 middling-class politics in Bath ceased to be of importance in national politics. While this probably had more to do with developments at the national rather than the local level, the fact remains that the Chartists through their acts of commission and omission have to bear some responsibility for the defeat of Roebuck and his disappearance as a charismatic leader of the local middling class and the effect this had in accelerating the decline of that class.

conflict and the poll books in
...an England

The starting-point for this essay is J. R. Vincent's *Pollbooks: How Victorians Voted*[1]—an important contribution to our understanding of the role of class in nineteenth-century history, which appeared too late for me to discuss at any length in chapter 1. The essay itself is a postscript to the one on Bath. A postscript suggested by Vincent's book. In some ways Mr Vincent's argument is similar to my own. He also uses evidence from the poll books to support his contention about the nature of political conflict in the first half of the century. My main disagreement with his analysis stems from the use he makes of the occupational lists of voters he has abstracted from them.

As I understand it, the socio-economic basis of Vincent's argument is as follows:[2]

> As a working hypothesis which at least fits a number of phenomena which would otherwise be puzzling, it may therefore be suggested that while the Industrial Revolution produced some proletarians in some factory districts, over the country in general the economic growth with which it was associated worked for quite a long time in favour of a wider distribution of small property and a diminution of the relative power of large property.

But Vincent does not stop here. He goes on to argue that the poll books show that voting was not determined by economic class in a Marxist sense or by social stratification along a spectrum running from rich to poor. Instead he considers that[3]

> The essential division was between distributed property (mainly urban) and concentrated property (mainly rural), between capitalist agriculture and distributist urban petty production and exchange, between an urban 'free peasantry' and the great capitalists who ruled the only real Marxian proletariat that England had, the labourers in husbandry.

This conclusion about the economic determinant of political behaviour does not follow logically from the initial hypothesis about the spread of petty production in the early years of industrialization in England. There is no *a priori* reason why a wider distribution of property among a set of petty producers should lead to a decline in the significance of economic class in a Marxist sense or of social stratification in influencing political behaviour. One would expect a wide distribution of property ownership in a newly developing economy to complicate the political relationships between social classes and social strata rather than to eliminate them.

Vincent's conclusion seems to be greatly influenced by his simplified and misconceived version of Dahrendorf's model of class conflict. However, it should be clear by now that Dahrendorf's model is a complex development of the Marxist model and not merely a rejection of it. On the other hand, Vincent's model is much less sophisticated than the Marxist one and is two steps backwards from Dahrendorf. Let me briefly re-state the essence of Dahrendorf's theory in order to try to clarify the theoretical differences between the Vincent and Neale models.

According to my understanding of Dahrendorf, the crucial characteristic of classes is that they are conflict groups arising out of the authority structure of imperatively co-ordinated associations. Dahrendorf also shows how conflict arises or is muted as a result of a complex of authority/subjection relationships in a wide range of associations in political, economic and social life. He also shows how Marxist class conflict is an example of superimposition of conflict; a case in which authority/subjection relationships between individuals are much the same over a range of associations and are dominated by the authority/subjection relationships arising from the economic relationships which characterized industrialization in western Europe in the mid-nineteenth century, namely the relationships between capital and labour in industrial enterprises. All that Vincent does is to substitute political conflict between two classes, the membership of which is determined by the ownership of different types of property, for the Marxist conflict between two classes, one property-owning, the other property-less. In Vincent's model the two classes contend with each other over the structure of political authority in much the same way as they do in the Marxist model and no other classes or strata are involved. In both cases the authority structure appears exclusively as a function of property relations, whereas the authority structure of associations which is at the root of class conflict in Dahrendorf's theory, and which I attempt to incorporate into my own model, is not necessarily or exclusively a derivative of property relations. There is the further point that what for Dahrendorf would be a quasi-group is for Vincent a class, yet it is difficult to see how a quasi-group which lacks cohesion—'Nothing keeps people apart like small property,' writes Vincent—can generate a conflict group which can properly be called a class, and Vincent has nothing to say about the generation of social class consciousness in these circumstances. The theoretical structure of Vincent's model is weak, it is certainly not that of Dahrendorf, while his determinant of conflict is closer to that of Marx than to Dahrendorf's.

Whether, in analysing the process of change in the early nineteenth century, one chooses to work with any one of the Marxist, Dahrendorf, Vincent or Neale models should depend on the test of empirical verification. It is in this connection that Vincent uses the poll books. However, since the poll books contain no record of the political behaviour of the unenfranchised, the absence of class conflict of a Marxist kind in early nineteenth-century England cannot be demonstrated by an analysis of them. (They might with care throw some light on the relationships between aristocratic, bourgeois and other candidates and their supporters.) On the other hand if one *can* find in the poll books support for the view that class relationships of a Marxist kind, as well as antagonistic relationships between rich and poor, were at work in influencing the political behaviour even of that very select group possessing the franchise, then Vincent's simplification must be regarded with considerable scepticism.

The empirical basis for Vincent's model is derived from an occupational analysis of voters. He finds that in general the votes of urban dwellers, whether tailors, merchants or gentlemen, were distributed among candidates and parties in such a way as to show that there was no class basis for voting behaviour. *To arrive at this conclusion Vincent has to equate occupation, which is a stratum, with social class and insist on the homogeneity of the occupational groups he uses.* Conversely he emphasizes the unimportance of income, wealth and differences in property relations as divisive factors *within* occupations, and denies that any one or all of these factors provided the starting-point for the emergence of social classes as conflict groups *within* those occupational groupings based on poll-book classifications. It is true that Vincent explicitly denies that he is making any assumption about homogeneity. Nevertheless he states with great conviction that, 'Though their fortunes might vary considerably upward or downward, *all* shoemakers shared in a body of social opinion about what kind of people shoemakers were, *which in turn derived from an objective economic homogeneity natural to skilled small producers competing in a free market*.'[4] And it is suggested in much of the text that through the use of his 'imaginative understanding' he chooses to regard occupations as homogeneous and regards occupational groups as classes. Throughout the book Vincent writes about occupational groups as entities and on one occasion asserts: [5]

> No group was linked by the cash nexus, or by the relations arising from production, except in a tenuous and indefinite way. . . . *The characteristic relation was that of vendor and customer, not employer and employee.* Conflict might emerge instantaneously, over a particular transaction, or reflectively, over jealousy of inequality, but not automatically and constantly, through the antagonism of differing groups competing for the rewards of the general flow of production in which they participated.

It is quite clear that in Vincent's model occupations are *not* divided along class lines however class might be defined, i.e. whether defined as a stratum, as a product of property relations, or as a product of authority structure. It should be apparent to any critical reader that the whole of Vincent's analysis hinges on his identification of social stratum with social class and on the assumption of occupational homogeneity.

This assumption about occupational homogeneity is questionable. Take the evidence in Vincent's own chapter on 'The Distribution of Capital at Death'. In it there is a table which Vincent uses to show that, 'The big shops apart, the shopkeepers were not on the whole much better off than the skilled workers'.[6] Table 4 which follows is adapted from it.

Table 4 shows that even in rural Cambridgeshire there was considerable differentiation within the ranks of skilled workers and shopkeepers as well as between shopkeepers and skilled workers.

TABLE 4   *Distribution of capital at death, Cambridgeshire 1848–57*

	Shopkeepers (%)	Skilled workers (%)
Under £20	1·6	19·3
£21–50	10·3	17·2
£51–200	34·9	40·0
£201–450	17·4	15·1
£451–600		
£601–1,500	19·8	5·5
£1,501–8,000	15·8	
£1,501–3,000		2·7
	99·8	99·8

Over one-third of skilled workers left wealth equal to less than one year's income, i.e. less than £50 (I wonder how much was in tools and furniture), while only 2·7 per cent left between £1,500 and £3,000, a capital stock which places them in the category of employers of substantial amounts of labour. Among shopkeepers the distribution was skewed in the opposite direction. Over one-third left more than £600 while nearly 16 per cent left over £1,500. When one bears in mind that charitable societies were able to set up men and women as shopkeepers and petty producers with capital loans averaging three guineas then any shopkeeper or petty producer with wealth in the range £1,500 to £8,000 was well set up indeed and in a stratum quite apart from the generality of skilled workers, shopkeepers and shopworkers.[7] Furthermore, a shopkeeper who left wealth of £5,000 at death left 250 times as much as one-fifth of skilled workmen and between 25 and 100 times as much as a man leaving a sum close to the modal amount. A skilled workman who left £3,000 left between 60 and 150 times as much as skilled workmen in the lowest stratum. These differences in wealth from 1848 to 1857 *within* occupational groups are of the same order of magnitude as those for the whole population in 1936. In the later period the 1 per cent of the population who were very rich owned 55·7 per cent of the national wealth. They possessed capital of more than £10,000 which was 100 times higher than the upper limit of £100 for the modal group owning 4·2 per cent of the national wealth.[8] I am inclined to think that differences of this order over the community as a whole are not only economically but also socially and politically significant. I hold to this view more strongly when the differences exist *within* occupations and regions. The political implications of such a stratification ought not to be dismissed out of hand.

Furthermore, Vincent's belief, that it is sufficient for his purpose of identifying political interest only to distinguish between very great landed wealth and the rest, ignores the fact that the economic and social horizons of the majority of people were and are restricted. Labourers, shoemakers and others occupying the lowest social strata in their day-to-day activities, did not generally aspire to £10,000 a year, a houseful of servants and a place at court, and one suspects that few of them were ever in conflict with the whole system of privilege and class.[9] On the other hand they could and did compare themselves with other workers employed in similar occupations, with their employers and with other groups close to themselves. A man on £30 a year might have dreamt occasionally of £10,000 and might have felt a diffused rage against those who possessed what he lacked, but he was more likely to think he had a right to £50 as earned by a workmate and to envy the £150 earned by his employer whose advantage was determined by the capital he possessed and the power he exercised over his workers, and to resent that power. In short, conflict as well as harmony *within* society are as likely to be generated by immediate experience in imperatively co-ordinated associations like industrial enterprises as by distant aspirations, and it is between social strata in close contact but divided by the authority/subjection barrier that conflict is likely to be most intense.[10] In which case it becomes important to distinguish more than two broad strata in the distribution of wealth and property and to explore in some detail differences *within* occupations.

In fact there were two occupations, both instanced by Vincent as good examples of occupational homogeneity, in which differentiation according to source and size of income and power was so marked as to generate constantly recurring conflict not only at local but at national level. These were shoemaking and tailoring, and for a time at least shoemakers looked like an embryonic nucleus of organized labour preparing for sustained conflict with capitalists.[11]

Vincent's notion that there was an 'objective economic homogeneity' among shoemakers depends on the proposition that shoemakers were all independent producers and were, like tailors and other craftsmen, members of an urban 'free peasantry'. The way to decide whether this notion is valid is not to take a mere passing glance but to use a microscope. Therefore I propose to go into a little detail about one of the constituencies, the city of Bath, for which Vincent tabulates voting figures for the election of 1847. These figures are arranged to show that shoemakers, who are assumed to be members of a homogeneous occupation, expressed no significant preference for the Radical Roebuck as against the Tory Ashley. The conclusion we are expected to draw is that the political decisions of shoemakers cannot be explained by reference to social stratification or different positions of authority and subjection *within* the shoemaking industry.

A look at the industrial structure of Bath shows clearly that shoemakers were not objectively economically homogeneous, nor did they all exercise the same degree of authority.[12] In 1831 the city contained 529 shoemakers, and in 1851, 747 male shoemakers, 133 female shoemakers and 308 'shoemakers' wives', a total of 1,225 persons engaged in shoemaking at mid-century. Some of these were independent producers, but in 1831 the majority worked for some ten or a dozen master shoemakers with establishments employing between thirty and sixty workers. A Union of Cordwainers existed as early as 1803 and there were strikes, some of which were well organized, in 1804, 1805, 1808, 1813 and 1824. In 1803 and 1804 the local society worked in conjunction with a national body with headquarters in London, and proposed to withdraw all labour from the city in order to compel employers to increase wages and restrict the number of apprentices. The local society of cordwainers remained in existence for the next forty years; and two years before the 1847 election, for which we are asked to adopt the notion that shoemakers were a homogeneous class of petty producers, a master shoemaker was reported to have said 'that for the last few months he had been obliged to submit to the exactions of a society of shoemakers who took advantage of the plentiful supply of work to charge exorbitantly for it'.[13] Thus it is difficult to avoid the conclusion that shoemakers were a militant and well-organized group of workers employed by and negotiating with relatively few employers with whom they *were* in continuous competition for 'the rewards of the general flow of production in which they participated'. What is more this competition, which gave rise to industrial conflict *within* the shoemaking industry, was also reflected in the way shoemakers voted in the 1847 election. Of the 108 shoemakers who recorded a vote 68 (63 per cent) voted for Roebuck and 38 (35 per cent) voted for Ashley. Clearly shoemakers showed strong overall support, almost two to one, for Roebuck and the Radical cause. (In St James the ratio was 5:2.) Moreover, when the voting figures for the parishes of Walcot and St James are analysed according to contemporary estimates of gross rental for the houses and property which entitled voters to the franchise, it becomes clear that the bulk of Roebuck's shoemaker supporters occupied houses with a gross rental of less than £19 per annum and were barely qualified to vote, whereas nearly half of Ashley's shoemaker supporters occupied houses having a gross rental of over £30 per annum. Indeed, Ashley's shoemaker supporters included two men with property valued at £91 and £141 per annum. The distribution of voters according to gross rental is set out in Table 5.

These figures suggest that Ashley's supporters included all the wealthiest shoemakers in the city—men who were master shoemakers and employers of labour—as well as those most likely to be self-employed in the largely conservative parish of Walcot which was a large and relatively wealthy parish. Other Ashley supporters among shoemakers probably included those persuaded by the Whig/

TABLE 5   *Votes of shoemakers in the parishes of Walcot and St James in 1847 according to estimated gross rental of houses and property*

Estimated gross rental (£ p.a.)	Roebuck		Ashley	
	Walcot	St James	Walcot	St James
10–19	18	1	3	1
20–29	7	5	8	
30–39	1	4	3	1
40–49			2	2
50–59	1		1	
60–89				
Over 90			2	
Total	27	10	19	4

Sources: *Bath Poll Book 1847*
Highway Rate Book, Walcot 1847
Poor Rate Book, St James 1839

Tory alliance, which promoted Ashley's nomination, that Ashleyism
—a ten-hour day backed by a modicum of welfare legislation—was
a better bet than Roebuck's demand for a wholesale transfer of
political power. A few of the others may have been Dissenters
upset by Roebuck's support for the Maynooth grant and an Irish
Poor Law, and his opposition to Sabbatarianism and sectarian
control of education.

The shoemakers who voted for Roebuck mainly consisted of those
who barely qualified for the franchise; they were probably journeymen, and those most likely to be independent producers living in
houses with gross rentals of between £20 and £39 per annum in
strongly Radical parishes like St James. Roebuck also had the
support of Chartist shoemakers with a proletarian social class
consciousness like Thomas Bolwell who had decided to sink their
differences with middling-class Radicals in a last desperate attempt
to wrest power from the hands of the upper and middle classes. In
short there is enough evidence to suggest that class relationships
of a Marxist kind were among those factors influencing the political
behaviour of shoemakers as measured by the exercise of the
franchise. However, most shoemakers did not have a franchise to
exercise—only 16 per cent of them are listed in the poll books. The
poll books, therefore, can tell us nothing about their social class
consciousness nor their activities, if any, as a political class.

There is also sufficient evidence relating to tailoring, hatting,
coachmaking and brassfounding to suggest that in all these trades
in the city of Bath there existed a workshop or manufacturing
organization in which the unit of production employed anything
between 20 and 130 workers. In addition there were manufactories
in wool, iron, glass and soap using water or steam power and
employing labour on a scale sufficient to cast doubt on the univer-
sality of an urban 'free peasantry'.

The largest single group of workers most nearly corresponding
to Vincent's concept of an urban 'free peasantry' was that made up
of workers in the building trades. Even so, during periods of high
unemployment, members of this group had a good chance of joining
the urban proletariat of non-agricultural labourers who made up
24 per cent of the city's workforce. Their voting behaviour in 1841
shows that, builders and plumbers excepted, men in the building
industry showed a high preference for Roebuck and the Radical
cause. The proportion in each trade voting Radical was as follows:

Percentage voting Radical
(number in category in brackets)

Plasterers	75 (24)
Carpenters	69 (62)
Labourers	67 (37)
Masons	66 (37)
Architects	66 (6)
Painters	64 (31)
Plumbers	46 (13)
Builders	41 (12)

The record not only shows the Radical preferences of shoemakers and building workers in the elections of 1847 and 1841 respectively, it also shows something of the relationships between property values, the whole urban ecology and political behaviour.[14] An analysis of the votes of more than one thousand plumpers in the 1841 election in the parishes of Walcot and St James shows beyond doubt that stratification based on property rentals and the type of community in which men lived were important factors in shaping voting behaviour. The results of this analysis are summarized in Tables 6 and 7.

In the compact central parish of St James, largely populated by independent artisans and tradesmen, nearly four voters out of five were Radicals—as was the case from 1832 to 1847. Of those who plumped for the Radical cause 92 per cent were occupiers of property with gross rentals of less than £60 per annum—75 per cent with gross rentals of less than £40 per annum—and only one in five voters occupying property so valued was prepared to plump for the Tory candidates. The Tory minority on the other hand drew nearly 21 per cent of its vote from men occupying property with gross rentals of more than £60 per annum, in which strata Tory plumpers almost matched the number of Radical plumpers. Even so the pressures to conform to the prevailing Radical ethos in the parish must have been great and committed Tories were not easy to find.

The parish of Walcot was a much larger, richer, dispersed and consequently a much less homogeneous parish than St James. Its inhabitants also showed a very different pattern of voting. Firstly there were slightly more Tory than Radical plumpers. Of these, 37 per cent compared with 21 per cent in St James occupied houses with rentals of more than £60 per annum. Indeed, in every stratum occupying houses with rentals of more than £40 per annum there were more Tory than Radical voters; in all, 107 Radicals as against

TABLE 6 *Estimated gross rental of houses occupied by plumpers in the parish of Walcot in the Bath election 1841*

£ p.a.	Radical		Tory	
	no.	%	no.	%
10–19	162	35·5	81	18·1
20–29	90	19·7	45	10·0
30–39	96	21·0	71	15·9
40–49	45	9·9	47	10·5
50–59	16	3·5	35	7·9
60–69	11	2·4	20	4·4
70–79	4	0·9	36	8·0
80–89	6	1·3	25	5·6
90–99	4	0·9	20	4·4
Over 100	21	4·6	67	14·9
Total	455		447	
Total plumpers	488		490	

Sources: *Poll Book 1841*
Highway Rate Book, Walcot 1841

Notes

1 Plumpers are those voters who gave both votes to either the two Tory or the two Radical candidates. Radical plumpers also include four voters who voted only for Roebuck.

2 Voters not allocated to any category of gross rental are those rated on business premises only, i.e. stables, shops, public houses, warehouses, and those untraceable in the rate books.

3 When a voter was recorded as rated on two or more properties only the highest rated property was recorded.

4 When two or more voters were rated on the same property each was recorded at the full estimated gross rental.

5 An estimated gross rental of £10–19 placed the property in streets like Avon Street or Lower Camden Place. An estimated gross rental of over £100 placed the property in areas like St James Square, the Circus or the Royal Crescent.

250 Tories. In strata below £40 per annum there were 207 Tories but 348 Radicals. Thus 76 per cent of Radical plumpers but only 44 per cent of Tory plumpers occupied houses with rentals of less than £40 per annum. Perhaps the most striking thing about both sets of figures—those for Walcot and St James—is that whereas the Tory vote was widely distributed over all strata the Radical vote was concentrated; in both parishes Radical support scarcely extended above the three lowest strata, i.e. above the £40 limit, and almost

TABLE 7 *Estimated gross rental of property occupied by plumpers in the parish of St James in the Bath election 1841*

£ p.a.	Radical		Tory	
	no.	%	no.	%
10–19	43	23·5	9	17·0
20–29	50	27·3	9	17·0
30–39	44	24·0	9	17·0
40–49	13	7·1	10	18·9
50–59	18	9·9	5	9·4
60–69	4	2·2	4	7·5
70–79	5	2·7	1	1·9
80–89	3	1·6	1	1·9
90–99				
Over 100	3	1·6	5	9·4
Total	183		53	
Total plumpers	189		55	

Sources: *Poll Book 1841*
Poor Rate Book, St James 1839

Note

Voters not allocated are those untraceable in the rate books and two Tory voters from the Williams family who were rated on parts of the family brewery property which had a total gross rental of £474.

one out of three Radical plumpers barely qualified for the franchise. In Walcot, however, Radicals were more likely to be found among those who barely qualified for the franchise while in St James Radicals were more likely to occupy houses with slightly higher rentals. Among the very rich, i.e. those occupying houses with gross rentals of £100 per annum or more, houses in St James Square, the Circus and the Royal Crescent, only one in five was a Radical plumper. Thus stratification along a spectrum rich to poorer was undoubtedly an important factor influencing voting behaviour.

This evidence also suggests that to regard all the recipients of the franchise under the Reform Bill as 'middle class' is either to misread the record or to use the term so broadly as to strip it of meaning. In the first chapter I suggested that some understanding of the distance separating a man on £200 a year from one on £5,000 is best gained from reading works like encyclopaedias of domestic economy. I now add that a 'true' understanding of the gulf within the 'middle classes' and of their great diversity can best be got from looking at and in houses in the Royal Crescent valued at £150 to £200 a year and comparing them with houses in Lower Camden Place valued at £12 to £16 a year. It seems to me that the gulf separating the worlds of the occupants of the two categories of houses must have been virtually unbridgeable and that words cannot describe it.

What I have endeavoured to show is that there are good reasons for doubting whether totalling occupations as recorded raw in the poll books is an aid to the identification of political motivation or any help in establishing the existence of social classes as conflict groups. This is not to say that they cannot usefully be used in a more sophisticated fashion. What it does mean is that without more detailed analyses of the economic, social and authority structure of constituencies and a close acquaintance with the ins and outs of constituency politics, the poll-book figures ought not to be used by research workers on the assumption of occupational homogeneity. I also believe that they cannot be used to support the contention that social stratification and a growing proletarian social class consciousness were unimportant in shaping voting behaviour and influencing political action even among the select minority possessing the franchise. As I have shown, the city of Bath did contain social strata including working men who approximated to the Marxist working class but who had little choice but to support middling-class politics and politicians. The city was also the home of a Vincent-type urban 'free peasantry' and a middling class. However the source of their social class consciousness was not property as such but their relationships to authority in all its guises. In fact the city possessed such a complex economic, social and authority structure, as well as a complete range of early nineteenth-century ideologies, that no monistic explanation of the political behaviour of its citizens is likely to be adequate. I suspect that much the same might be said about most of the other constituencies listed in Vincent's book.

This chapter is a revised version of a paper read to a history seminar at Monash University, Melbourne, in April 1969.

H. S. Chapman, class consciousness and the 'Victorian' ballot

In chapter 1, I suggested that historians who see no use for theorizing of the kind attempted in that paper could find themselves committed to an approach to history based on the notion that biography is the essence of history.[1] I include this chapter to suggest that biographers are themselves rarely if ever free from some pre-existing conceptual framework which gives shape to their biographical end products, and to suggest that they and the historians who use their biographies are more the victims of such pre-existing conceptual frameworks when the latter are never made explicit. I also wish to show that it is possible to put a good deal of factual flesh on at least one little-known member of the middling class and to make greater sense of his life by employing the framework and concepts of the five-class model. At the same time this chapter will develop the theme of the interplay of middling-class men and ideas throughout the English-speaking world in the first fifty years of the nineteenth century. In this way it will serve as a case study of one of those executive councillors reduced to anonymity in the tables in chapter 5.

The accepted history of the adoption of the 'Victorian' or 'Australian ballot' as told by Professor Scott shows clearly the influence of the three-class model of social structure on the interpretation of what many historians would regard as objective data.[2] According to this conventional view the Victorian ballot legislation of 1856 was the result of the presence and influence of men with a working-class Chartist background gaining new political significance in a country and a social environment conducive to a proletarian social class consciousness. The argument here is similar to the argument concerning the relationship of a proletarian social class consciousness to the making of the Charter in England. Professor Scott, who first outlined what is now the accepted history of the 'Victorian ballot', also recognized that the man who did the work in drafting the ballot clauses, H. S. Chapman, was neither a Chartist nor a proletarian. According to almost any measure of social stratification in the mid-nineteenth century Chapman was upper middle class.[3] He was a successful lawyer earning some £5,000 annually. He lived in a large house in St Kilda. He was a member of the old Victorian Legislative Council and an ex-colonial judge and colonial secretary. It is almost axiomatic that such a man should have been opposed to the ballot or at best and for peculiar personal reasons indifferent. Professor Scott's interpretation of the evidence enabled him to side-step the problem of why Chapman was involved in the introduction of the ballot into Victoria, and the problem his involvement poses for the wider question of the relationship of social class to ideology and to the creation of political institutions. He attributed personal psychological motives to Chapman which cannot be found in the record. It was Scott's view that Chapman was politically unexciting and lacking in strong political convictions and concerned only to translate the intention of the majority in the Legislative Council into something workable in practice. He was simply a skilled and worthy lawyer who merited commendation for his strong sense of public duty.[4] This view was based on inferences drawn from two slender pieces of evidence culled from the official record, insufficient and inaccurate knowledge of Chapman's life and an inadequate analytical framework. Professor Scott's view has passed into history. In doing so it has helped to conceal from historians and students of history the widespread influence of quasi-groups and social classes other than the conventional middle and working classes in England and her colonies in the early nineteenth century.

A closer examination of Chapman's life, interpreted within the framework of the five-class model, should help to weaken the traditional interpretation and suggest fresh lines of inquiry in colonial as well as in English history. It will also rescue Chapman from oblivion.

Chapman's father was a minor government official employed in the Barrack Department. He lived in a yellow-brick terrace house in Kennington from whence he commuted daily to his office across the river. He had had some technical training in a Thames-side ship-yard, had experienced penury and unemployment, had married when he was thirty-two and, after the birth of his only son Henry Samuel in 1803 and during the period of war-time inflation never earned more than £300 a year. During the period of uncertainty caused by reductions in military expenditure at the end of the

Napoleonic Wars, Chapman senior feared for his job. Henry Samuel had to leave school at fifteen with only eight years of education to take up a position as a clerk in Esdaile's Bank at 28s. per week. Thereafter, from 1818 to 1841, Henry Samuel Chapman had a succession of jobs; clerk to a bill broker, commission agent in the Atlantic trade, journalist, correspondent for the Assembly of Lower Canada, book reviewer and pamphleteer, assistant commissioner on the enquiry into hand-loom weaving, and eventually at the age of thirty-nine he became a barrister. Even as a barrister in the early 1840s he rarely earned much more than £300, and for that reason never married until at thirty-nine he qualified for the Bar. He possessed no capital and owned no property.

The rest of his family were in no better state. His grandfather, once a prosperous merchant in the American trade, had been ruined by the Revolution. His uncle lived permanently in the East Indies alternating between periods of prosperity and depression and never making enough to afford a return to England. His two elderly maiden aunts lived in genteel poverty on the geographical and social fringes of society in Bath.

Thus by birth, occupation, income and social status as indicated by Webster's classification, Chapman was close to the very bottom of respectable society.[5] On £300 in 1841 he was in the social stratum which could afford only a maid of all work, and to achieve even that he worked himself to death, conscious all the time that prolonged illness could ruin and degrade him and his family for ever. In 1842 he wrote:[6]

You know I have nothing but the proceeds of the labour of my head and hands, and at 39 years of age I find the Bar very up hill work. I have certainly met with success for the short time I have been in practice, and if I were ten years younger or had a few hundred a year, as most men who go to the Bar have, I should feel certain of success but my expenses of circuits, chambers, clerk and books amount to upwards of £200 a year before I can earn one shilling, so that the deficiencies of my professional income I am compelled to make up by the pen. Now to do this I am obliged to condemn myself to incessant labour. I am never at rest. I can hardly walk with my wife or play with my child, without a sacrifice of the time which should be devoted to earning an income. Nobody has any idea of the severity of that labour which knows no remission, and whilst my mind has been worn out and my body in a painful state of fatigue by excessive toil I have over and over again been regarded by those about me as one who knew no other pleasure than toil at the book or the pen. My illness of last winter was the result of this close application and of nothing else. In a more pecuniary point of view a second illness of this kind would throw me into difficulties that I might never recover.

One problem this detailed knowledge about Chapman raises for those who operate with the three-class model is that of deciding how to categorize him according to social class. Clearly he was neither bourgeois, nor proletarian, nor aristocrat. Perhaps, if the term 'middle class' is substituted for 'bourgeois' and used very loosely he might be classified accordingly. But if this is done then the terminology loses its significance for the Marxist model and two questions must be asked and answered. The first is, what are we to understand by the term 'middle class' so used? The second is, what of importance about Chapman is held to be subsumed in that term? It seems to me that there are no satisfactory answers to such questions and that there can be none since the three-class model was basically a Ricardian abstraction from reality, adapted by Marx to forecast the outcome of historical development, not to describe the social structure of England as it was in the period before 1850.

Clearly Chapman cannot be handled nor his contribution understood within the traditional classification of the three-class model, nor can the facts be allowed to speak for themselves, because, until there has been some sifting of the data, we do not know what the facts are. To sift the data requires a conceptual framework. But the framework most readily at hand does not fit. Try the five-class model.

Objectively Chapman had most of the characteristics of the upper social stratum of those social strata which were the recruiting grounds for the quasi-group which for a short time in some places produced a middling class. Chapman was of this middling class for as well as fretting about his lowly economic position he was resentful of his exclusion from power and authority, and felt most keenly the consequent frustration of his strong motivation to high achievement. By the early 1830s Chapman's social class consciousness was that of the middling class. As a result he became politically active in the Radical cause in Lower Canada, in London and in Bath. In

England he was violently opposed to the power of the aristocracy and other sections of the upper class. He wished to turn the House of Commons into a representative and responsible body, to abolish the House of Lords and to curb the veto of the Crown. The key to all this was to be the ballot. In Canada he wished to abolish the Legislative Council and to subject the power of governors to popular control. The key to this was also the ballot. Thus in regard to Canada as well as to England the idea that the ballot was a necessary condition for political freedom was one of the central notions of Chapman's ideology. Moreover, where, as in Canada, political conditions seemed to obstruct moves towards political liberty, Chapman also advocated and justified the use of force to overthrow established authority. In Victoria in the mid-1850s Chapman had become a man of some substance. He was also an ex-member of the colonial political and administrative élite. Nevertheless, these notions had such powerful roots in his basically middling-class consciousness that he was incapable of totally rejecting his past. I set out the following chronology of Chapman's political activities to show the strength and development of this social class consciousness, and the way in which it led him into sustained political activity throughout the English-speaking world.

In the late 1820s and early 1830s Chapman attended the Radical debates held in the Free Mason's Tavern, listened to John Austin's lectures on jurisprudence and took to speaking in the Radical cause in Canada. In 1832 he took part in J. A. Roebuck's campaign in Bath. In the following year he returned to Montreal to found the Daily Advertiser, as the first daily newspaper in Canada.[7] With his partner, Sam Revans, the compositor son of an apothecary and another member of the midding class, Chapman used this paper as a weapon with which to expose and attack the interests of the English Ascendancy in Canada—the governor's court and the big mercantile interests—and became increasingly committed to the politically and economically under-privileged and exploited, a majority of whom were French. The paper survived for less than eighteen months and was destroyed by powerful interests. As Chapman explained, the Daily Advertiser

cannot be supported without advertisements; and although its circulation was rapidly increasing and especially among a class

to make it a good advertising medium, those who hold the
advertising support in their hands will not support a paper which
interferes with their political views. . . . Had we adopted the
political views of the Mercantile body we are convinced fortune
was at our feet . . . . [However] we did not sign the petition
against the Resolutions;[8] we did not denounce the *Vindicator*
and *Minerve* when they expressed their detestation of Lord
Aylmer;[9] we never called the Canadians all sorts of names, we
never denounced the Assembly as seditious and treasonable. . . .
All our articles had a Radical tendency.[10]

This Radical tendency also meant that in its editorial policy the
Daily Advertiser espoused the cause of migrants against English
shipowners and against Canadian landlords. It meant, too, that
Chapman gave his full support to Wakefield's proposals for
systematic colonization in the belief that it would destroy the economic basis of aristocratic privilege. It would do so by concentrating
settlement and getting rid of credit sales of land and replacing them
by cash sales. This latter would enable the owner-occupier to raise
a mortgage to acquire working capital. In short, strict government
control of land sales would 'raise up a bold and really independent
yeomanry' as a bulwark against aristocracy.[11]

Chapman also made the pages of the *Daily Advertiser* open to
Papineau and his Radical supporters and, when the establishment
newspaper, the *Gazette*, gave strong support to the view that
employers should use all the influence and power they had to direct
their employees to vote against Papineau and the Radical cause,
Chapman wrote a powerful and bitter editorial: 'Loudly do we
protest against such a recommendation. . . . Far better do away with
the franchise than to demand its abuse . . . we say now, if blood
come of these elections, upon the *Gazette* do we charge the fatal
exciting cause.'[12]

Chapman's Radical commitment brought him into contact with
Papineau, and other leaders of the popular movement in the
Assembly in Lower Canada. He, like O'Callaghan and Roebuck,
argued that the impetus to conflict in Lower Canada derived from
the clash between the rival political principles of aristocracy and
democracy, as embraced by opposing classes, and not from racial
differences and aspirations as was maintained by the English
Ascendancy in Canada. Chapman's fullest exposition of this view

is in his analysis of the 1834 election.[13] The argument and evidence advanced by Chapman for this phase of the struggle is persuasive and, since historians have yet to subject the results of this election to any penetrating analysis, difficult to refute.[14] When his paper collapsed, and because of his known adherence to ultra Radicalism, he was sent by the Assembly of Lower Canada to England to act as a paid intermediary between it and its friends in the House of Commons. In this capacity he renewed his contact with J. A. Roebuck, also employed by the Assembly to argue the case for representative government in the House of Commons. Then Roebuck in the House and Chapman outside it kept the Canadian question before the country until the Canadian rebellion temporarily frustrated the possibility of ordered progress to representative and responsible government, and terminated Chapman's employment.

For as long as he was employed by the Assembly, Chapman maintained a flow of letters to E. B. O'Callaghan, editor of the *Vindicator*, in which he reported on political developments in England. Greatly influenced by the course of events in Bath and Radical successes in the election of 1835, Chapman forecast the inevitable political success of his own class in England. So convinced was he of the sure triumph of 'movement' Radicalism that he was led willy-nilly to advocate extremist policies as solutions to the Canadian problem. His advice to the Canadians was that the English government, under constant pressure from the Radicals in Parliament, was so weak that it would give way to threats of force and would even acquiesce in a bloodless *coup d'état* if it should be followed by efficient administration by the new rulers.

I am persuaded [he wrote] that whensoever any colony demonstrates that it is determined to manage its own internal affairs, by some such act as seizing on the offices, and suitably filling them, they will be allowed for ever after to manage their own affairs. Some little noise would be made here, attended with blustering; but Parliament would never sanction any costly interference. And the Ministry daring to propose anything of the kind, would quickly seal its own fate.[15]

This was scarcely credible and Chapman seemed to realize this himself since a week later[16] he emphasized that if the Canadians were to get anything at all it would not be through a sense of justice, but the operation of fear . . . [thus] Each honest man in Canada should keep his rifle in order, and his powder dry. Lamentable will be the occasion which shall instigate them to gain by force what, through the legitimate work of their institutions, they may require. But if the Government rejects the authority of the only power which controls it, and makes it responsible, the people must assume the authority which numbers and force give them.

This public statement was a clear incitement to treason.

The extent to which these reports and opinions on English politics were seen to embody a Radically progressive and revolutionary ideology is indicated by the opinions expressed about him a year or so later when the Canadian question was still very much alive. The occasion was his appointment to the post of assistant commissioner on the inquiry into hand-loom weaving. These press opinions and Chapman's own words create a very different impression about the strength of Chapman's social class consciousness and political commitment than that suggested by Professor Scott for the later period.

Mr. H. S. Chapman [declared one newspaper] has done more more than any man living, not excepting Mr. J. A. Roebuck and Mr. L. J. Papineau, to saddle England with the expense of several millions sterling to put down and keep down rebellion in Canada. . . . His correspondence from London . . . contributed more than anything else to deceive and corrupt the minds of the people in the District of Montreal, and bring on the rebellion.

And again,[17]

We have no hesitation whatever in denouncing [Chapman] as one of the ringleaders of the late rebellion in this Province, and whose occupation it has been for many years, to bring about a revolution in these parts of Her Majesty's dominions.

There can be little doubt that Chapman was culpable for, as Professor Manning has argued, 'Papineau's most serious miscalculation lay in the assumption that the Radical group in Parliament would soon be in the ascendant in the English political world . . . and Henry Chapman, in his letters to O'Callaghan, supplied plenty of misleading information and speculation to nourish these hopes.'[18] It was he above all others who spread the idea that the British government would not and could not act in Canada in the way in which it did. And it was he with O'Callaghan of the *Vindicator* who spread the belief that it was possible to get reform in Canada by exploiting the home government's fear of revolution and by writing about revolutionary action without actually preparing for a revolution. One gets the impression that after the revolutionary débâcle in Canada in 1837 and 1838 Chapman carried a considerable burden of guilt around with him—but this is not in the record. His only consolation was in the letters of appreciation from English and French Radicals which survive in his papers, one of which said:[19]

> None but men in our situations—subject to daily
> misrepresentation and calumny—exposed to and suffering from
> the persecuting power of a Government never sincerely the
> friend of liberty and always foremost to crush those who
> presume to oppose or expose its iniquities—can fully appreciate
> the value of those services which you and our other friends,
> in and out of Parliament, have conferred both on ourselves
> and on Canada.

The outbreak of fighting in Canada ended Chapman's employment by the Assembly of Lower Canada. Fortunately he had already branched out into two activities, which conjointly were to give a new direction to his life, although for the moment they were to thrust him deeper into the thick of the Radical protest and into commitment to advanced opinions and activity. The first was writing, the second was his preparation for the Bar.

Chapman, as well as writing on behalf of the Canadians, wrote for payment in journals, like the *Edinburgh Review* and the *Westminster Review*. He also wrote, throughout 1835 and 1836, for Roebuck's *Pamphlets for the People*. These were published in the form they were, to avoid the Newspaper Stamp and as part of a comprehensive Radical campaign for the freedom of the press.[20] But they were also an attempt to establish a vehicle for the ideas of the Radical faction. Chapman wrote twenty-seven articles for them. His first two contributions were arguments for the ballot, and later articles often included a discussion of the ballot as part of a general programme of legal reform necessary for the establishment of effective representative institutions. They indicate a sustained belief in the importance of the ballot. Chapman was thoroughly committed.[21]

The fullest and clearest expression of Chapman's political ideology, however, is contained in an article called 'Preliminary reforms'.[22] Following Bentham, he wrote, 'The object of Reform is to obtain good government, that which secures to the great body of the people the greatest aggregate of happiness . . . of the several instruments of government, by far the most important in its effects upon the happiness of the community is the body in which the power of making laws resides—in other words, the Parliament.' Parliament, however, was not representative of the people and, like all Parliaments, was concerned solely to promote the interests of the class by which it was chosen. Thus it followed 'that good government cannot be attained but by an extension of the suffrage to the great body of the people'. From this also followed a number of supplementary legal reforms, necessary to make the House of Commons an efficient instrument of good government. Minimum preliminary requirements were:

(1) an extension of the suffrage to all occupants,

(2) an abolition of property qualification,

(3) secrecy of suffrage, by means of the ballot,

(4) the abolition of the present complicated system of registration,[23] and the reduction of the expenses of elections; and

(5) a more equal distribution of members, according to population and territory,

(6) the duration of Parliaments to be shortened; and

(7) the tax on knowledge to be abolished.[24]

Where Chapman dissented from this general programme he said so. And when he thought some order of priority was essential he emphasized it. The only point on which he dissented was on the length of the shorter Parliaments.

Radicals traditionally supported triennial Parliaments. Chapman, at this time, preferred annual ones. On the question of priority he wrote:[25]

It must not be supposed that the Reforms above specified, are set down in the order of their importance. Of the whole six

measures, the Ultra-Liberal deems the Ballot of the greatest
moment. The present limited franchise, joined with the Ballot,
would be far preferable to an extension of the Suffrage without
the protection of the Ballot, a measure fraught with evil to the
dependent classes of the community, which none of the
anticipated advantages are likely to compensate.

Thus for Chapman as for all Philosophic Radicals, and not ex-
cluding J. S. Mill, the ballot was crucial; the key to political
progress.

In addition to this seven-point Radical Charter which preceded
the Chartist Charter[26] by two years, Chapman also urged the
incompatibility of a representative lower house with a hereditary
upper one. He argued that the 'only Radical remedies are abolition,
election by the People, or depriving the Lords of their veto'. He
also pointed out that similar care would have to be taken to curb
the use of the royal veto. Only with a Parliament so reformed would
it be possible to get the better laws necessary for the greatest good
of the greatest number.

The years 1832–8, in which Chapman aligned himself with the
most progressive political group in England, probably marked the
peak of united middling- and working-class support for the politics
of Philosophic Radicalism. It also marked the peak of Chapman's
involvement. After 1835 the Parliamentary Radicals failed as a
group, and Roebuck and others failed as leaders. In Roebuck's own
constituency, the organization of which was so much praised by
Chapman, working-class and middling-class Radicals were at
loggerheads. Moderates wished to associate with Whigs, and
artisans were hostile to Roebuck's support for the Poor Law.
Furthermore, the revived Tory party was drawing support from
liberal defections brought about by Roebuck's proposals to abolish
the House of Lords, and by non-conformist hostility to Roebuck's
opposition to Lord's Day Observance. At the next general election,
in 1837, the Radical faction was almost annihilated.[27] Thereafter
erstwhile Radicals further weakened the Parliamentary Radical
opposition by accepting office.[28]

Thus, by 1837–8 Chapman, like other Radicals of his own class,
was in a dilemma. His support for movements advocating a transfer
of power to his own class had twice been frustrated—once in
Canada and again in England. Furthermore, the annual vote on

the ballot, the one instrument likely to achieve a real transfer of power, showed clearly what little hope there was.[29] The forces of traditionalism and reaction were too great. What could he, or any other Radical, do?

One possible course of action open to him was to associate himself with the working-class inheritors of the Radical programme. But there is no evidence that he even considered this. Like most other Philosophic Radicals, Chapman felt himself to be something of a philosopher king, fit to govern benevolently but cut off by taste and aspiration from the mass of the governed. The good laws, which he thought Parliament, reformed according to his plan, should pass, were fundamentally those designed to lift the incubus of aristocrats, placemen, sinecurists, pluralists and monopolists from the backs of men like himself, leaving them free to achieve political, social and economic equality with other men through their own unaided efforts. They were not laws designed to serve the more collectivist interests of the working class. Thus there was no hope, politically or otherwise, for Chapman through association with working-class political movements of proletarian persuasion, just as there was no longer hope for him in political Philosophic Radicalism.

The other, more hopeful, course of action was to persist in preparing for the Bar and to lend open support to those Radical measures which could still attract Whig support, i.e. to take his own pragmatic advice to take whatever could be got. So Chapman continued to study and write.

In 1841 Chapman was called to the Bar. At about the same time his new writing gained him less notoriety and some acclaim. He became a leading popular propagandist for the Anti-Corn Law League and for Wakefield's movement for systematic colonization.[30] These activities brought Chapman into increasing contact with men in responsible positions and began to offer attractive opportunities. He thought increasingly of advancement by non-political channels. But as yet he had not completely severed his connection with the political activities of the Philosophic Radicals and, although less active in Radical politics, he was an active member of the Political Economy Society. He was also in touch, in a conspiratorial way, with the exiled Canadian rebels and gave considerable assistance to Lord Brougham in his attack on the Durham Ordinance which brought about Durham's return from Canada.[31]

Yet success was as evasive as ever. His post as assistant commissioner enquiring into the condition of hand-loom weavers was only a temporary one. And, after his marriage in 1841, he found it necessary to subsidize his legal practice from his writing.[32] These difficulties in earning a living, his interest in the New Zealand Company, his editorship of the *New Zealand Journal*, and glowing reports of the possibilities of a lucrative practice in Wellington from his ex-partner Revans, plus the promised half share in the latter's newspaper, led Chapman to make plans to emigrate to practise at the Wellington Bar. He anticipated an income of between £1,000 and £1,500 per annum, which with £300 per annum in total expenses would leave a large surplus for investment in land at a 20 per cent rate of profit.[33] There seemed to be no doubt in Chapman's mind that success was just around the corner.

Then (1843) came the vacant judgeship in New Zealand. This was Chapman's chance. He had already written on the problem of the administration of law in New Zealand.[34] He now decided to apply for the security of government service. So he applied for and was appointed to the judgeship at Wellington with an income of £800 annually.

From this time onwards Chapman seemed to have turned his back on his active political past. Instead he determined to administer the law impartially, and to contribute his mite towards the creation of the new Radical society from a colonial judge's bench instead of through the press and political parties. This, of course, was permissible for a Benthamite and wholly consistent with the later tenets of Philosophic Radicalism. Nevertheless, it did represent a shift to a more pragmatic position than that advocated in the 1835 Radical Charter, which, if implemented, would have brought about a wholesale transfer of power in England and given great opportunities to men like Chapman.

The pragmatic, perhaps opportunist, approach with its personally favourable results was itself not without perplexities. Chapman's ambition was fed by success, as well as by his growing family of sons and, for the next nine years, through his father and friendly contacts close to the Colonial Office, he sought preferment. Less than a year after his appointment to New Zealand he wrote,[35]

Now Charles Buller will be sure to be Colonial Minister before many years, and when he is I am nearly certain he would ask me to take office under him. It would not surprise me were

he to offer me the Under Secretaryship, either with or without
a seat in Parliament for that I should think I should be disposed
to give up my Judgeship.

In his less ambitious moments Chapman was prepared to settle
for a better paid judgeship in New South Wales, which, in his
view, would lead to the office of chief justice, a knighthood, and
£2,000 a year, although he would 'rather get back to England at
£1,000 or even £800'.[36] Not all of Chapman's time, however, was
given over to writing for and about promotion, for, although his
judicial duties were light, he spent his time as a Benthamite should.
He established rules of procedure for the Wellington Court and,
in co-operation with Chief Justice Martin, laid down a system of
procedure for the Supreme Court of New Zealand, which became
the forerunner of the existing Code of Civil Procedure. Through his
judicial decisions he created confidence that the judiciary was not
a tool of the administration and helped to force Governor Grey
to clarify his land policy, particularly in connection with the
FitzRoy grants.[37] At the same time he enjoyed himself as a small
landed proprietor. Nevertheless, Chapman, who was essentially a
political and public man, had to wait nine years in Wellington
before his expectations of promotion were fulfilled.

When promotion came it was not of his choosing and resulted
in throwing him back into the vortex of politics, only this time
(1852) as colonial secretary in Van Diemen's Land.[38] In this capacity
he was the nominee officially appointed to manage a largely
representative legislative body, and the representative of an
authoritarian system of government paid (£1,200) to support an
unpopular policy of transportation. For the first time in Chapman's
life, his ambition conflicted with his basically Radical principles and
it did so not because he became a wealthy man but because he
switched positions in the authority structure of society and became
a member of the colonial élite.

The choice was a painful one. Chapman had been seeking
promotion, and, although he would have preferred a judgeship, to
have refused an already gazetted appointment would have con-
demned him to the Wellington bench for life. Yet who, looking at
the Australian political scene at the beginning of 1852, could have
doubted that the end of transportation was in sight? Chapman
certainly did not.[39] New and more representative constitutions were

coming into force everywhere. In Van Diemen's Land, a majority of the newly elected council was opposed to transportation, and in England Molesworth, who had moved for the discontinuance of transportation in May, was coming to the fore as a Radical leader soon to get cabinet rank (January 1853). On the other hand Denison, the lieutenant governor, was known to have publicly expressed doubts about the home government's policy on transportation, and had yet to demonstrate the intransigence he adopted on the question six months later.[40] In these circumstances Chapman hoped to play for time.

> My hope is [he wrote] the question is by this time settled at
> home—as there is a rumour to that effect, and if not I hope
> my letters will prevail. You see I have a rather delicate part to
> play, but I have confidence in myself, and I believe I shall come
> out with credit, both in the eyes of the Home Government, and
> of the people. Hitherto, I have succeeded in this and the
> difficulty of this present question does not discourage me.[41]

Unfortunately, Denison was not co-operative. The elected members would not wait for the results of their earlier petition, and insisted on proceeding with their plea to the Crown for the cessation of transportation. So the fifty-year-old Chapman, forced to decide on what he felt to be a non-issue—since the real and favourable decision would be taken elsewhere—acted in a way which he knew would be followed by dismissal. When the House divided on the motion for the petition to the Commons he absented himself from it.[42] But even then he sustained himself with the belief that the home government would reinstate him. It did not, and after hanging about the ante-rooms of the Colonial Office for over twelve months, Chapman relearned the lesson of his early manhood, the lesson of the conservative cohesiveness of those who held the centres of power and merely employed ambitious men like himself. He resolved never again to take office in an irresponsible government and subsequently, on three separate occasions, refused the offer of the chief judgeship, treasurership and colonial secretary-ship of Victoria.[43] When he heard that Denison in Van Diemen's Land was likely to reach a reconciliation with the elected members, he confided his bitter sense of disillusion to his wife. In doing so he has allowed us a glimpse of his self image and revealed something of the deeper psychological motives for his own

G

important part in the negotiations for the ballot in Victoria two
years later. He wrote:

> If the popular party [in Van Diemen's Land] now pockets all
> insults I shall be inclined to stick to law and never stir one inch
> for popular rights, in a colony at least, again. My whole life has
> been a series of sacrifices to principle. In Canada it was hinted
> to me that if I should be disposed to act with the dominant
> party, I might have almost anything I asked for. In England
> I was always on the losing side, I mean so far as personal interest
> was concerned. If now the Council is to be mesmerised by
> Denison who has never lost an opportunity of insulting them,
> nothing will exceed my disgust.
>
> If I am cast adrift—depend upon it, I will bring about responsible
> government in a very few years and force the Governor to
> send for me to form the first responsible ministry. I am
> convinced this must take place in not many years. If I return
> as Secretary, it would have the effect of putting it off, but it
> must come and finally it is a reform I *must not oppose*. Depend
> upon it that whether in office or out of office my function—my
> *mission* as some would call it, is the development of free
> institutions. I must see that they are not too hurried—that they
> are calmly and prudently considered but to shut the door of
> reform and place my back against it, is what I never will do.[44]

Chapman arrived in Victoria in October 1854. Within six months
he showed the authorities where his interests lay by offering his
services free of charge to defend the men charged with treason for
their parts in the Eureka affair. In fact Chapman led brilliantly
for the defence and, as if defending his own Radical past at the
Bar of Victorian opinion, made nonsense of the government's case.
His client, the American negro Joseph, was acquitted. Thereafter
the government found it impossible to get a single conviction. Its
case collapsed.[45] Thus, Chapman had quickly established himself as
an anti-government man in the eyes of the public. He was also
able to avoid taking up a position of authority with the colonial
administration because in the next ten years in Victoria he
established himself in a successful legal practice. At the same time
Victoria moved rapidly towards representative and responsible
government. His successful law practice (£3,000–£6,000 per annum),

plus the recognition he had gained as a man of principle as well as of legislative experience, enabled him to re-enter politics via the Victorian Legislative Council in 1855. As far as his electorate at South Bourke was concerned he was returned as a member who had the support of Nicholson, the leader of the democratic faction, and was pledged not to take office until the new constitution came into force. In his programme he expressed strong support for a speedier administration of the law, a national system of education, representative government, closer settlement and the rapid establishment of railways. In answer to questions he said that he favoured an amnesty for the Eureka prisoners who were still being tried, and the introduction of the ballot.[46] As far as Chapman was concerned he was largely going over old ground, the ground which English Philosophic Radicals had covered at least twenty-five years earlier. It is true that the land question was new and was one on which Chapman had changed his mind as a result of his New Zealand experience of the Wakefield system.[47] It is also true that his experience in the colonies had brought him to a realization of the important role governments should play in the construction of railways. But these were extensions of his thoroughly Benthamite and Philosophic Radical background rather than contradictions of them.

In this manner Chapman, an ambitious middling-class Philosophic Radical, came to be in the Victorian Legislative Council when it decided to introduce the ballot into the Electoral Act, setting out the conditions for the first election under the new constitution.

The story of Chapman's part in this event as told and interpreted by Professor Scott is unsatisfactory. His main evidence for concluding that Chapman was indifferent over the ballot and politically uncommitted is that he made only 'a very moderate' speech in favour of the ballot motion and did not deny or take exception to a remark, passed in the Legislative Council, that the ballot clauses 'were not those of honourable members who advocated the system but of those who were opposed to it.'[48]

What actually happened in the Victorian Legislative Council is as follows. Chapman emerged as one of the few members (nineteen out of sixty-six) who voted consistently for responsible government and the ballot.[49] In doing this he showed his continued adherence to those political beliefs formulated during his early manhood. Then, on the first day of the debate on Nicholson's motion to incorporate the ballot in the Electoral Act, he initiated a procedural move to ensure a full discussion of the motion. On the second day he delivered his own pro-ballot speech.[50] In it he made it clear that he was in no doubt about the desirability of the ballot. He said Nicholson had shown the need for the ballot, and argued, although the evils of elections were not so bad in Victoria as in England, that the problem of intimidation and coercion did exist. He also countered O'Shannassy's argument, that a 'perfect' system could not be produced, by likening ballot legislation to laws against crime, and by throwing scorn on the view that because one cannot have everything one might as well have nothing at all. Then, distinguishing between the position of the elected representative and individual voters, he claimed that the ballot would allow the latter to serve their consciences and the community without fear of coercion. It is clear that Chapman was wholeheartedly in support of the ballot motion. It is equally clear that the remark, which is alleged to show that Chapman was neutral, if not hostile on the ballot question, was not directed at him. What Dr Greeves, the member responsible, actually said was,[51]

> Honourable members opposed to the ballot had endeavoured as far as they could to falsify their own views by trying to make that workable which they had said was not so. Even the ballot clauses of the bill were not those of honourable members who advocated the system, but were due to honourable members opposed to it. Any reflections on the bill were due, not to the House, but to those honourable members who, introducing the clauses, had failed to pay attention to them in Committee.

The last sentence should make it clear what Greeves was getting at. He was referring to the ballot clauses as they then stood in the Bill at the Third Reading. And, in his statement, he was praising the work of the anti-ballot members and criticizing the laxness of the pro-ballot members, in committee. His was not a claim that the member responsible for drafting the original clauses was opposed to them. Indeed the extent to which Chapman was known to be close to Nicholson is indicated by the Argus's speculation that if Nicholson could form a ministry, Chapman would be the attorney-general.[52] As attorney-general it would have been his task to draft the necessary ballot clauses.

Chapman's own story is that[53]

Nicholson came to me and asked me to draw the ballot clauses for him. In order to do so I examined every system of ballot to which I could obtain a reference. In the end I discarded them all in favour of reliance on what I deemed to be a natural human propensity. Instead of making the voter write in the name of the favoured candidate or put a cross against his name I determined that he should strike out his opponents.

And for many years after, in Victoria and elsewhere, this is just what the voter did. Nevertheless, another version of this incident, that of Vincent Pyke, one of the goldfields representatives, credits Chapman with a more intimate and positive role. According to Pyke, a meeting of Nicholson's supporters was held at the old Council Club, where it was agreed that the government should not be allowed to get away with its opposition to the ballot. Chapman was at this meeting and offered to draft the necessary clauses.[54] Whether Chapman was invited, or whether he offered to draft the clauses does not materially affect the result—he did draft them—but it should influence the light in which the historian sees Chapman's political inclinations. Pyke's version suggests that Chapman was of the Nicholson and democratic faction, and not outside it. There is another letter which suggests that Nicholson, the man who was fêted throughout England for having introduced the ballot into Victoria, was much more of a front man than Professor Scott acknowledged, and which also shows that there are more by-ways into the relationship between social class consciousness and political institutions than indicated in our discussion of Chapman. This letter was probably published in a New Zealand newspaper in the 1890s. It argues that even the initiative on the ballot motion was not Nicholson's but that of William Kerr, town clerk of Melbourne. It reads:[55]

In the draft of Mr. Nicholson's address Mr. Kerr had inserted a clause strongly advocating the introduction of the ballot. To this clause Mr. Nicholson strongly objected in the first instance, but being talked over by Mr. Kerr on the subject, who insisted on retaining the clause, he consented at length, although somewhat reluctantly, to its insertion in his address, and it was to this fortunate circumstance that he owed all his subsequent fame.

Thus what needs to be emphasized is that in drafting the ballot clauses Chapman did not act against his beliefs or his interests, or in any laggardly fashion. On the contrary, he acted in accordance with an ideology deeply rooted in his own person and social class situation. His political education, gained through working with the English Philosophic Radicals and with Canadian Radicals in some of the most spectacular protest movements of his day, had already led him to make explicit those principles.[56] And what he might have forgotten about the strength of reaction had been relearned through his recent experience of the ruthlessness of arbitrary government. It is true that Chapman had brought his last experience upon himself by his own expanding ambition. But this ambition was itself only the personalized aspect of his ambition for the political collectivity—the people. Philosophic Radicals, and Chapman was one of them, wanted excellence for all men. They also wanted it for themselves. It may well be that they wanted it for all men because they wanted it for themselves. Yet the fact remains, they did want it for both. The way to achieve it, they thought, was through representative and then responsible government, and education. They believed it possible to educate men to a rational awareness of enlightened self-interest, to give them good, i.e. representative government, and then to leave them to pursue personal excellence restrained only by reason and enlightenment. Thus there was nothing incompatible between personal ambition, high aspirations and Philosophic Radicalism. In fact, one was a necessary condition of the other. Chapman's fault, or lapse, had been to let ambition and confidence blind him to the dangers of compromise with an imperfectly responsible and representative system. This Van Diemen's Land lapse apart, Chapman was politically consistent, although in his later years mellowed by age and success.

Mellowed or not, Chapman was not content with the ballot. In July 1856 he pointed out the potential dangers to the ballot in the new Parliament. He urged the need for a simplification of the franchise on the basis of a residential qualification, expressed a strong belief in the value of triennial Parliaments, and opposed the property qualification. He was sceptical about the value of a second chamber and opposed state aid to religion. Furthermore he indicated that it would be his intention, to 'advocate a reconstruction of the electoral districts, with a view to a fair and equal representation of the people' and to press for 'administrative reform' to provide those surpluses necessary to finance development, law reform, education and the unlocking of the land.[57]

It fell to the second Haines ministry reluctantly to establish universal suffrage and remove the property qualification. But it was Chapman's pleasure, as attorney-general, literally to fight through the Assembly a Bill providing for the redistribution of seats according to population, to help draft legislation for stricter accounting procedures,[58] and to take a hand in introducing state financing and control of railways into Victoria. Each of these is a story in itself.

This story, however, is almost complete. All that remains to be said is that John Stuart Mill, once the intellectual doyen of Philosophic Radicals, on learning of Chapman's and Victoria's achievement remained sceptical. Times had changed and, in his view, the ballot was no longer necessary, even in England. According to Mill, open voting had an important moral and educational role to play in so far as it could lead to attempts by men to justify themselves to their fellows through the use of reason. He thought, too, that another Radical panacea, payment of members, would lead to the growth of a class of professional politicians. Above all, he said, the true test of the democratic intentions of Victorians would be the steps they would, or would not take to ensure representation of minorities.

> The only thing which seems wanting to make the suffrage
> really universal [he wrote] is to get rid of the Toryism of sex,
> by admitting women to vote; and it will be a great test how
> far the bulk of your population deserve to have the suffrage
> themselves their being willing or not to extend it to women.[59]

Thus, in his lifetime Chapman was told that, as a Philosophic Radical, he had not done those things he ought to have done, and had done those things he ought not to have done. Subsequently historians have decided that he did the things he did, not from any deep conviction about them or commitment to them, but merely because he wished to keep the peace. This kind of judgment allows him to be fitted cosily into the traditional conceptual framework which opposes middle to working class. But it is my contention that such a classification and interpretation does less than justice to Chapman and those others whom I have dubbed the middling class. Furthermore, by ignoring the notion that the basis of social classes as conflict groups is the distribution of power, it directs attention away from important areas of conflict and the consequent generation of social class consciousness and, thereby, away from important sources of change and development.

The colonies and social mobility: governors and executive councillors in Australia, 1788-1856

Introduction

Some of the sting was taken out of the early nineteenth-century Radical movement by the creation of job opportunities in the colonies for at least some of the aspiring professional and petit bourgeois members of the quasi-group from which a stronger middling class might have come.

The publication of the first three volumes of the *Australian Dictionary of Biography* seemed to provide a starting-point for beginning to test this hypothesis at least in an aggregative descriptive fashion. What follows is simply an attempt to measure some of the social origins and characteristics of men, who for the most part were capable of being characterized as members of the middling set of people or quasi-group, but who, since they also constituted the executive and administrative *élite* in Australia during its early years, became themselves the nucleus for a new colonial ruling class possessing authority and coercive power.

We claim no high order of analytic or explanatory power for our findings. Therefore, we hesitate to make many inferences from the facts of social origin and characteristics about the determinants of executive and administrative decisions and actions. However, we do believe that our approach is valuable for what it suggests ought not be said about Australia's rulers during the first seventy years of its existence under English control, as well as for the light the results throw on aspects of social mobility in Great Britain in the eighteenth and early nineteenth centuries.

In the next part of the chapter we set out briefly the origins and the main functions and powers of these executive councils and our reasons for believing that their members had a special administrative and political status. In the penultimate part we describe some of the procedures used to gather and interpret the data and discuss some of the problems involved in categorizing our subjects in terms of occupation and social stratum. The final part contains summaries of our attempts at quantification and tentative interpretations of some of the data so assembled.

Executive councils and their members

Governor Phillip and his successors in New South Wales until 1825 were issued with Commissions and Instructions, which gave each individual governor complete authority over all other officials in the colony.[1] Subject to the limitations laid down in their Commissions and Instructions the early governors had complete, though certainly not unchallenged, control of the convict colony. There was no council to advise, guide or control the governor in either legislative or executive matters.

In order to carry out their instructions the early governors adopted the practice of issuing daily General Orders which were, in effect, the colony's only legislation. However, in response to growing opposition to the existing administrative framework and the criticism that the governor had no right to legislate without the authority of an Act of Parliament, J. T. Bigge was commissioned to investigate the state of affairs in New South Wales.[2] The upshot of his investigation and report was the Act of 1823 which included the provision for a Legislative Council to consist of not more than seven nor less than five members. Though the 1823 Act included many sections relating to legislative and judicial procedures it did not mention an executive council, since both Commissioner Bigge and the British government had decided that the nature of the convict colony necessitated the maintenance by the governor of a strong and independent executive authority. However, the business of government in New South Wales was becoming far too extensive for one man to handle effectively. Consequently various *ad hoc* executive appointments were made until 1825 when friction between the governor and his officials forced the decision to regulate and define their relationship by the creation of executive councils in New South Wales and Van Diemen's Land.[3]

The functions of these executive councils varied little from the time they were created until the time of responsible government. Governors were instructed to consult and advise the executive council 'in all things' and that no 'power or authorities' were to be exercised by them except with the 'concurrence and advice' of the executive council. If urgent action was necessary then the governor could first move independently of the council and consult it later. Trivial matters did not have to be taken before the council nor did issues which might result in 'material prejudice' to 'Our Service'. The governor presided over and determined the council's business; he could also suspend members if he thought it necessary as well as making temporary appointments in the event of death, resignation or departure. In the main, however, it was the secretary of state who determined which officials should sit in the council and any change in membership made by the governor had to be confirmed by the Colonial Office.

Executive councils with similar functions were set up in the other Australian colonies: in Western Australia in 1832, in South Australia in 1836 and Victoria in 1851. In these three colonies the governor was given an executive council from the time of foundation of the colony except that in Western Australia delays in the issuing of instructions meant that the governor functioned as a local autocrat from 1829 to 1832.

It is difficult to determine the extent to which the governor was influenced by his councillors or the reverse since the direction of influence depended very much on the character of the governor and the way he interpreted his instructions. For example, Governors FitzRoy of New South Wales and La Trobe of Victoria held frequent meetings of their executive councils and tended to depend on their advice while with Governors Hotham, Gipps and Darling it was rather the reverse; the council was neglected or its advice ignored. Darling was sharply rebuked by the secretary of state who wrote:[4]

On referring to the Journals of the Executive Council . . .
I perceive that a large proportion of the most important business
of the colony is transacted without the advice of that Body. I must
recall your . . . attention to the language of your general
Instructions upon this subject, which, I trust, will, for the future
be much more closely observed.

In a similar fashion Denison, the Governor of Van Diemen's Land in 1852, seemed to consider the executive council as superfluous and regarded the government of the colony as being vested in himself and his colonial secretary.[5]

Clearly governors could and did act in opposition to the wishes of their executive councils but, since a full explanation for such an action had to be sent to the secretary of state, there were limits to their freedom of action. Similarly if a governor exercised his power of suspension he had to seek confirmation from the Colonial Office and, as Governors Darling and Bourke at least realized, suspensions of executive councillors were not invariably supported by the secretary of state.[6]

These checks on the powers of governors meant that policy decisions within the colonial context were generally made by the governor assisted by members of the executive council. Even in situations such as that described by the colonial secretary of Van Diemen's Land the governor found it necessary to confide in and consult with the colonial secretary and it was important for him to get the consent if not the advice of the other members of the executive council. In general executive councils were frequently called upon to report on petitions presented to the sovereign and, at the governor's request, to prepare and scrutinize legislative proposals. They also made decisions in connection with the suspension of top officials, the issuing of reprieves and pardons, and the approval or disapproval of land grants. In New South Wales after 1842 the executive council investigated and reported upon such matters as immigration, transportation and the franchise law, and generally its reports were carried into operation.[7]

In addition it must be remembered that most executive councillors were also administrative heads in their own departments in which they had considerable responsibility. Many decisions within these departments were made without the official consulting the governor and much routine administrative work was in fact carried out by the executive officials.

Membership of the executive councils varied somewhat in each colony though all included at some time a colonial secretary and colonial treasurer. The advocate general and the senior army officer became a member of each colonial executive except in Van Diemen's Land and South Australia respectively, while clergymen, customs collectors, surveyors general and others were included in different executive councils at different times.[8] The size of the councils varied from a minimum of three to a maximum of eight members. In New South Wales and to a large extent in the other colonies with the exception of Victoria the executive councillors were also members of the legislature and so could cast their vote on legislative issues as well as bringing their influence to bear in executive decisions. In Western Australia and South Australia, from 1832 to 1839, and from 1836 to 1843 respectively, members of executive councils were also the sole members of legislative councils.[9] Thus there can be little doubt that the governor and his executive council, whether or not they agreed on all general or specific policies formed at least the nucleus of the early colonial political and administrative *élite*.

Broadly speaking, historians and other commentators writing about the character of sections of this *élite* have been content to select cases and on the basis of their selection make general statements of a quantitative nature which describe this *élite* in one of two ways; the Sancho Panza, failed gentry way, or the Samuel Smiles, successful careerist way. Generally neither way of describing the *élite* is well documented nor based on anything more than a narrow selection of cases. Our impression is that the Sancho Panza view is the more popular. A few examples will show what we mean.

In the 1830s one writer's view was that colonial executive officialdom was composed of 'briefless barristers, broken down merchants, ruined debauchees, the offal of every calling and profession'.[10] In the 1880s another commentator noted that in the 'good old times' a colonial governor was regarded as 'an eccentric individual with an ambition not much higher than that of Sancho Panza. Frequently he was the discredited scion of an illustrious house and the pest of the Colonial Office.' The naval and military men from whom the governors were chosen, had only the recommendation of 'several years' service by land and sea'.[11] More recently it has been argued that the majority of the early officials in Van Diemen's Land (only one of those described, except for the governors, was an executive councillor) were not of 'high calibre' and, being second-raters, they had been dumped by their patrons and influential friends in that isolated penal colony.[12]

The chief advocate of the Smilesian position is Professor Auchmuty who concluded that during the first half-century of settlement in Australia only two of the early governors, Brisbane and Bourke, came from 'established families'. The others were of 'fairly humble origin' and had 'either themselves or in their fathers' generation forced their way upwards in a society which was far more fluid than we are today likely to admit'. These governors had 'made their way in the world mainly through their own ability, but largely because that ability was recognized in the circles where influence on appointments could be exercised'. They were a group of able, competent men and, though some of them may have gone to sea at an early age, still they showed by 'our standards an amazingly high level of education'.[13] In his study of governors of Western Australia, P. J. Boyce also concluded among other things that although they had some connections none of them would have been well known in England and that they were largely from middle-class professional families or the Irish gentry and most were moderately well educated.[14]

One important point to note about all these views is that although they relate to Australia they also reflect opinions about the structure and nature of English society in the late eighteenth and early nineteenth centuries and give expression to widely different views about the nature and meaning of emigration from England in that period. The rest of this chapter will endeavour to throw some light on these problems.

Method of categorization

In order to carry out our own survey, we first compiled a list of all those who had ever been a governor and of those who had ever filled an official position with a place in any one of the executive councils in all the Australian colonies for the period 1788–1856. In this period 126 men served in one capacity or another. Forty-six of these were governors, the rest were executive councillors. We were able to get some information on 43 of the governors and on 64 of the 80 executive councillors; of these 21 were colonial secretaries, 7 treasurers, 9 advocates-general, and 27 were holders of various official positions which we have classed as 'others'.

Our main source of information throughout was the *Australian Dictionary of Biography* supplemented where necessary by Percival Serle's *Dictionary of Australian Biography*, Johns's *An Australian Biographical Dictionary*, Mennell's *Dictionary of Australian Biography*, *Dictionary of National Biography* and *Australian Encyclopaedia*. In addition, we used individual biographies and information provided by N. B. Nairn and the staff of the *Australian Dictionary of Biography*, who also put us in touch with many contributors to the ADB who were often able to supply us with details lacking in the original articles.

Our next task was to draw up a questionnaire which originally consisted of forty-one questions, each question including a number of alternative responses. As the work progressed and as it became clearer what type of information was available in the ADB, various questions and alternative responses were changed or discarded and the final questionnaire was the result of our original design adjusted by familiarity with the biographical material and the technical requirements which were demanded by us and the computer for ease of storage and calculation. Our first list of countries in questions 12 and 13 was enlarged by the addition of, for example, India and the West Indies; new occupational and educational categories had to be included, while our original question 14, which sought to reveal a subject's income, wealth and the amount of land owned, had to be discarded. Question 32 originally asked the subject's ordinal position in his family, but was altered to his position among his father's sons since this latter information was more frequently given in the ADB articles.

Before proceeding to our results it is necessary to make clearer and add certain qualifications to the way in which our material was organized.

First, the term 'governor' was applied in a wide sense to actually commissioned governors, and to lieutenant governors and acting governors who administered a colony during a commissioned governor's absence.[15] Thus the term 'governor' applied to all those officials who were at some stage or another at the top of the administrative ladder. Councillors who were acting governors at one time but held another official position, for example the colonial secretaryship, were recorded as 'governor' in question 6. By classifying in such a manner we have a continuous run of the top administrators as well as placing such men in a category which reflects the peak of their administrative careers in the Australian colonies.

In order to gain consistency in determining a subject's occupation and social stratum we formulated a number of general rules which applied when there was any doubt at all about categorization. If a subject had more than one occupation in his country of origin then the last position he held, provided that he held it for more than a year, was the one which was acknowledged on form A.[16] Certain difficulties arose over the occupational status of both army and naval officers; if a subject was either one of these and held no other employment and did not serve in an *administrative* capacity in any of the British colonies (though he may have been stationed or fought there) then he was categorized simply as 'army officer' or 'naval officer'. Even though a few army officers were also engineers they were listed as officers since they worked on army pay and under army direction. However, so that we could enumerate the total number of people who had served in the colonial administrative service, army or navy officers who had done such service were listed as 'government employees in the colonial service'.

Categorization for a subject's occupation in the Australian colonies also needed a guide line since it was quite common for a subject before or after he became an executive councillor, or even while he held the latter position, to be employed in a variety of ways. Similarly executive councillors who were also lawyers presented a problem as to whether they should be classified as 'government employees' or 'lawyers'. In all cases the most important point taken into consideration was the length of service. If a lawyer held his position on the council only occasionally and then for a relatively limited period of time he was classified as a lawyer. When we were unsure about placing a subject in any one occupation because he was employed in a variety of ways and the time period and importance of each was not clear, then he was classified as 'other'.

Social stratification was determined according to the categories on form B. In many cases the authors of articles in the ADB were asked to categorize the subjects' parents according to social stratum on the basis of their own detailed knowledge. If a subject arrived in the colonies as a child then his social stratum in country of origin was taken to be the same as that of his father.

Approximations are evident in the answers to three of our questions. Years spent in the colonies and the executive councils (questions 10 and 11) were recorded as whole years only. Thus one year means anything up to a year, between one and two years is recorded as two years and so on. Dates of birth and death (questions 4 and 5) which are marked in the ADB with question marks are accepted as being as accurate as possible under present circumstances.

The number of a subject's children (question 37) is the total number of legitimate children a man fathered regardless of how many times he was married.[17]

Though 12 per cent of our subjects married more than once there was only one category for their age at marriage (question 36) so the figure we entered here was the age at which they first married.

Summaries and interpretation of data

As we have already indicated, there were 126 men who served either as governor in the period 1788 to 1855–6 or as executive councillor in the period 1825 to 1855–6. Information of one kind or another is available for 107 (85 per cent) of them. For the purpose of analysis and report and for the reasons given in the section on executive councils and their members we have chosen to regard our subjects as members of a single group identifiable by the fact that each of its members exercised constitutional executive and administrative power and that their appointment and dismissal was the prerogative of the Colonial Office or its predecessor, the Department for the Colonies. Thus our sample does not include those men who assisted governors in carrying out their duties before 1825.

All of our subjects were born between 1737 and 1827 and were remarkably long-lived; their average age at death was sixty-nine and the average length of life of those born after 1800 was over seventy years. As well as living long they also married late. The average age at marriage was thirty-three and almost a quarter of them postponed marriage until they were more than thirty-six. When they first arrived in the Australian colonies they were, on the whole, no longer young; the average age on first arrival was nearly thirty-seven. After their arrival they spent an average of eighteen and a half years in Australia, just over five of which they spent in one of the executive councils or as governor. Forty per cent of them stayed and died in the colonies.

As was to be expected, all of them were white and British but not all were born in the British Isles. Of the group whose birthplace is recorded (ninety-four), 10 per cent were born outside the home islands in India, the West Indies, Portugal and at sea, 56 per cent were born in England, 15 per cent in Scotland, 17 per cent in Ireland and 1 per cent in Wales. Compared with the proportions of the national groups in the population of Great Britain (see Table 1) the English were very slightly over-represented, the Scots substantially over-represented, and the Welsh and the Irish very much under-represented. Indeed only six (14 per cent) of forty-three governors were born in Ireland and, as far as we could ascertain, none was a Roman Catholic.

H

TABLE 8 *Birthplace of governors and executive councillors in Australia 1788–1856*

Birthplace	Governors and executive councillors (94) (%)	Distribution of population of UK (%)	
		1781	1831
England	56	54	55
Wales	1	4	3
Scotland	15	11	10
Ireland	17	31	32
Outside British Isles	10		

A breakdown of the contingents from England and Scotland shows an even greater degree of concentration of origin. Of the fourteen born in Scotland, eight came from the central Lowlands, and of the fifty-three born in England, twenty-three (43 per cent) came from the counties of Kent, Surrey, Middlesex, Essex and London, whose share in the total population of England in 1801 was 19·5 per cent, and only three (6 per cent) from counties north of the Trent with 37 per cent of the total population. In all, over a third of all governors and executive councillors whose county of birth is known (ninety-one) came from the Home Counties and the Lowlands of Scotland.

As we have said, 40 per cent of our subjects stayed and died in the Australian colonies. A further 10 per cent died in other English colonies and 47 per cent returned to die in the British Isles—29 per cent in the Home Counties. Only three out of fourteen Scots and three out of sixteen Irishmen returned to die in their country of birth.

Information about religious affiliation was available for only fifty-five of our subjects. According to our classification 76 per cent were Anglicans, 13 per cent Presbyterians, 7 per cent Non-conformists and 4 per cent Roman Catholics. These proportions are roughly similar to the proportions of these four religious groups in the total population of England, Wales and Scotland. However, the inclusion of Ireland would substantially increase the proportion of Roman Catholics in the total and lead to a considerable under-representation of Roman Catholics in our sample.

According to our classification of occupation in country of origin,

41 per cent of all governors and executive councillors (44/107) were army or navy officers many of whom had had colonial experience. (Sixty-five per cent of governors and 28 per cent of other executive councillors were army or navy officers.) Another 26 per cent were government employees almost all of whom had had substantial administrative experience in other British colonies—of the forty-one governors, nine had been governors or lieutenant governors in other colonies, at least three others had had considerable administrative experience and two were engineer officers. The next largest occupational groups were lawyers, 9 per cent, and ministers of religion, 6 per cent. These figures suggest, therefore, that about eight out of ten of Australia's ruling bureaucracy were drawn from the military, naval, government, legal and religious professions, all of which were themselves conducive to bureaucratic attitudes and values. On the other hand there were no bankers or manufacturers and only two merchants in this ruling *élite*. Furthermore, only two of the governors and executive councillors in almost seventy years had had any close connection with the land as farmer, owner-occupier, steward or landowner before moving to the Australian colonies.[18]

Our occupational analysis also throws some light on the changing basis for recruitment into the colonial service and emphasizes in particular the importance in this respect of the introduction of executive councils in eastern Australia in 1825. In New South Wales until 1825 and in Van Diemen's Land until 1824 all governors were army or navy officers. Thereafter, until the introduction of responsible government, only four out of nine governors in New South Wales and three out of seven in Van Diemen's Land were, according to our classification, army or navy officers. Of the non-military governors appointed in these two colonies after 1825, eight out of a total of nine had had previous administrative experience in other British colonies. Thus the balance of appointments to the top administrative and executive posts was shifted more towards the career 'civil servant' and away from the career officer. Of the forty executive councillors in eastern Australia on whom we have information, only eight were army or navy officers before coming to Australia. Indeed, in New South Wales and Van Diemen's Land (Tasmania) combined, between 1825 and 1855, the proportion was as little as four out of twenty-eight and, of these, three had resigned their commissions some years before they first sat in an executive council.

In Western and South Australia the pattern of development in administrative and executive appointments after 1828 and 1836 respectively was more reminiscent of the early history of eastern Australia. In South Australia five out of the first eight governors were army officers. In Western Australia the first two governors were officers. Thereafter they were drawn from men with experience in other colonies. A higher proportion of executive councillors also came from the military—eight out of twenty-four compared with eight out of forty in eastern Australia. However, of the eight, two had resigned their commissions some years before accepting appointment to an executive council and one executive councillor, J. S. Roe in Western Australia, was on forty years' leave from the navy! Overall, a third of all executive councillors had either been government employees, many with colonial experience, or lawyers before arriving in Australia. And, in general, one can say that the growing preference in the Colonial Office for making appointments from the non-military professions and from career administrators is clearly evident in our occupational analysis. As was to be expected, most, that is eighty-five or 79 per cent of our subjects, once in Australia, took up employment according to our classification as government employees in the colonial service. Only a handful remained employed as army or navy officers, ministers of religion or lawyers.

The occupational classification of our subjects was used as the basis for classifying them according to social stratum. Our main guide lines for this operation are set out in form B. However, we also gave subjective weighting to other information about rank, other occupations, descriptive or literary comment, and the advice of contributors to the ADB. We also attempted a social stratum classification for the fathers and mothers of our subjects. We were successful for only twenty-seven mothers, but were able to classify ninety-nine (93 per cent) of our subjects and eighty (75 per cent) of their fathers. Our decisions about classification are summarized in Table 9.

As was to be expected, very few governors and executive councillors had their origins in social strata IV, V and VI. Some came from social strata I and II but two-thirds came from social strata III which, by the 1830s and 1840s, was also the main recruiting ground for the middling class. However, we did have difficulty in determining the boundaries between social strata II and III, and since our subjects included few men who for lack of information could properly be described as big employers of labour or men outstandingly successful in their professions we prefer to treat these two social strata as one and to rely more on occupational categories as guides to the social origins and social mobility of our subjects.

We have information on occupation for our subjects in country of origin and for subjects' fathers for seventy-seven (72 per cent) father/son pairs. The occupational distribution for these two groups is presented in Table 10.

TABLE 9 *Social stratum of governors and executive councillors in Australia 1788–1856*

Social stratum	Distribution			
	column I Subjects (99)		column II Subjects' fathers (80)	
	no.	%	no.	%
I	15	15	16	20
II	18	18	23	29
III	65	67	38	48
IV	1	1	3	4
V				
VI				
Unknown	8		27	
Total	107		107	

TABLE 10 *Occupational distribution for seventy-seven father/son pairs*

	Fathers	Sons
Landowner	9	
Army officer	17	29
Navy officer	2	7
Minister of religion	17	4
Government employee	6	21
Lawyer/solicitor	5	10
Land steward/Tenant farmer/Land agent	3	1
Antiquarian	1	
Architect/draughtsman	1	1
Doctor/surgeon	3	2
Economist	1	
Teacher/tutor	2	
Merchant	4	1
Other commercial/industrial proprietor	3	
Student		1
Army (OR)	1	
Navy (OR)	1	
Cook	1	

The distribution presented in Table 10 suggests that there were two streams of social mobility which were channelled through four professions to provide the men who constituted Australia's political and administrative *élite* during our period. The first stream is made up of movement out of landowning and the Church; probably this movement represents a stream of downward social mobility at least as far as landowning is concerned, but not one of the sons affected was a discredited scion! The second stream is out of commercial and industrial activities and out of the lowest social stratum. This looks very like upward social mobility; the son of a millowner, a draper, a merchant, a cook, a master gunner, a sergeant major or a private tutor probably regarded his own status as an army or navy officer as superior to that of his father. Fathers too, no doubt, thought so when their sons achieved even higher status as governor or executive councillor in one of the Australian colonies. The funnel, or was it a sieve, through which this *élite* had to pass was clearly made up of the army, the navy, government service in England or in one of her colonies, and the law; thirty fathers but sixty-seven (87 per cent) sons were in these four professions.

However, a further aspect of social mobility is brought out by comparison between the professions of fathers and sons which is not tabulated here. It is that twenty-six (34 per cent) sons went into the same profession as their fathers—of the eighteen army officers and other ranks among the fathers, sixteen had sons who went into the army. Moreover, even when sons did not follow fathers it is our impression based on all our attempts at categorizing, that most of our subjects were at least second-generation members of the middling set of people or quasi-group referred to earlier. In this connection the differences in social stratification between fathers and sons, shown in columns I and II in Table 9, is more the result of the fact that fathers were classified at the height of their careers and our subjects early in theirs than it is an indication of real downward social mobility. Thus almost 80 per cent of fathers and 84 per cent of sons were in the professional occupations listed as suitable for inclusion in social strata II and III and scarcely any fell into any of the other occupations so listed. Most changes in social status were, therefore, the result of promotion or demotion within the ranks of a handful of professions rather than movement into and out of a wide range of occupations or movement across the boundaries between social stratum I and other social strata.

This suggests to us that the San Gimignano model of social structure is a good fit for late eighteenth- and early nineteenth-century England.[19] However, according to our classification, all our subjects at the height of their careers were in social stratum I and it would not be difficult to show wholesale upward social mobility over the two generations.

No doubt it is historians' impressionistic awareness of the downwardly mobile among our subjects which has given rise to the Sancho Panza view with its emphasis on terms like 'second-rate', 'discredited scion', 'offal of every calling' and so on. Yet in our terminology, 'downwardly mobile' has no such connotations. We recognize that downward mobility may result just as much from misfortune or the mere fact of being a younger son as from any innate inferiority or second-ratedness. We must, therefore, reiterate that the main message of our calculations is that the majority of the ruling *élite* in the Australian colonies were men from a few professions in social strata II and III whose fathers were also in this same group of professions in social strata II and III. That is, they were at least second-generation members of the middling set of people.

We also hazard the interpretation that as a group they were more highly motivated by considerations of a rational, calculative and prudential kind and were thereby more highly achievement motivated and more given over to the idea of work and success than were men in either higher or lower social strata. We infer this from two sets of undeniably objective evidence: age at marriage and number of children in family.

Table 11 summarizes a series of calculations of age at first

TABLE 11 *Mean age at first marriage of governors and executive councillors in Australia 1788–1856*

	Mean age
First marriage* (78)	33·11
First marriage† (77)	32·59
Marriage of those first marrying before 1829 (34)	30·50
Marriage of those first marrying after 1830 (43)	34·25
Marriage of governors (33)	33·63

* Includes one man first marrying at age 73.
† Excludes one man first marrying at age 73.

marriage of all those for whom this information is available: seventy-eight (62 per cent) of all governors and executive councillors.

Comparisons of the mean marriage age of our subjects with those recorded by investigators studying other groups show clearly that governors and executive councillors had an exceptionally high average age of marriage. In Peller's study the mean marriage age of men in European ruling families in the period 1800–1849 was 28·4.[20] In Hollingsworth's study of British ducal families the mean age of marriage of the cohort born 1730–79 was 28·6.[21] In our study the mean age for the group marrying before 1829 who were born in the period 1738–1803 was 30·5, for those who married after 1830 it was 34·25. In Wrigley's study of Colyton in Devon[22] the mean marriage age for men was:

	No.	Age
1770–99	93	27·6
1800–24	67	25·6
1825–37	59	25·9

Tranter's study of Cardington in Bedfordshire in 1782 records a mean age of marriage for men of 26.[23] Therefore, the mean age at first marriage of Australia's political *élite* was much higher than that of either the English or European aristocracy or the English rural labourer and village dweller. Furthermore, the distribution of age at first marriage (Table 12) shows that only 18 per cent married before the age of 26 whilst 36 per cent either never married or postponed marriage until they were more than 36.

TABLE 12   *Age at first marriage of governors and executive councillors in Australia 1788–1856 (n = 107)*

Age	20–25	26–30	31–35	36–40	41–45	46–50	Over 50	Never married	Not known
No.	15	19	20	12	3	8	1	7	22
%	18	22	24	14	4	9	1	8	

A further calculation of the age of marriage of those in social strata III and IV shows the mean age to be 33·9 (fifty-one) compared with the mean age of 31·5 for those in social strata I and II (twenty-two).

The late marriages contracted by our subjects influenced the number of children born to them. For those whose number of legitimate children is recorded (seventy-four) the mean number of children born was 4·51. Table 13, however, summarizes our attempt to show the influence of period of marriage and mean age at marriage on the number of children born.

TABLE 13 *Period of marriage, mean age of first marriage and number of children born to governors and executive councillors in Australia 1788–1856*

Period of marriage	Mean age at first marriage	Number of children born
1763–1867	32·59 (77)	4·51 (74)
Before 1829 (31)	30·51 (31)	5·77 (31)
After 1830 (33)	35·78 (33)	3·89 (33)

Estimates of family size for other groups in roughly comparable periods are as follows. In Cardington, Bedfordshire, in 1782 there were between 5 and 5·5 baptisms per family.[24] In Colyton in Devon the completed family size of women marrying under 30 in the period 1770–1837 was 5·9.[25] The number of births per father among Europe's ruling families in the period 1800–1849 was 5·2 and the average family size of sons of British ducal families who were born 1720–1829 was 4·92.[26] In England as a whole the average size of completed family of cohorts marrying in the period 1861–9 was 6·16.[27] Our estimates for the average number of children born to members of the Australian political *élite* marrying between 1830 and 1867 is 3·87. Since our figures are for total legitimate births unadjusted by mortality rates in infancy and childhood, and since the other estimates used here for purposes of comparison sometimes incorporated the effects of mortality to arrive at estimates of family size then it is likely that our calculations over-estimate the mean relative size of family of our subjects by at least 20 per cent.[28] Therefore, even if some allowance is made for under-recording of births in the ADB, it is clear that the maximum possible average size of completed family for our subjects could never have been so high as for other social groups. Since, also, the average completed family size in England was still as high as 4·81 for cohorts marrying as late as 1886 it seems legitimate to hazard the opinion that these members of Australia's ruling *élite* were successful Malthusian men whose life style had kept down the burdens and charges upon them which they would otherwise have incurred through early marriage.[29] As early nineteenth-century precursors of the prudential middle classes of the later nineteenth century they were undoubtedly an exceptional group.

As far as we can judge from a very much smaller sample of our subjects, they were also exceptional in regard to education. We were able to obtain information on school education for only forty-four (41 per cent) of our subjects. Our summary of the information is in Table 14.

TABLE 14   *School education of governors and executive councillors in Australia 1788–1856*

	No. (44)	% of sample (44)	% of total (107)	Governors only (18)
Privately educated	12	27	11	3
Public school	5	11	5	1
Grammar school	9	20	8	5
Some mixture of private, public, grammar	2	5	2	
Naval or military academy, or shipboard education	7	16	7	3
Combination of naval or military with either or all of private, public, grammar	9	20	8	6
Unknown			59	

As can be seen from Table 14, our subjects were mostly educated in the ancient grammar schools or in a sequence of schools which at some stage included education in a naval or military academy. Indeed, 36 per cent of our small sample were educated in the latter manner and 20 per cent in grammar schools. Our sample, however, is weighted in favour of governors. Eighteen out of the forty-four were governors. Thus we have information on 43 per cent of all governors of whom only one was wholly a public-school man and three privately educated. The rest (fourteen out of eighteen) were educated in grammar schools or in naval or military academies or on shipboard. The proportion of privately-educated and public-school men in the sample is thus considerably higher for executive councillors, i.e. 50 per cent. However, the large number of 'unknowns' could well reflect the probability that the educational status of the vast majority of governors and executive councillors was so lowly as not to find a place in the record. To say this, however, is not to say that the level of education was a lowly one for, as we shall see, a high proportion of our subjects had some form of post-school education.

One type of school which figured largely in eighteenth-century England but which is completely absent from the educational backgrounds of Australia's governors and executive councillors is the Dissenting academy. Since there were only two Congregation-alists, one Calvinist Evangelical and one Moravian among our subjects, this is not surprising. But it does confirm in a negative fashion that eighteenth- and early nineteenth-century England provided few opportunities outside industry and commerce for the energies and enterprise of members of the Dissenting sects.

The number of firm responses to our question on 'higher' education was greater than that on school education. Of the 107 subjects for whom we managed to obtain some information 36 per cent had no formal education beyond school level, 34 per cent were unknown, but 29 per cent (thirty-two) were educated at a university, the Inns of Court or both. In fact these thirty-two represent 25.3 per cent of all our 126 subjects. Their places of 'higher' education are listed in Table 15.

TABLE 15   *Places of higher education of thirty-two governors and executive councillors in Australia 1788–1856*

	Governors (n = 43)	Governors and Exccutive Councillors (n = 126)	% of Total (126)
Trinity	2	10	7.9
Cambridge		8	6.3
Oxford	1	3	2.4
Edinburgh	2	2	1.6
Aberdeen	1	1	0.8
Inns of Court	2	8	6.3

By way of elaboration of the raw figures in Table 15 we note that of the twenty-four listed as attending a university, six also spent terms at the Inns of Court and that at least six others were under-taking their studies for professional purposes, to gain entry into the Church or the law. Indeed, of the thirty-two with higher education, seventeen studied for the legal profession and at least three intended to enter the Church. A further striking fact about our subjects is that while there were only sixteen Irishmen among the governors and executive councillors, six of them had been educated at Trinity (two in preparation for the law), three at Trinity and the Inns of Court, one at Oxford, and one at the Inns of Court. In all, eleven out of sixteen had received a 'higher' education, six of them in law, and most of them finished up in Victoria.

Thus, beyond all doubt, our subjects had experienced a longer and more vocationally oriented education than the general population and they can only be regarded collectively as second-rate in regard to education if one assumes that those who went to Eton and Harrow, Oxford and Cambridge were by definition first-rate and that men educated at English grammar schools, in naval or military academies, and at an Irish university or the Inns of Court could never be first-raters. However, since education at a military academy or the Inns of Court was likely to be the consequence of revealed ability and a career motivation, and education at a public school and an ancient university frequently a confirmation of a way of life, we suspect that what little we could discover about the education of our subjects points to the notion that many of them were able men for whom education was an aid to upward social mobility. Certainly there were some among them who struggled against great odds to perform well and achieve efficiently and sometimes honestly in Australia; among them Grey in South Australia, Gipps and Deas Thomson in New South Wales, Roe in Western Australia, and Chapman in Van Diemen's Land. Moreover, in connection with this question of the calibre of our subjects when measured, as it frequently is, by reference to inefficiency, incompetence and corruption, we consider that none of the evidence adduced shows that they were *more* corrupt, inefficient or incompetent than officials in England where there was massive corruption and inefficiency in all aspects of parish and town government, in the administration of the Poor Law, in the granting of sinecures, pensions and places, and in all walks of life from the highest to the lowest.[30]

One other way in which the governors among our subjects were distinguished from other sections of the English community from which they came is that an unusually high proportion of them were eldest sons. We have information on position in order of sons for thirty-one of forty-three governors. Twenty-two of the thirty-one were eldest sons. A comparison with other groups is summarized in Table 16.

Again, although we do not wish to make too much of these calculations, they do suggest that top colonial administrators were differentiated not only in respect of place of origin, occupation, social stratum, schooling, age at marriage and number of children, but also according to position in family. Two possible explanations of the high proportion of eldest sons among governors occur to us. One is that eldest sons in Great Britain grew up in families which had high expectations for the eldest son, and that eldest children as a group were treated in such a way so as to motivate them to perform well at every stage of their development. Consequently, eldest sons might have been more highly achievement motivated than younger sons.[31] A second possibility is that parents in the middling strata of society sought more assiduously to educate and place their eldest sons than they did younger ones. Perhaps what was at work was some combination of both influences.

The question of placement through patronage was of course an important one in a society in which scarce positions were still allocated through connection and influence, and our guess is that almost all our subjects at some time in their careers gained some advantage from an act of favour by someone with more influence than themselves. So far, however, we have made no attempt to quantify this aspect of social mobility in relation to our subjects. What we have done is try to determine whether our subjects derived any improvement in worldly wealth, position or status from their marriages. Of the list of forty-three governors probably forty were married and we found sufficient information on twenty-one wives to classify them, by their fathers' occupations, into one or other of

TABLE 16   *Proportion of eldest sons among Australian governors 1788–1856*

	Ratio of younger sons to eldest sons		
	Younger sons	:	eldest sons
British ducal families born 1680–1872	1·70	:	1
British ducal families born 1830–1939	1·54	:	1
Executive councillors (32)	1·46	:	1
Governors (31)	0·40	:	1

our social strata. Our findings were that governors in social stratum I tended to marry women from the two social strata beneath them; governors in social stratum III either married into their own or a higher social stratum and the single governor in social stratum II married into his own social stratum. Only in five cases out of the twenty-one could we find evidence of the husband making direct occupational or mercenary gain through marriage. Of the five mentioned, Bligh, Stephens and FitzRoy were helped or enabled by their wives' relatives to gain employment. Phillip acquired land, and Macquarie money. Also Brisbane probably gained through his marriage to an heiress. Unfortunately there was little information on the wives of our subjects who held office below position of governor; out of a probable total of sixty-one wives we could only classify eighteen of them. The trend was much the same as for governors, at least for subjects in social stratum III who tended to marry women from their own or a higher social stratum. As with the governors there were very few subjects in social stratum II— only five; three of these married into social stratum III, one into I and one into II. We could find evidence of only four subjects in the non-governor group who benefited materially from their marriages. One subject acquired money and in the other three cases the wives' relatives were instrumental to some degree in aiding the husbands to find employment. On the basis of these observations, incomplete as they are, it would be difficult to argue that governors and executive councillors used marriage as a means of improving their fortune and status, though admittedly the group which would have most needed these improvements—those subjects in social stratum III—were also the only group which, to some extent at least, tended to marry into a higher social stratum.

The results of this very restricted survey are presented in Table 17.

The social profile of governors and executive councillors which emerges from our survey suggests that they were mainly at least second-generation members of a middling set of people who lived either in the Home Counties or the Lowlands of Scotland and were members of the Anglican or Presbyterian Churches. For the most part they had been educated to 'secondary' level either privately or in grammar schools or in some way incorporating a spell at a military or naval school or academy. A large minority of them

TABLE 17 *Marriages of governors and executive councillors in Australia 1788–1856 according to social stratification of wives*

Governors (43)

Social strata of governors	Social strata of wives					
	I	II	III	IV	V	VI
I (9)	2	2	5			
II (1)	1					
III (11)	6		4			1
Total (21)	9	2	9			1

Executive councillors (83)

Social strata of executive councillors	Social strata of wives					
	I	II	III	IV	V	VI
I (—)						
II (5)	1	1	3			
III (13)	3	2	8			
Total (18)	4	3	11			

had been either to university or the Inns of Court to study for the Church or the law. The small Irish contingent was almost wholly university educated. In the main they had had to make their own way in the world and they did so either as an officer in the army or navy, as a government employee or through the law. Many benefited at some stage in their careers from some act of favour but few married either money or influence. Those who were in the army, navy or government service tended to have had experience in senior administrative or technical posts in some other British colony before being appointed to an executive post in Australia. Probably as a consequence of preference for a higher social status rather than a lower one and the necessity for them to make their own way in the world they had a greater tendency to postpone marriage and to have fewer children than most other social classes. Only a small proportion of them ever re-married. Governors also seemed to have derived some advantage from being themselves eldest sons. Once in the colonies they tended to forsake all occupations except those connected with government service which for them was the road to higher status and maximum achievement. Physically they appear to have been tough and lived to a good age. A large minority of them died in Australia. Of those who returned to the United Kingdom, a majority retired to the Home Counties—few of those who were born elsewhere, for example, in Ireland or Scotland, retired to their country of birth. On the whole they seem to us to have been men who would have been much respected by Samuel Smiles and incomprehensible to Sancho Panza.

Élites *in early Australia*
Form B
Classification for social stratum

Social stratum

  I Landowners employing tenant farmers.
    Senior clergy (bishop and higher).
    Senior army and naval officers (above rank of lieutenant-general or captain).
    Governors and members of executive council.
 II Owner-occupiers employing labour (more than 4).
    Tenant farmers employing labour (more than 5).
    Land stewards or agents.
    Manufacturers employing more than 25.
    Large bankers, merchants, judges, lawyers and other professions.
III Lesser clergy, junior army and navy officers.
    Lesser professional groups: teachers, clergy, doctors, clerks, government employees.
    Small shopkeepers, small employers of labour.
    Owner-occupiers or tenants not employing labour.
 IV Artisans and higher domestic servants.
  V Skilled and semi-skilled labourers in manufacturing industry.
 VI Unskilled labourers in urban and agricultural trade, lower domestic servants, street traders, unemployed, etc.

6

'Middle-class'[1] morality and the systematic colonizers

My starting-point in this chapter is the integrationist models of mid- and late nineteenth-century English society associated with the names of Peter Cominos and Steven Marcus.[2] Both writers describe nineteenth-century English society as one in which sexual mores and practices, and the sexual identity of men and women, were functionally integrated into the social and economic structure of society. I propose to try to relax some of the premises underlying their arguments in order to portray the middle strata of society as less ideologically homogeneous and, therefore, more flexible and capable of generating change from within than Marcus permits, and able to choose from more alternatives than Cominos is willing to allow. I hope to show that mid-Victorian society was much less rigidly articulated than is suggested by both writers who largely work within the conventions of the three-class model. This is important not only for understanding what life was 'really' like but also for understanding how change came about.

First a look at the main organizing theme of each of the works to be discussed.

Peter Cominos begins with the assumption that what he calls 'respectable sexual ideology' was integrated in a comprehensive system of relationships.[3] Component beliefs of respectable sexual ideology were: the only purpose of sexual intercourse was the propagation of the species in marriage, physical desire in women was almost non-existent, contraception permitted the gratification of mere sensual appetites and frustrated the only legitimate purpose of sexual intercourse, reason and feeling were diametrically opposed, sensual man was the enemy of civilized man. These beliefs were rationalizations arising out of the tensions set up within respectable man. According to Cominos there were only two choices for the man who sought 'the status of comfort' and 'the comfort of status'.[4] These were continence and the sublimation of the sexual appetite in work, or incontinence accompanied by descent into the lowest stratum, the 'residuum'. Respectable man resolved the resulting tensions through strength of character. Strength of character meant choosing continence both before and after marriage as well as conformity to the other beliefs of respectable sexual ideology.

Peter Cominos does not stop there. He says:

> The mere narration of the process ... did not in itself yield the historical meaning of the gospel of thrift in semen. To understand the process historically is to ascertain the function of continence in a comprehensive system of relationships. More specifically the gospel of continence reveals its meaning when it is related to (1) the dynamic quality inherent in the structure and functioning of the Respectable Economic System, the compulsion to accumulate and re-invest capital, (2) Respectable thought about the purpose of political economy, and (3) the degree of integration of the virtue of continence into the Respectable Social System.

By way of expanding on the first two of these themes Cominos repeatedly asserts that the prevailing sexual ideology was the product of the economic system. Thus:

> The realization of the dynamic quality (an inherent compulsion to accumulate and re-invest capital) *produced derivative economic virtues and vices* ... In congruency with the dynamic quality of the economic system were not only the economic virtues, but their summation in a highly exaggerated form of the disciplined and ascetic life.

And again,

> It is certainly necessary here to avert any confusion between what appears to have been that exaggerated asceticism just described and which *derived from the structure and functioning of the economic system* and the asceticism and disciplined life which derived from the imperative need for self-control and self-discipline in the formation of a 'permanent political society'.

And, in answer to his own question, 'What has all this to do with the gospel of thrift in semen?', he wrote, 'The economic virtues and vices—*derivatives of the dynamic quality inherent in the structure and functioning of the economic system and vindicated by the political economists—included the sexual virtues and vices of continence and incontinence.* ...'[5]

Of course there is more to Cominos's article than this. There are qualifications, asides and elaborations. Nevertheless, the central organizing thesis seems to be that the sexual ideology of the English 'middle classes' in the middle of the nineteenth century was an integral part of their economic ideology and was derived from the capitalist mode of production, most particularly from its need for saving and capital accumulation. Thus the corollary of thrift in capital was thrift in semen.

In outlining one of the organizing themes running through Steven Marcus's work I do not intend to discuss anything he has to say about the relationship of pornography to literature. My main interest is in his own avowed purpose:

> to add a further dimension to Weber's great work on the relation between modern forms of economic and social organization and the kind of character that was necessary to create those forms and to perpetuate them—namely I have tried to demonstrate that the theory should include an account of how sexual energies were enlisted in and affected by the change.[6]

Marcus admits that a good deal of nineteenth-century sexual ideology represented a hangover from earlier periods and that 'the impulses and fantasies of pornography are transhistorical'. Nevertheless, he also believes

> that in our society sexual beliefs, practices, and institutions were more susceptible to radical alteration than their counterparts in economic and social activity; another way of putting it is to say that in our society the fundamental organizations of economic and social behaviour have been more resistant to radical change than have the institutions which govern and express sexual beliefs and behaviour. From this point of view, then, sexual moral beliefs and certain forms of sexual practice take on the surprising appearance of a superstructure, to which the more resistant institutions of economic and social organization function as a substructure.

What happened in the course of the eighteenth and nineteenth centuries was a restructuring of personality and the development of a character which was 'more armoured and more rigidified, a character capable of sustained executive action, yet a character also less spontaneous, less openly sexual'.[7]

Marcus also argues that the capitalist mode of production and the economics of capitalism were such dominant influences in shaping sexual ideology that not only the practices but also the fantasies of normal and abnormal sexuality were couched in the terminology and imagery of economic practice and ideology.[8]

According to Marcus economy, economics, class and sexual ideology were so tightly bound together in a mesh of inter-relationships in the mid-Victorian period that change had to wait on influences from outside. Whereas Cominos sees the changes in sexual ideology which occurred at the end of the nineteenth century as being part of a general revolt against authority, Marcus gives the chief role in achieving a breakthrough to Freudian psychology and the novelists. Other aspects of the breakthrough merely followed the first two.

In these accounts of nineteenth-century ideology, deviations from the sexual norms are to be found only in the very lowest or very highest strata of society. Cominos, although recognizing the dual morality implied in the differences between the norm of absolute continence and the double standard is content to see these two attitudes as variants of the same basic ideology. The implication is that there was only one sexual social class consciousness among the 'middle classes' and deviation was class (stratum) determined. (The argument is very similar to that about the political element in social class consciousness discussed in the earlier essays in this collection.) Similarly it is claimed that the economic component of Victorian 'middle-class' ideology was what Marx said it was, namely an inherent compulsion to accumulate and re-invest capital in an economy in which capital accumulation was the be all and end all of economic activity.

It is my purpose in this section to draw attention to 'middle-class' deviations from 'middle-class' ideology which have considerable importance not only for our description of Victorian society but also for understanding more about the central problem of how change came about.

In the matter of sexual ideology we know enough about two of its beliefs to claim that there was a strong minority ideology within the ranks of the 'middle classes'. These two beliefs are those about the sexual impulse in women and contraception. As both Cominos and Marcus show, it was one of the sexual conventions of the nine-teenth century that women had virtually no sexual impulse. It is also argued that deviation from this ideological norm was both class (stratum) linked and a characteristic of the world of prostitution and pornography. Yet the facts are, that some very respectable nineteenth-century figures expressed a belief in the existence of a strong sexual impulse in women irrespective of social stratum, respectable women did admit to strong sexual impulse, and there was a literature which sought to spread this notion. The significance of this is that respectable women, not just the sex-object women of pornography, were regarded by some men as being like men in this respect. The sexual identity of some women incorporated the same idea. This in itself was a liberating and humanizing notion and, if not a retreat from the 'Toryism of sex', was at least a refusal to advance further. On the wider question of the relationship of sexual ideology to class (stratum) the mere existence of this minority suggests that either the connection between socio-economic position and sexual ideology did not always work in the manner required by the two models, or there must have been groups *within* respectable society whose experience and response to their socio-economic position was not that predicted by either model. Thus, although Havelock Ellis and Marie Stopes were exceptional in the late nineteenth and early twentieth centuries, they were not unique, and both built on a long-established non-pornographic minority tradition.

Ellis, for example, drew attention to English opinion expressing belief in the idea of a sexual impulse in women in the work of Michael Ryan in 1837 and Dr Elizabeth Blackwell in 1894.[9] Other English opinion from the first half of the nineteenth century not noticed by Ellis is to be found in William Godwin's *Of Population* in 1820 and in the writings of Alexander Walker in the 1840s.[10] Mary Wollestonecraft, still widely read in the late 1820s, argued that even if women were not naturally voluptuous or as passionate as men, they could become so. And in 1869 J. S. Mill, discussing the Englishman's view that women are by nature cold, implied that he thought they were not.[11] So one could go on referring to respectable opinion which points to the existence of a sexual ideology at odds with that generally attributed to the 'middle classes'. These minority beliefs were frequently expressed in conjunction with politically Radical opinions.

But what of the women themselves? What evidence do we have of sexual practice within the 'middle classes' contrary to the prevailing norm which might help to soften the picture of the ideal type constructed for us by Marcus? The short answer is, very little.[12] But even that little is enough to suggest that some Victorians could have enjoyed both sensuality and affection within marriage, and could have been precursors of the generation who responded so vigorously to the work of Marie Stopes. Moreover, the beginning of active propagandizing for contraception suggests that many 'middle-class' Victorians were seeking for a mid-way between the worlds of continence and incontinence discussed by Cominos.

This English movement for contraception within marriage began in the nineteenth century with Joseph Townsend, Methodist minister of Pewsey in Wiltshire. It descended from him through Bentham to Place, and from Place to Carlisle, who published and sold 10,000 copies of *Every Woman's Book* by 1828. Dr Knowlton's *The Fruits of Philosophy* first appeared in 1832 and thereafter sold about 1,000 copies a year until the Bradlaugh/Besant trial in 1877–8. In 1854 Dr Drysdale published his *Physical, Sexual and Natural Religion*, a book recently described as a 'trumpet-blast against sexual abstinence, prostitution and poverty. Theme and arguments alike are a bold anticipation, half way through the nineteenth century, of many of the tenets of the so-called "new morality" of our own day.'[13]

The fact that fertility rose slightly during the mid-nineteenth century should not be regarded as evidence that while these books were written, published and read their advice was ignored. English fertility, even at its highest, never reached levels as high as those in contemporary underdeveloped countries. What we would like to know is how far these publications in the early nineteenth century assisted in keeping alive, in an urbanized and fragmented society, knowledge of what was previously known and practised even in rural areas.[14] Furthermore, the methods advocated, even if skilfully and regularly practised, were not always reliable. Even so there were differences in fertility between social strata for marriages contracted as early as 1851–61 which can only be explained by the growing practice of contraception.[15]

Irrespective of the influence on practice of these writings, their publication was symptomatic of a growing pressure to find a third way out of the dilemma—respectable continence or disreputable incontinence—symptomatic of a new notion of respectable incontinence. Propagandists for birth-control also tended to be politically Radical.

According to advocates of the extreme version of the norm of continence this third way posed a greater threat to conventional morality than the double standard. Hence the war against the neo-Malthusians.[16]

> There is [wrote T. L. Nichols] another theory of sexual morals, worse, if possible, than this (the double standard), but more logical and consistent. It is the one *widely taught by a large and very active school of social reformers in England and elsewhere, under the name of Free Love,* by which the names of freedom and love are both perverted; or Sexual Religion; or Social Science.
>
> The doctrine is that sexual union, from the age of puberty, is the natural requirement and right of every person, male and female, and that nothing ought to prevent its free and frequent exercise; and that to avoid too great an increase of population, the inconvenience of children to the unmarried, and too many to the married, means should be used to prevent conception. . . . This doctrine is simply one of unrestrained, universal, promiscuous intercourse, extending to every person of both sexes; and it is at open war with the conventional morality of society, which tries to guard the purity of some women before marriage, by the sacrifice of others to the Moloch of masculine lust, and the morality of religion, which insists on chastity both of men and women, in and out of marriage.

The second 'middle-class' deviation from respectable or official ideology is a deviation from ideas about the nature and functioning of the economic system. In order to grasp its full significance, however, it will be necessary to enquire into the accuracy of the Cominos/Marcus notion about the economic component of 'middle-class' ideology.

The essence of this notion can be reduced to three major propositions :

(1) The objective of economic activity was the accumulation of its own product—capital.

(2) The economy was dominated by scarcity, particularly the scarcity of capital. It was of overriding importance, therefore, to take stringent measures to save, re-invest and accumulate capital.

(3) The economy was a self-perpetuating closed one in which intake and output were always in balance.

In order to clear up any confusion between fact and thought it is important to note that nothing in these propositions describes with any degree of accuracy the actual dynamic factors in the English economy of the eighteenth and nineteenth centuries. It is true that few economic historians would dispute the view that capital accumulation did have an important role to play as *one* of the factors causing the economic growth of Britain in the nineteenth century. It is, however, a commonplace among them that this economic growth was achieved with low rates of investment per annum, compared, say, with investment rates in other countries at comparable stages of development and in Britain in the twentieth century.[17] Moreover, in the hundred-year period preceding the high peak of the norm of gentlemanly continence all the evidence suggests that there was a bigger supply of capital in England than at any other time. Hence the fall in interest rates in the eighteenth century.[18] Indeed, a comparison of recent work on capital investment in the cotton industry and in building suggests that at the end of the eighteenth century almost as much capital had been invested in building the city of Bath for consumption purposes as had been invested in the cotton industry for productive purposes. There was no general shortage of capital for either.[19]

As well as conceding only a limited role to capital accumulation during the early stages of England's industrialization, recent work in economic history has resulted in a substantial list of other 'dynamic qualities'.[20] Furthermore, during the period of the high peak of the norm of gentlemanly continence, in the late nineteenth century, the rate of capital investment declined, and, if the work of many economic historians is anything to go by, energetic entrepreneurial activity necessitating concern for saving, investment and capital accumulation was on the wane.[21] Of all the obstacles to economic growth capital scarcity and inadequate saving were of least importance, and capital accumulation was of immediate concern to only a small minority of the population.

What then of the economic component of a 'middle-class' ideology in the mid-nineteenth century? The principal economists whose writings were the basis of economic beliefs in the mid-nineteenth century were: Adam Smith, Ricardo, Malthus and J. S. Mill. All four were more concerned with the objective of increasing human welfare than with accumulating capital for its own sake.[22]

It is true that in all their analyses capital and capital accumulation were regarded as making vital contributions to economic growth.[23] But, so were land and labour and a favourable framework of law and institutions. Adam Smith added the extent of the market, the division of labour, and *laissez faire*. Malthus added consumption by an unproductive section of the population and slow population growth. Ricardo emphasized improved productivity in agriculture and free trade. J. S. Mill had something to say about all these factors and added to them: Wakefield's field for the employment of capital and labour, knowledge, and the influence on production of differences in social organization. The end result of all this was that political economists envisaged economic growth and, therefore, increases in consumption and standards of living, as the consequence of all of these factors and not of any one of them alone.

Perhaps the best way to clarify how political economists of the first half of the nineteenth century envisaged the economy is to look briefly at the Ricardian model since it was central to political economy until well into the second half of the nineteenth century.[24]

This model began with the premise that there were three factors of production: land, labour and capital, producing three types of income: rent, wages and profit, accruing to three classes in society: landowners, labourers and capitalists. The starting engine was the capitalists' expectation of profit. There were, however, two spanners in the works: the labour theory of value and the law of diminishing returns.

The starting engine caused growth to begin and capitalists invested to bring land and labour into productive use. Once growth had begun it increased the demand for labour, stimulated population growth and increased the demand for food. However, land was limited in area and subject to diminishing returns per unit of labour input. In the absence of innovation in agriculture, any increase in the demand for food could only be met through the cultivation of inferior marginal land. This would necessarily raise rents on existing cultivated land and increase production costs. As a result of this and the increased demand for food the price of food would rise. According to the labour theory of value, price always tended to equal the labour cost of production. Therefore, money wages (the price of labour) would rise to meet the higher cost of foodstuffs necessary for the production and re-production of additional supplies of labour. Thus, the consequence of growth was a rise in rents and in money wages. Therefore, the share of the national product going to capitalists in the form of profit would fall. This smaller share going to profit would have to be divided among an increasing stock of capital.

The rate of profit would fall. The starting engine, profit expectation, would cease to stimulate investment and the rate of economic growth would slow down until 'the very low rate of profits will have arrested all accumulation, and almost the whole produce of the country, after paying the labourers, will be the property of owners of land and the receivers of tithes and taxes.'[25]

Thus would be produced the stationary state regarded by J. S. Mill as an attractive possibility and by Ricardo as an undesirable but very distant prospect. A distant prospect because free trade would give Britain unrestricted access to new sources of foodstuffs and, thereby, maintain the rate of profit. On the other hand, mere saving and more capital accumulation would not produce further growth.

According to Ricardo, the chief influence on the rate of profit and, thereby, on capital accumulation was the efficiency of labour in agriculture. The way to overcome the low efficiency of labour was not via more capital accumulation but through free trade. 'Nothing, I say', wrote Ricardo, 'can increase the profits permanently on trade with the same or increased capital but a really cheaper mode of obtaining food.'[26] Therefore, although Ricardo allocated pride of place to profit expectation as the starting engine he was clear that saving and accumulation could not guarantee growth. Most economists of the period agreed with him.

The basic message of political economy to the people of England throughout the nineteenth century, which was derived from the Ricardian orthodoxy, was that living standards could only rise with the introduction and spread of free trade. If there was any axiom of political economy entering the psyche of Victorian men and women it was this: free trade—Cobden and Bright were the culture heroes of mid-nineteenth-century England not Marx, and Victorian England was the first great consumer society.

There was, however, one other component in mid-nineteenth-century economic thought which was probably the basis for a popular belief that capital accumulation was vital for economic growth. This was Say/Mill's Law. The essence of this was that supply created its own demand and there never could be too much capital in any economy. As the third edition of James Mill's *Elements of Political Economy* put it in 1844, 'There were sufficient investment outlets at home and the labour and capital of a country cannot prepare more than the country will be willing to consume. . . . Every country, therefore, contains within itself a market for all that it can produce.'[27] But economists were neither unanimous nor consistent in adherence to this doctrine. The main division was between those worried about booms and the depressionists concerned with slumps. The former spoke in terms of over-investment, the latter in terms of over-saving. According to A. K. Cairncross, the popularity of the depressionist view can be gauged 'from the comment of Mill on his famous proposition that "demand for commodities is not demand for labour". "Even among political economists of reputation", Mill said, "I can hardly point to any, except Mr. Ricardo and M. Say, who have kept it constantly and steadily in view." '[28] Indeed, those who argued in terms of over-saving at mid-century included Fullarton, Giffen, Leone Levi and even Mill.[29] Thus there seems to be some truth in Cairncross's view that in all probability Hobson, who implied there was a universal dogmatic adherence to Say/Mill's Law, 'in his eagerness to play the heretic, exaggerated the unanimity of the public.'[30]

It is my purpose in the remainder of this chapter to look at one of the theoretical offshoots of the depressionist over-saving school which, in conjunction with those minority attitudes in regard to the ideology of continence discussed above, led to the development of a strong minority ideology focusing around yet a fourth choice for the 'middle classes' at mid-century. This choice was systematic colonization.

It is a peculiarity of the Marcus/Cominos approach that both authors write about nineteenth-century attitudes to sex in relation to political economy without referring to Malthus. Yet, in his population theory, Malthus said more about the connection between economic growth and sexuality than most other nineteenth-century economists. Beginning with the two postulates 'that food is necessary to the existence of man', and 'that the passion between the sexes is necessary, and will remain nearly in its present state',[31] Malthus built a complete edifice of capitalist institutions and sexual conventions. Private property, monogamy, chastity, self love, as well as violence, oppression, falsehood, misery, every hateful vice and every form of distress, flowed from the clash between these two basic drives. Moreover, since the passion between the sexes was uncontrollable, except, within the middling ranks of society, by restraint accompanied by vices of the worst kind, there could be no permanent improvement in the living standards of the mass of mankind.

The truth of this is irrelevant for our purpose. What matters is that men believed it. While some did so because it met their needs to keep themselves in power, to preserve their purses, and to deny the claims of Utopians like Godwin and Condorcet, Spence and Hodgskin, its widest appeal sprang from the fact that Malthus spoke for several generations of the middling strata whose real condition he mirrored. For men on fixed incomes or meagre salaries the war-time years of high prices had been bad ones. It is true that there had been some respite for them during the period of falling prices after 1815, but the 1830s and 1840s were especially difficult. During these years mortality in childhood had begun to fall and the size of surviving families to increase. At the same time the rate of growth of the manufacturing sector of the economy was not as good as it might have been and respectable employment for the growing number who had been touched by aristocratic mores was not easy to come by. In these circumstances there must have been thousands who recognized themselves in Malthus's description of a man of liberal education, but with an income only just sufficient to enable him to associate in the ranks of gentlemen who[32]

> must feel absolutely certain, that if he marries and has a family, he shall be obliged, if he mixes at all in society, to rank himself with moderate farmers, and the lower class of tradesmen. The woman that a man of education would naturally make the object of his choice, would be one brought up in the same tastes and sentiments with himself, and used to the familiar intercourse of a society totally different from that to which she must be reduced by marriage. . . . Two or three steps of descent in society, particularly at this round of the ladder, where education ends and ignorance begins, will not be considered by the generality of people as a fancied and chimerical, but a real and essential evil.

For everyone who read and identified himself with this portrayal there must have been many more who arrived at the same view from bitter experience.[33] For them the norm of gentlemanly continence, accompanied though it may have been by the liberal exploitation of a glut of young and impoverished women from the lower classes, had little to do with saving and capital accumulation but everything to do with consumption and the status implications of the performance or achievement norm.[34] As Cominos so rightly said, they desired 'the status of comfort and the comfort of status'.

Moreover, there was one group of neo-Malthusians who repeatedly drew attention to the sexual problem of these people with the avowed object of showing how sexual passion could be satisfied by the young, chaste and marginal gentleman without at the same time curtailing his consumption; the comforts of bed, board and status could be his for the asking. These men were the 'systematic colonizers'. What is more they argued their case using an economic conceptual framework which had high consumption as its objective and regarded capital as being super-abundant rather than scarce. The scarce factor in their model was what Wakefield called the field for employing capital and labour—the field of production. The other two factors, capital and labour, were in excess. To put their case as simply as possible, they saw the economic problem in the late 1830s and early 1840s as the result of a glut of capital and a glut of people in a narrow field of production. And, they argued, unless the government took quick remedial action to found colonies on Wakefield's model, then for men of what they called the 'uneasy class' there could only be celibacy followed by continence in marriage, and, for women, enforced chastity for the respectable and prostitution for the rest. According to Wakefield this was already the case. He wrote: 'Amongst the middle class, amongst all classes except the highest and lowest, moral restraint is a confirmed habit. Hence, immorality without parallel in any other country.'[35] About the effect of chastity and maternal and sexual frustration on the women of the 'uneasy class' he had this to say:[36]

There is not in the world a more deplorable sight than a fine brood of English girls turning into old maids one after the other; first reaching the bloom of beauty, full of health, spirits and tenderness; next striving anxiously aided by their mothers to become honoured and happy wives; then fretting, growing thin, pale, lifeless and cross, at last, if they do not go mad or die of consumption, seeking consolation in the belief of an approaching millennium, or in the single pursuit of that happiness in another world, which this world has denied them.

But there was worse to come and the ultimate result of the excess of capital and labour and the consequent corruption of morals would be 'commotions and civil wars, which dry up the very springs of national greatness'.[37]

Thus, the urgent need for government-sponsored schemes of emigration, whereby surplus capital, the result of over-saving, and population, the result of sexual passion, would be shifted to new and bigger fields of production, and respectable men and women would be able to conform to the norm of gentlemanly continence yet live a legitimate and a more sexually relaxed existence since they would be nicely proportioned one with the other. In a very short time each colony 'would be an immense nursery'.[38] England would be saved.

One of the leading propagandists for systematic colonization was H. S. Chapman. The norm of gentlemanly continence was stamped all over him and was everywhere about him, yet the economic component of his ideology centred on the belief that capital was super-abundant. Moreover, he repeatedly advocated high wages and the importance of high levels of consumption, and in his capacity as assistant commissioner on hand-loom weaving wrote, 'To preach contentment to potato-fed people is to preach perpetual degradation'.[39] In his private life he was a bon-vivant, who considered himself not cut out for the business of making money in business. 'To me', he said, 'commerce is disgusting, unless with large capital, so as to make it a matter of science.'[40] All in all, if we are to believe the Cominos/Marcus models and ideal types of mid-nineteenth-century England, Chapman was a most unlikely figure. It is my belief that there were many like him.

What Chapman had to say in the 1840s reflected the ideology of a portion of that middling set of people whose exclusion from a share in authority was made worse by the sexual frustration which accompanied their struggles to achieve and improve their status according to the performance norm.[41] Moreover, it was a drive for power and the passion between the sexes which gave form to his economics rather than the reverse, and a desire to consume rather than to accumulate which was the mark of his economics.

In a review of a pamphlet by Ross D. Mangles, *How to Colonize*, Chapman made it clear that he accepted the premises of the author in regard to the sexual problems of the great unmarried, which were compulsory celibacy and prostitution, and added:[42]

Who, for instance, does not feel the pressure of numbers in some shape or other? In the professions—in commerce—in all

the higher kinds of service or employment, civil as well as
military—all are full to overflowing. To provide for families
is the pressing difficulty of the middle class. Every head of a
family feels painfully the perpetual danger to which he and his
are exposed, of falling into a lower grade of society than that
to which he belongs.

Hence the importance of colonization.

In the *New Zealand Journal*, eight months later, he was even
more explicit in his rejection of 'moral restraint':[43]

Celibacy has its miseries as well as its vices : into these we do
not mean to enter; we think it unnecessary, since we have a
confidence in a very superior power to Malthus, and believe
that none were sent into this world in vain; and, although
this philosopher may choose to deny food to many at his
imaginary board, we deny that nature has done so ... we
believe that if the procreating portion of the people were led to
exchange a miserable, degraded existence for one of comfort,
plenty, and independence, it would prove a true, although
latent safety valve.

These words of Wakefield, Mangles and Chapman show that
just as the neo-Malthusians saw birth-control as an alternative to
continence and incontinence, so too, the systematic colonizers saw
systematic colonization as an alternative. We can best judge the
size of the minority for whom they spoke by reference to the
circulation of journals devoted to colonization. In 1841 the circulation of such journals was nearly 2,600, to which must be added a
circulation figure of 2,500 for the *Spectator* which, under the
editorship of Rintoul, was a great advocate of colonization. This
was a substantial readership, equivalent to half the readership of
The Times.[44]

The kind of fantasy that followed reading one of these journals—
a fantasy that colonization was sexually therapeutic, an alternative
to celibacy and prostitution, is in the letters of a young Oxford
shop assistant written just before his voyage to New Zealand in
1853. He wrote to his friend:[45]

You must have heard of Castle-building in the air. For instance
I go to bed tonight and lying awake, give reins to my
imagination. We go to Australia and get amazingly rich in a

remarkably short space of time and return home. I come down
to Oxford and possibly punch the heads of one or two obnoxious
persons, make them open their eyes in the shop at my riding
up on horseback or in a carriage and buying a lot of books.
Then I marry a beautiful lady, settle down in some delightful
country seat and beget lots of angelic little Cochrans. . . . Your
own castle would most likely be of a slightly different style of
architecture, one of its distinguishing features might possibly
be the astonishing of 'Betsey' by driving up in a chariot and
four and whisking her off amidst the cheers of the assembled
multitude amongst whom your attendants are showering five
shilling pieces.

A few weeks later he added, 'I do not see that in order to throw
off Mrs. Grundy's yoke it is necessary at the same time to become
a degraded wretch.'[46]

In this fantasy there is emphasis on the rewards of chance rather
than performance,[47] on consumption rather than saving, and on
aping the life of the aristocrat rather than that of the successful
bourgeois. There is also some suggestion that there might be sexual
fulfilment in marriage when accompanied by high levels of
consumption. Overall, the fantasy is one of release rather than
constraint—a release from sexual frustration through emigration
and colonization. There can be little doubt that the systematic
colonizers knew their early Victorians.

One result of the tensions experienced by growing numbers of
the middling strata was the development by the systematic colonizers
of an innovation in economic theory, running counter to the
Ricardian orthodoxy and to Say/Mill's law, which was to give
rise to a new component in 'middle-class' ideology.

Leading advocates of systematic colonization—Wakefield, Chapman, Rintoul, Buller and Mill—argued that the Ricardian
stationary state had in fact set in and that the period of the 1830s
and 1840s was characterized by an excess of both capital and labour
in relation to the field for employing both. Wakefield had been
concise and clear about this as early as 1833.[48] He reiterated the
point in his edition of *The Wealth of Nations* in 1835.[49] Despite
the views of modern theoreticians, contemporaries were convinced
that he had made a significant contribution to economic theory.
It was, said one of them,[50]

Mr. Wakefield who first clearly explained the important part
played by the field of production in determining the condition
of a people. This is no doubt implied in, or is rather a corollary
from the received doctrine of rent, and necessarily flows from
what the leading economists lay down on the subject of rent,
wages, and profits, but it was there latent, like [word
illegible] in ice. Mr. Wakefield was the quasi-chemist who
first disengaged it. He worked out the doctrine more in detail
and therefore more clearly than they have done; showing most
successfully and clearly that in relation to the field of
production, wages and profits may fall (and therefore rise)
together; that capital may be in excess (in relation to the field
of production as well as labour), and that therefore it is not
merely unwise to check, but is actually wise to promote the
removal of capital as well as labour to the new and more
productive field.

Following Wakefield's formulation of the notion of the field of
production it was left to propagandists and politicians like Rintoul,
Chapman and Buller to develop it into a conceptual framework
which came close to being a theory of long swings in economic
growth. The high point of the development of their ideas was
contained in a speech delivered in the House of Commons by Charles
Buller in April 1843.

At the beginning of 1843, when signs of recovery from the
disastrous years of 1841-2 were all too few, the time seemed
opportune to press the government to initiate a government-
sponsored scheme of emigration. Charles Buller, as the most able
Parliamentarian among the systematic colonizers, planned to open
the debate in the House. Chapman, acting as his secretary, collected
essential information on the colonies for him, and then, following
Buller's dictation, wrote out his speech. Rintoul was then called in
to put it into good English. On the Sunday before the speech was
to be delivered, Buller read this prepared draft to a select band of
four: Wakefield, Rintoul, Mill and Chapman. Each was selected
to attend this briefing because he was considered to have special
qualifications fitting him to judge the speech and make suggestions.
Chapman's version of this foursome was that 'one was the father
of the principles—another was not ignorant of the principles and
was a most acute critic—a third was a profound economist—a

K

fourth was supposed to be master of the facts and their application'.[51] It seems, therefore, that Buller's speech on 6 April was made with the full approval of these four intellectual leaders of the movement, and that it was a sort of politico-economic manifesto presenting the considered economic, as well as the political/cultural, viewpoint of those Philosophic Radicals who were also ardent supporters of systematic colonization. It certainly contained the most developed form of the thesis previously advanced by Wakefield, Rintoul and Chapman. As Mill said, they spoke for 'the ten pound electors— the greatest sufferers of all by low profits and an overcrowded field of employment'.

According to Buller there was a universal distress. But he was careful not to regard this either as unparalleled or desperate. He also observed that in spite of this distress 'We are a richer people, with more of accumulated wealth, more of the capital of future commerce, than we ever possessed at a former period.'[52] Nevertheless, he held to the opinion that although wealth was accumulating it was doing so at a less rapid rate than before, and that the situation had all the marks of a glut.

> That a smaller amount of useful and profitable enterprises are
> being carried on now than five or six years ago—that there is
> less employment for capital, and that business brings in smaller
> profits—that there are more people out of employment, and that
> the wages of those who are employed are less than they used to
> be. The supply of many goods is now almost, if not quite, as
> redundant as ever.

This situation, he went on to say, was not to be explained simply in terms of the cyclical over-production of 1841–2. It would have developed even had there been no short-term over-production in these years. The cause was more deeply seated than that. It was

> that there is a permanent cause of suffering in the constant
> accumulation of capital, and the constant increase of population
> within the same restricted field of employment. Every year
> adds its profits to the amount of capital previously accumulated;
> and certainly leaves the population considerably larger at its close
> than it was at its commencement.

Nevertheless, argued Buller, in the long run the growth of international demand, new discoveries of raw materials and improvements in technology, particularly in agriculture, tended to enlarge the field of employment. Consequently, 'the condition of the great mass of our countrymen has as regards mere physical circumstances, indisputably gone on improving from century to century since the Norman Conquest'. In arguing in this way Buller showed that he accepted that, in the very long run, free trade and competition would produce sustained growth. But, it was as clear to Buller as it is to us, that in this kind of long run, some eight hundred years, we are all dead. So he turned his attention to 'shorter term' frictional problems. The sort of problems which would arise during periods of adjustment in the relationship between capital, labour and the field of employment. These 'shorter term' frictional problems were not to be confused with the short-term problems of crises of over-production, although they were aggravated by them. The 'shorter term' problems Buller had in mind resulted from long period lags in innovation either in markets, discoveries or technology. It was because of these long period lags that the rate of growth of the field of employment was not the same as the rate of growth of labour or capital accumulation. In Buller's own words:

> It is as indisputable that this enlargement of the field of
> employment, though in the long run greater, is not so steady
> as the growth of capital and population; and that in the intervals
> that elapse ere fresh employment is found, competition in a
> restricted field, oftentimes reduces both wages and profits, and
> occasions periods of distress.

It seems that what Buller and his advisers were moving towards was a theory including some kind of long swing in economic growth, the course of which was determined by what we have come to regard as Schumpeterian innovations. These innovations were unpredictable and irregular. In such a model there is no *a priori* reason why free trade should maintain a constant relationship between capital and labour and the field of employment. Furthermore, the failure of free trade to ensure the correct relationship, whatever it might be, does not result simply from institutional or political obstacles, it results from the inability of free trade, or market forces, to guarantee a steady flow of innovation. In short innovation is unpredictable, and in modern terms growth is unbalanced growth and free trade is a poor device through which to get balanced growth in any thirty- or forty-year period.

It was Buller's view, as it was Wakefield's, that the period in England, since 1815, was deficient in innovation. The economic result was much loose capital seeking speculative outlets overseas. The failure of much of this speculative investment acted as a further deterrent to safe and useful investment. Furthermore, capital became concentrated in the hands of 'great capitalists content with a rate of profit at which a smaller capital would not produce a livelihood. This constant swelling of population and capital up to the very brim of the cup', said Buller, 'is the permanent cause of uneasiness and danger in the country.'

By 1843, therefore, the leading advocates of colonization as a theory of growth for empty continents with political/cultural objectives designed to ease the lot of the middling strata of English society, via their search for some domestic economic rationale, had also produced the germ of a theory of growth for advanced countries. This theory shifted both free trade and capital accumulation to the positions of necessary but not sufficient conditions for growth. In their model they emphasized the notion that there was a divergence between the rates of growth of capital, the field of employment and the rate of innovation. Both capital and population had accumulated too rapidly. They emphasized the need for government to play an important part in innovation and argued that colonization was a vitally necessary innovation; it would provide investment outlets and create markets. They failed to develop this model more completely because they remained constrained by their general belief in the efficacy of market forces and because innovations and the business upswing after 1843 reduced the pressure to abandon more of orthodox political economy. Nevertheless, in 1870, Mill was still of the opinion that systematic colonization was essential for England's welfare and deplored the fact that her hands were tied because control of colonial land had been passed over to local legislatures.[53]

What is especially important for us to notice is the remedy the systematic colonizers proposed for the problem they identified. It was not that men should save more, not that they should accumulate for accumulation's sake, and not that they should take refuge from reality in some idea of a self-enclosed economic system. In fact they neither did nor advocated any of the things that economists and popularizers of political economy are alleged to have done and advocated according to the Marcus/Cominos model. Of course, performance, capital and free trade were necessary to growth. Yet all three together were incapable of producing it, and without growth there could be no increases in consumption and no easing of the stresses resulting from 'moral restraint'. As the colonizers saw it, the missing necessary component was the field of production or the field for the employment of capital and labour. To remedy this deficiency meant going *outside* the merely national economic system, calling upon governments for massive assistance with a pump priming concession of crown land, and encouraging the export of surplus capital.

As far as we know the advocates of systematic colonization lived according to the norm of gentlemanly continence and met most of the demands of 'moral restraint'. However, like the neo-Malthusians, they also challenged the Malthusians and the norm of gentlemanly continence. They argued that men could remain gentlemen *and* satisfy the passion between the sexes *and* increase their levels of consumption. In developing and spreading these beliefs they did much to build up the foundations of Empire and contributed to a dominant element in late nineteenth-century 'middle-class' ideology—the idea of Empire.

The 'middle classes' in the nineteenth century included such a wide range of social strata that they cannot easily be fitted into conceptual frameworks derived from the three-class model. Even when these classes appeared to have congealed into a single homogeneous 'middle class', suffocating itself in a blanket of respectable ideology, there were still many important minorities and deviations from respectable ideology whose relationships with social strata and social class have yet to be determined. One thing seems clear; deviant beliefs about the sexual impulse in women, the practice of contraception, and systematic colonization were all frequently held in conjunction with the politically Radical beliefs characteristic of the middling class. This points to the possibility that not only the history of the period before 1850 but that of the whole of the nineteenth century is best interpreted within a model of social class more akin to the five- than the three-class model, and with the aid of more than one 'ideal type'. Certainly the discussion of the ways in which Victorian sexual mores and fantasies were integrated, if they were integrated, into a comprehensive system of relationships is still very much an open one. And, if one must isolate a single feature of the socio-economic system in order to derive the 'historical meaning' of the norm of continence, it seems to me that it would be best simply to look at its connection with the desire for comfort, status and achievement noted but passed over by Cominos. These drives and desires, like the 'Toryism of sex' were not derived from the capitalist system. All were pre-capitalist in origin and probably provided the motivation for the development of capitalist society. It is also possible that capitalism acted upon them and used them for its own ends. Nevertheless, these drives could also be or become anti-capitalist. They could even induce ardent capitalistic free-traders like Chapman, Rintoul and Mill to advocate government intervention to regulate the economy by exporting surplus capital and *creating* markets! One wonders just how many Victorians were Victorian and how functionally integrated Victorian England was.

7
Working-class women and women's suffrage

This essay was written early in 1965 before the final formulation of the five-class model and before the recent surge of interest in women's liberation led to a considerable re-writing of the history of women and women's movements in the nineteenth and twentieth centuries. I include it here as originally published in 1967 because nothing that has been written since has invalidated the main line of argument and because it shows how, lacking an explicit theoretical framework, I was then groping for an adequate model of social change incorporating relationships of authority and subordination, the concept of class as a political rather than an economic category and the role of dependence and deference in inhibiting conflict. The major contribution of recent writers on contemporary women's movements is that they have made explicit that the issue between the sexes is essentially about the loci of power in a patriarchal society, that it is consequently a political issue in the widest sense and, therefore, in the terminology of the five-class model a class conflict. In writing thus they have moved the social class consciousness of increasing numbers of women to a new political awareness. If women in the past were merely members of loosely knit quasi-groups many are now class-conscious members of a new political class. And, if I were to re-write any part of this essay on the relationships between male working-class movements, working-class women and women from the middle and upper classes, I would make more of the clash resulting from the relative authority positions of men and women in a paternalistic society, and more of the conflict between the privatized but deferential attitudes of women like Emmeline and Christabel Pankhurst and the more proletarian and non-deferential positions of the Women's Co-operative Guild and Sylvia Pankhurst. I see more clearly now that the Suffragettes were the Philosophic Radicals of the women's movement with only some of their strengths but with all of their weaknesses.

It is with this consideration in mind that I reformulate my conclusion about militancy being a tactical error. Militancy was an error but not because it was militant. It was an error because it was militancy directed to obtain objectives too narrowly defined. The militants directed their energies only to efforts to get access to the Parliamentary centre of power for nationalistic and racial objectives both of which were fully incorporated into the prevailing ethos of the patriarchal society which the militants merely wished to join. At the end of their careers as militants, Christabel and Emmeline Pankhurst were no longer concerned with the wider 'liberation' issues involved in the women's movement nor aware that a necessary condition for the emancipation of women was the 'liberation' of men. Consequently militancy led to a great misdirection of energy dividing woman from woman and women from men instead of uniting them for concerted action to attack the roots of women's subjection in family, economy and society. It was Teresa Billington Creig's awareness of this development that led her to write in 1913:

> The movement is still separated from the real life of the women of the nation, it is still a thing apart, detached. . . . The worst result of this policy is that the majority of Suffragists have been left crudely ignorant and fearful of the very problems they must finally solve. . . . The movement now has no more interest than a puppet play, pathetic, pitiful, heroic, ridiculous, but a play only.

This is the real conclusion of this essay.

Introduction

Recently the part played by working-class women in the emancipation and women's suffrage movements has been emphasized. This emphasis suggests that, in some areas, they played a positive and initiatory role in the women's movements of the late nineteenth and early twentieth centuries. On the wider question of emancipation one historian has asserted that, 'It was during the industrial revolution moreover, and largely because of the economic opportunities it afforded to working-class women, that there was the beginning of that most important and most beneficial of all social revolutions of the last two centuries, the emancipation of women.'[1] Yet another, commenting on the more restricted question of women's suffrage, and finding the original stronghold of the Suffragettes in the Lancashire textile areas, made play with the form of Annie Kenney's written question to Sir Edward Grey to imply that the militant initiative in 1905 came from organized women trade unionists.[2] While a third, writing of the women's suffrage movement, 'into the leadership of which the Oldham mill hand Annie Kenney then brought a working-class element,'[3] expressed the same idea even more firmly and inaccurately.

These views seem to reflect and perpetuate the belief that during the course of the nineteenth century exploited working-class women slowly, but inevitably, emerged as a self-conscious social class exerting progressive and emancipist influences on the climate of opinion and that after organizing themselves into trade unions, working-class women became members of militant pressure-groups endeavouring to compel governments to act to remedy some of the social problems of industrialization. When this failed they infused the women's suffrage movement with a new vitality, leadership and militancy to draw attention to the plight and position of women generally. Expressed in this form these views suggest that kind of naïve belief in economic determinism, frequently and wrongly attributed to Marxists, but which is often found in the writings of non-Marxist economists.[4]

As explanations of the emancipation movement in general, and of the militant agitation for women's suffrage in particular, however, such views conflict with the assessments of contemporaries and of earlier liberal, Marxist and socialist historians. Contemporaries either kept up the pretence, as H. G. Wells put it, 'that the vote for women was an isolated fad, and the agitation an epidemic madness that would presently pass', and that it seemed, 'as if it were a disconnected issue, irrelevant to all other broad developments of social and political life',[5] or they were convinced that both the emancipation and the women's suffrage movements were reflections of the malaise and aspirations of middle- and upper-class women.[6] Elie Halévy was, perhaps, the historian most committed to a belief in the intellectual and upper-class basis of both. 'The origin of the feminist movement,' he said, 'was intellectual not economic, bourgeois not proletarian.'[7] The most scathing was G. D. H. Cole, who held that 'the militant suffrage movement was largely psychopathic'.[8] The most recent Marxist contributor has claimed that the women's movement was one 'which from the start was middle-class in its leadership, and . . . had but little contact with the lives and problems of women of the working class . . . who were beginning to realize that their aims were identical with those of the working-class movement as a whole.'[9]

In this area, as in others, there is little agreement about the nature of the inter-relationships between economic development, class and ideology. One reason for this may be the variety of meanings which can be and have been attached to the terms emancipation, feminism and women's movements, and the general terminological looseness which until recently has been associated with the whole subject.[10] It is the purpose of this paper to bring some precision into a small part of the discussion. The aspect of the women's movement which will be examined is that which is contained in the demand for the franchise and, more particularly, the part played by working-class women in the origin of the militant, Suffragette phase of this demand. Special attention will be given to the incident involving Annie Kenney's question to Sir Edward Grey, and to the relationship between the WSPU and the cotton unions. This is necessary since Annie Kenney's question, her connection with the cotton unions, and the relationship between the cotton unions and the suffrage movement have been offered as evidence of considerable working-class commitment to, and initiative in, the suffrage movement. That is, they have been used as indicators of significant developments in the political attitudes and alignments of working-class women.

Working-class women and the suffrage to 1867

From the early days of organized working-class movements some working-class women were active in them and often formed separate branches or societies. In some areas women established their own benefit societies, in others they joined trade unions. They took part in strikes and riots. Everywhere they were active in co-operative societies. In the political sphere Female Reform Societies came into existence among cotton spinners in 1817, in Bath women chaired and spoke at Chartist meetings,[11] and in Sheffield the Female Political Association, a remnant of Chartism, passed a resolution advocating female suffrage in the early 1850s.[12]

Nevertheless, it would be difficult to argue from evidence of this kind that male-dominated working-class movements were as equally committed to female as to male suffrage, or that this amounted to the beginnings of the movement either for emancipation in its widest sense, or of a mass movement of working-class women for a reform of the suffrage. Even as impulsive movements in any or all of these directions they were abortive. Almost inevitably so since during the early nineteenth century the most demagogic of Radicals likely to reach the mass of working-class women were hesitant on the issue of female suffrage, and inclined to restrict their demands to manhood suffrage.[13]

Even the Philosophic Radicals, the fountain-head of Radical inspiration, were divided. James Mill, 'who, in spite of Malthus, had begotten more children than he could afford on a female whom he despised', argued conventionally against giving women the vote. Bentham, politically more consistent and a bachelor, spoke up for universal suffrage.[14]

Furthermore, the weight of convention and the mere task of living deadened any massive response by women to such hesitant leadership. The fact was that women's role 'was confined to giving moral support to the men, making banners and caps of liberty which were presented with ceremony at reform demonstrations, passing resolutions and addresses, and swelling the numbers at meetings'.[15] Consequently, and as George Holyoake puts it,[16]

In 1840 there were no signs of an agitation for the civil rights of women. Only small numbers of women knew how few the rights of their sex were, or had any desire to increase them. The majority did not know, in any intelligent way, whether they had any civil rights at all. . . . Women desire a share in the suffrage. They are taxed, and therefore they claim a right to vote. But where are women's political unions—self-oriented and self-sustained? If they want political rights, why do they not ask for them?

The truth is, of course, that even in the male dominated working-class agitation for manhood suffrage and for the Charter as a 'bread and butter' question only a minority of the working class was politically active. Experienced and politically literate leaders were few, the working class was not homogeneous and leadership frequently came from members of the middle classes and from demagogues. Consequently the period of 'gestation' for the growth of a distinctive working-class political party was so long and difficult that it almost died at birth.

In the women's case the persistence of the traditional sex role of subservience and dependence was added to class attitudes of deference, indifference and apathy. These, reinforced by the narrow range of experience available to the uneducated, made it difficult for working-class women to perceive newer and higher goals, and created almost insuperable obstacles to effective mass political action. So, throughout the Industrial Revolution and the whole of the nineteenth century, working-class women, as wives, daughters and citizens, remained dependent in law and in fact[17] despite the assertion of Engels that capitalism meant that 'no basis for any kind of male supremacy is left in the proletarian household'. Indeed the revolt of Annie Kenney, one of the very few working-class girls to become closely associated with the leading Suffragettes, was in part inspired by a revulsion against the inferior position of women in working-class households in those textile areas which are often held to have been favourable to the growth of independence among working-class women.[18]

Thus, although it is possible to trace some interest and participation in working-class movements, and in their demands for universal suffrage, by working-class women, it seems unlikely that they exerted any sustained or active demand for women's suffrage. This demand when it came, as an extension of Radicalism, was inspired by the writings of William Thompson, intensified by the agitation started by the Manchester Women's Suffrage Committee over J. S. Mill's amendment to the 1867 Reform Bill, and extended through the legalistic clash over the definition of the word 'man' as used in the Bill. Thereafter the initiative remained with women from the middle classes, and the intelligentsia.[19]

Women, a depressed class

The political apathy and weakness of working-class women can be explained in terms of broad cleavages in society arising from differences between classes and the sexes. But unless it is clearly recognized that there was, and is, differentiation within the working class, and that sex was itself a factor moulding opinion within the working class and influencing differentiation within it, the role of working-class women in the suffrage movement and their relationships with other sections of the working class cannot be comprehended.

The extent of differentiation according to sex in the second half of the nineteenth century is clearly illustrated in Table 18.

TABLE 18   The manual working class, England and Wales 1867

Social class	Average weekly wage for men	Proportion of men	Total employed women
		%	%
Highly skilled and most highly skilled	28s.–35s.	21·1	2·2
Lower skilled	21s.–25s.	39·0	21·8
Unskilled 'A' domestic servants,* agricultural labour	14s.–20s.	37·3	48·4
Unskilled 'B' and 'C'	12s.	2·7	27·6

* No wage figures for domestic servants.
Source: adapted from G. D. H. Cole, *Studies in Class Structure*, p. 56.

The facts are clear. Twenty-seven per cent of working-class women workers were employed in occupations paying average wages of 12s. per week, and only a very small minority were in well-paid work. The significance of these wage differentials for class differentiation is also clear. Low wages meant that proportionately more working female heads of families, and their families, were poor or very poor. In the 1880s working female heads of families in eight central and east London parishes constituted between 3·2 per cent and 5·2 per cent of all heads of families, yet they made up between 8·1 per cent and 45·6 per cent of class 'B' in Booth's survey; i.e. 'The very poor, casual labour, hand-to-mouth existence, chronic want'.[20] And Rowntree attributed about 16 per cent of primary poverty in York to the death of the chief wage-earner. This meant that whole families were reduced to existing on 8s. 7d. per week in circumstances which made 21s. 8d. per week the poverty line.[21]

It is well known that poverty produces its own cultural patterns. Part of this consists of an adaptation to the acceptance of casual work and low expectations, and the extinction of vitality.[22] Consequently women workers, whether heads of families or wives and daughters of low-income labourers, particularly in London, readily accepted employment in enterprises producing low-priced, poor-quality products, and whatever wage might be offered. While some women, in these conditions, were able to retain their self-respect, many more revealed all the characteristics of subjection. They became nervous, timid and shiftless.[23]

In most trades women were 'sweated'. If employed as domestic servants or shop assistants they were tied to, and dependent on, their employers. That is, their relationship to their employers was different from the overall relationship of labour to capital. They sold their labour, it is true. But the wage was so low, the restriction on women's employment so great, the subjection to authority in work so ingrained, and their places of work so dispersed that they were unable to emerge as a political class. Thus they were truly at the bottom of the reserve army, a drag on the upward movement of wages, and as such felt to be a threat to the living standards of more highly paid workers.[24] As a *Votes for Women* editorial reported : [25]

> The women of the country are deeply dissatisfied with their position. They stand at the very bottom of all—however miserable the lot of the most wretched and poverty-stricken man, there is always one being in the world more miserably placed than himself, and that is the woman who stands in the nearest relationship to him. . . . The average wage of the working girls is about 7s. (Haggerstone in the East End.) In times of special distress, brought about by unemployment, employment schemes are started to help men. The women are left out. During the last fifty years, while the wages of men have been steadily rising, the wages of women have either remained stationary or gone down. The dirtiest and most unpleasant work that has to be done in the world is done by women. The so-called sweated trades are women's trades. Women who are left as widows have to earn the living of the family, and look after the little ones, cook, wash and mend for them, nurse them when they are sick, and play the part of father and mother as well. They become the home workers, who get paid less than a penny an hour for their work.

Thus working women, particularly as heads or members of low-income families, differentiated by sex and discriminated against through wages, were a sub-class. The position of the members of this class can only be paralleled in more recent times by that of coloured immigrants in Britain and negroes in the USA. There was, however, the saving difference that beneath the dirt their white skins were a passport to upward social mobility and some measure of equality, although for long the marks of class seemed as indelible as those of colour. There can be no doubt that there were many, themselves on the margin of subsistence, who agreed with Charles Booth that 'the poverty of the poor is mainly the result of the competition of the very poor',[26] and who felt, moreover, that the very poor were mostly women.

These women, like the generality of unskilled labourers before them, found their interests as wage earners ill served by existing working-class organizations. And it was not readily apparent to them that their interests as wage earners were always identical with those of the working-class movement as a whole.[27] When the long-delayed move to organize working women to protect themselves industrially, and then to urge their claims for political equality, did arrive, the organizing drive for both movements came from outside the ranks of working-class women and outside the ranks of labour.

Trade unions and women's suffrage

Trade unionism among women was slow to develop. The handful of women who, in 1834, joined the 'Lodge of Female Tailors' within Owen's 'Grand National' had grown by 1896 to 142,000, of whom five-sixths were organized in the cotton unions. Forty years later no more than 15 per cent of employed women were members of unions, and the majority were still in cotton. In these cotton unions, some of which, like the Card and Blowing Room Operatives, were predominantly women's unions, men then held and still retain control of union affairs.[28] One result of this was to retard rather than stimulate interest in the women's suffrage movement.

In every other industry the initiative for the little that was done to organize women in trade unions came from middle-class women. The channel along which it flowed, in the first instance, ran from the women's suffrage movement into trade unionism and not the other way. The lead was given by Emma Paterson,[29] the daughter of a headmaster in Hanover Square. She was secretary of the Women's Suffrage Association until her marriage and visit to America in 1873. On her return she founded the Women's Protective and Provident League in London and the National Union of Working Women in Bristol, both with the object of assisting working women to form trade unions. Under the influence of these organizations, whose active membership was largely middle-class, unions were formed among women employed as bookbinders, shirtmakers, tailoresses and dressmakers. Then, in spite of the resistance of Henry Broadhurst, and other conservative trade unionists, Emma Paterson took her place as a delegate to the Trades Union Congress from 1875 to 1886.

In 1891 the organization she had established changed its name to the Women's Trade Union League, and, in 1908, it was this body, led by Mary MacArthur, the daughter of a wealthy draper, ably supported by Sir Charles Dilke, which persuaded the government to put the Trade Boards Act on the statute book. The Parliamentary Committee and the TUC played little part. The reason given for their lukewarm attitude is that 'the Trade Boards Bill did not affect the great majority of trade unions; it was a measure mainly of value to the women trade unionists who certainly ought to have this protection, the men felt, but the men themselves at this time were more interested in other matters'.[30] They generally were.

But the main claim is that it was the cotton unions which provided the initiative for, and some element of working-class leadership in, the Suffragette movement. As it stands it is a claim which hinges on Annie Kenney's association with the Oldham Card and Blowing Room Operatives, and the link which she provided between it and the Pankhursts. Thus it is the nature of her association with both groups, and the role of the cotton unions which must be clarified.

A brief narrative of events is as follows. Firstly, there was the growth of cotton unions recruiting women and participating in demands for universal suffrage via the Charter and other nineteenth-century reform movements, but no evidence of any greater readiness, on the part of these unions, to demand the suffrage for women than was shown by other predominantly working-class organizations. In fact the leadership of these unions was all male. Secondly and separately, there was the agitation for the suffrage intensified by the activities of Lydia Becker and other middle- and upper-class founders of Women's Suffrage Committees. These were established in London, Manchester, Edinburgh and Bristol, after 1866 and in that order. After 1867 these committees kept up a running fight for women's suffrage with an intensity which varied with their leadership and the adroitness of the Parliamentary opposition to women's suffrage. The Radical barrister, Dr Pankhurst, was close to the centre of this movement in Manchester from its beginnings.

Until the end of the nineteenth century women members of cotton unions played no part as trade unionists in the demand for women's suffrage. The initiative for the effort to bring together the women cotton operatives and the suffrage movement was provided by Esther Roper, secretary of the Lancashire and Cheshire Women's Suffrage Society, and Eva Gore-Booth, daughter of an Irish baronet, who became secretary of the Manchester Women's Trade Council. These two women proselytized and organized the women textile workers of Lancashire for the suffrage movement from the late 1890s. It was their activity and not the initiative of cotton operatives which finally secured the petitions signed by 67,000 textile workers, which were presented to the House of Commons in 1901 and 1902. Thereafter votes were taken in union branches supporting the proposition that women's suffrage should be a trade union question. In 1902 David Shackleton, the newly elected Labour MP for Clitheroe, was reminded of his obligation to support the enfranchisement of those women cotton operatives who paid his salary. 'Then came a period of apathy on the men's part of the women's claims.'[31] In despair the Lancashire and Cheshire Women Textile and Other Workers Representation Committee issued the following manifesto in July 1904, after years of patient work under middle-class women's suffrage leadership.[32]

Fellow Workers—During the last few years the need of political power for the defence of the workers has been felt by every section of the labour world. Among the men the growing sense of the importance of this question has resulted in the formation of the Labour Representation Committee with the object of gaining direct Parliamentary representation for the already enfranchised working men. Meanwhile the position of the unenfranchised working women, who are by their voteless condition shut out from all political influence, is becoming daily more precarious. They cannot hope to hold their own in industrial matters, where their interests may clash with those of their enfranchised fellow-workers or employers.

The one all-absorbing and vital political question for labouring women is to force an entrance into the ranks of responsible citizens, in whose hands lie the solution of the problems which are at present convulsing the industrial world.

In view of the complicated state of modern politics, and the

L

mass of conflicting interests, the conclusion has been forced on those of the textile workers who have been working unceasingly in past years to secure the votes for women, that what is urgently needed is that they should send their own nominee to the House of Commons, pledged to work in season and out of season to secure the enfranchisement of the women workers of the country.

A committee has been formed of women in the trade from various Lancashire and Cheshire towns, whose duties are (1) to select a suitable and zealous candidate, and (2) to collect and be responsible for the spending of £500, which is the amount absolutely necessary for one candidate's election expenses. A balance sheet will be submitted to each town subscribing.

Anyone who wishes to better the position of her fellow-workers, and the thousands of women outside the ranks of the unskilled cotton operatives, who are being overworked and underpaid, should remember that political enfranchisement must precede industrial emancipation, and that the political disabilities of women have done incalculable harm, by cheapening their labour and lowering their position in the industrial world. What Lancashire and Cheshire women think today England will do tomorrow.

Yours fraternally,
Pro the Committee:
Sarah Dickinson
Selina Cooper
Sarah Reddish
Esther Roper
Eva Gore-Booth.

The next general election saw an attempt to run a local mason, Thorley Smith, as a Women's and Independent Labour candidate, but the Wigan and District Trades Council, on a miner's motion, decided to withhold its support. Consequently Smith had to depend for his campaign on the women and the funds of the Women Textile and Other Workers Representation Committee. He lost to the Conservative by 3,573 votes to 2,205.

Annie Kenney and the question

It must be emphasized once again that this election result was the outcome of nearly ten years of organizational work by Esther Roper,

Eva Gore-Booth and others of the committee. Annie Kenney, however, later wrote of 1905, when she was already twenty-seven years
old, 'I had never heard about votes for women. Politics did not
interest me'. Indeed her only interest outside work was in the
Oldham Clarion Vocal Union and reading Blatchford on topics
which carried with them 'the clear, fresh air of the countryside
and the simplicity of nature'. Thus, although she was, like 96,000
other textile operatives, a trade unionist, her eventual interest in
the suffrage movement did not spring from a deep or long involvement in working-class affairs or politics. It came from a chance
invitation to hear Christabel Pankhurst address the Oldham Trades
Council on the suffrage. Subsequently she developed a deep personal
attachment to Christabel,[33] who was to rescue her from the factory
and open up to her a whole new way of life.

Annie Kenney's slow growth to political action, if not to political
maturity, is in itself an example of the problem of the early days
to which Sylvia Pankhurst drew attention in 1908.[34]

> How wonderful it is [she wrote] in these days of vigorous,
> hopeful, enthusiastic work to look back upon that dreary and
> dismal time not yet four years ago ! How difficult it was then
> to arouse women from their apathy upon this question. How
> well-nigh impossible to get them to come down to the House.
> Old Suffragists had lost heart and energy in the long struggle,
> while new Suffragists did not understand Parliamentary
> procedure, and could not be made to see the reason for being
> there.

This was a plaint particularly relevant to working-class women and
their inability to help themselves. Even after Annie Kenney had
herself seen the political light, her first suffrage meeting, organized
for working-class women, was attended by an audience of two.

An indication of the continued flow of influence from suffrage
movement to trade unionism, emphasized above, is that Annie
Kenney, as a result of her work for the suffrage, was asked by a
trade union official at Blackburn to spend two weeks organizing
the girls there into a union. 'This pleased Christabel,' said Annie;
'she saw ready-made audiences to speak to and she advised me to
try and accept the offer'.[35] Annie carried out the task with some
success. But in doing it she came to realize that out of 96,000
women members of trade unions there was not one woman official.

Once more the initiative to change the situation was neither hers nor working-class. 'After a talk with Mrs. Pankhurst and Christabel on this subject', she wrote, 'they asked me to put my name down for election on the local (union) committee in Leeds'.[36] Her election to the committee was followed by correspondence classes through Ruskin College and her first acquaintance with the history of trade unionism. Thus the flow of influence was clearly from the middle-class Pankhursts to the working-class Kenneys, and from the suffrage movement into trade unionism.

The Pankhursts, having already broken with the LRC and on the lookout for mass support for the WSPU as a non-party, classless organization, were seeking ways to stimulate it among women textile workers. Annie Kenney was thus a very useful recruit. She was working-class and vocal but she would do as she was told. Thereafter she was deliberately used as a political mouthpiece by the Pankhursts to inaugurate the militant phase of WSPU activity. This they did in a way which gave the WSPU such an aura of widespread working-class support and working-class initiative as to lead latter-day historians to elevate Annie Kenney's question to Sir Edward Grey into the category of a historical fact signifying working-class involvement, initiative and leadership.

The truth is not so simple.

As Annie Kenney put it, 'Christabel Pankhurst *decided* that she and I would go to the Free Trade Hall meeting'.[37] And, as Christabel put it, 'Annie as the working woman—for this should make the stronger appeal to Liberals—rose first and asked. . .'.[38] What did she ask? According to Christabel the question was: 'Will the Liberal Government give votes to women?'[39] According to Annie it was: 'Will you, if elected, do your best to make women's suffrage a Government question?'[40] But only Annie of the two principals subsequently mentioned anything of the form of the written question, which was never read out at the meeting or referred to by anyone else who could possibly have seen it. She said in 1907, 'I wrote it [the question previously asked orally], signed it and sent it up with a statement that I was representing 96,000 women cotton workers of Lancashire and Yorkshire'.[41] This in spite of the fact that she was there at the behest of the Pankhursts and was afraid that one consequence of her action would be the loss of her position on the District Trade Union Committee.[42]

Sylvia Pankhurst later gave further emphasis to this incident by claiming that the oral question was one asking, 'What the Liberal Government would do for *working* women, and whether it was prepared to make them *politically free*', and that the written form was, 'Will the Liberal Government give votes to *working* women?', signed on behalf of the Women's Social and Political Union, Annie Kenney (Member of the Oldham Committee of the Card and Blowing Room Operatives). To this she added that as one of the 96,000 organized women cotton workers, *'and for their sake*, she earnestly desired that the question should be answered'.[43]

This version of both the oral and written questions, accepted by Phelps Brown and Turner, seems unlikely for a number of reasons. First, the WSPU and the two senior Pankhurst women, although anxious to attract working-class support, did not wish to align themselves exclusively with the working class. They were only interested in the class struggle for as long as it could assist them in the sex war for equality. The WSPU was never interested in universal suffrage.[44] But the form of the question, as expressed by Sylvia, brought class alignment and the class struggle into the forefront of policy. Second, Annie Kenney was at pains to show that the question was carefully phrased beforehand in order to make it impossible to answer without committing Sir Edward Grey to raise it in Cabinet or revealing Liberal chicanery. The question was to mark a shift from the old suffragist one, 'Are you in *favour* of women having the vote?' to the new form, 'Will you *give* us the vote?'[45]

Finally, by 1908 and 1911, when Sylvia made her version of the question public, she was already more committed to a policy of organizing working-class women in the East End of London for wider social ends than in women's suffrage itself.[46] This policy led her to take the initiative in founding, first the East London Federation and then the first British Communist party in 1920.[47] Thus, while her belief that the militant Suffragette movement was geared to the interests of the working class reflected her own intentions, her youthful suggestion that it reflected working-class initiative and leadership from its inception was a distortion of the truth. This she soon realized. Hence her initiative in the East London Federation and the Communist party. Her report of a conversation with Christabel emphasizes the degree of difference between WSPU policy and her own. According to Sylvia, Christabel said, 'You have a democratic constitution for your Federation; we do not agree with that.' Moreover, she urged, a working women's movement was of no value:

working women were the weakest portion of the sex; how could it be otherwise? '. . . Surely it is a mistake to use the weakest for the struggle. We want picked women, the very strongest and most intelligent! You have your own ideas. We do not want that; we want our women to take their instructions and walk in step like an army.'[48]

But at the time, i.e. 1908 to 1911, Sylvia's version of the written question was not without some propaganda value for her own movement. In her later history of the Suffragette movement, however, Sylvia made no reference to the form of the written question and stated that the oral question was, 'Will the Liberal Government give women the vote?'[49]

Thus Annie Kenney first, and then the question, were used by two of the emerging factions within the militant movement to advance their respective causes.

Then there is the claim that Annie Kenney's participation represented working-class leadership. Yet Annie was never a leader and early on ceased to identify herself with the working class. And although she always faithfully and enthusiastically executed whatever task was allotted her by the two senior Pankhurst women, there was little about her that was original, socially Radical or progressive. She showed no signs of the kind of charisma necessary for a popular leader. She had no personal following. In Sylvia's opinion she 'was essentially a follower. . . . Her lack of perspective, her very intellectual limitations, lent her a certain directness of purpose when she became the instrument of a more powerful mind. Her obedience to instructions ignored all difficulties.'[50] She believed, for example, that trade unionism had no further role in the millennial conditions of the 1920s, and that the function of voting women was to ensure that 'we shall keep our place at the first Great Power of the world and the Guardian of the Seven Seas'. She was more an example of the sycophantic, conservatively deferential section of the English working class who adored 'genuine county people'[51] than representative of the political aspirations of working-class women. That she was able to mould the Pankhursts' predominantly middle-class organization to serve or even reflect working-class interests is unlikely.

Thus it is important to see this incident and Annie Kenney within the whole chronology of the movement and in relation to other facets of it. What seems to emerge is, on the one hand, a picture of middle-class, upper-class, Radical and women's suffrage influence and leadership gradually extending into some areas of the industrial and political organization of women workers, but capturing the enthusiastic support only of the smallest minority. On the other hand, working-class and other socialistic organizations were unenthusiastic about incorporating the social and political aims of women into their programmes. Something has been mentioned already about the reluctance of trade unions in this respect, but other bodies also dragged their feet. With a few personal and notable exceptions the LRC's commitment to women's suffrage was nominal and by itself was insufficient to pass legislation.[52] It is true that the ILP, responding to the initiative of Keir Hardie, did incorporate the cause into its programme, but Hardie's Bill was lost in 1906. George Lansbury, who resigned to fight a by-election on the suffrage question in the East London constituency of Poplar in 1912, found that his stand on the question of women's suffrage had turned a majority of 863 into a minority of 731.[53] And it was only in 1906, rather late in the day and at 'pistol point', that the executive of the Fabian Society accepted an amendment to include in the Objects of the Society, 'The establishment of equal citizenship between men and women'.[54]

A working-class initiative

Nevertheless, there was one group of women from whom came a genuine working-class initiative in demanding the vote. It came from the Women's Co-operative Guild, which, although assisted from its foundation in 1883 by middle-class patronage, rapidly threw up its own leaders from among the rank and file members.[55] So the guild was the largest body of self-organized working-class women in the country when it obtained 2,200 signatures to a suffrage petition ten years later, and when in 1897 it organized guild conferences on 'why working women need the vote'. The papers on which these conferences were based were all written by guild members, one of whom was a labourer's wife and a well-known guild official who 'never attended a public school except for three or four months as a child' and had had to work to earn her living 'ever since she was able'.[56] In the same year the Annual Congress passed a resolution regretting that facilities were not given for the further progress of the Women's Enfranchisement Bill.

In spite of this early activity by the guild, little more was done until interest was revived by the example of the textile workers under middle-class and suffragist leadership, at the turn of the century. Then, in 1905, the guild initiated a declaration asking for votes for women which was signed by thirty-six societies including: the Northern Counties Weavers Amalgamation, the Yorkshire General Union of Weavers and Textile Workers, the Irish Textile Operatives Association, the Leicester Hosiery Union, and the Bleachers', Dyers' and Finishers' Association, among fourteen trade unions supporting the declaration. Subsequently the president of the guild, one of a deputation, pointed out to the Prime Minister that,[57]

> As married working women we depend, more than any other
> class, perhaps, on good laws. Our everyday home life is touched
> by law at every point. Our houses are both our workshops and
> our homes, so that Housing and Public Health questions are
> specially important to us. Our incomes are affected by taxation
> and by laws relating to Trade Unions, Accidents, Old Age
> Pensions, and all industrial laws that go to secure the health of the
> workers. We, as a body of working women, appeal to you to do
> your best to give us this common right—the right of the Citizen.

Guild members, however, were mostly married women with a status which gave them a special position in regard to the suffragist and WSPU demand for an extension of the suffrage 'on the same terms as men'. This formula would have left the majority of married women without the vote. Hence they expressed a strong preference for womanhood (and therefore adult) suffrage and, on this issue, found themselves more in agreement with socialist and labour opinion than with other suffrage societies and the WSPU. Their spokesmen claimed, therefore, that objection to limited Bills, i.e Bills extending the existing franchise to women, was not an invention of the enemy and that it would have been better 'if the vigorous life of the new movement had at first been poured from all quarters into the wide channel of adult suffrage, there would [then] have been no need for troublesome grubbing to make way for wandering streams'.[58]

The usefulness of working-class women to the WSPU

But Mrs Pankhurst brooked no opposition. With experience of Radical, suffragist, Fabian and ILP attitudes to women's suffrage behind her, and carried along by her own frustration, she had already broken with labour and the constitutional suffragists to establish the WSPU. This was a non-party, classless but centralized authoritarian body carrying out a militant yet, initially, a constitutional policy, which demanded an immediate, limited extension of the suffrage to women.

To make the claim of this minority movement impressive and effective it was necessary not only to use working-class Annie Kenneys but to capture the enthusiasms, if not the permanent support, of a mass of working-class women. This was necessary for two reasons. First, the usual government response to middle- and upper-class demands for women's suffrage was that there was no evidence of a universal demand for it[59] and, therefore, that the suffragist societies did not reflect the wishes either of the electorate or the mass of women. Hence Annie Kenney and then the 96,000 cotton operatives were useful in the same way as Keir Hardie and George Lansbury were useful. She and a scattering of others gave a working-class tinge to the platform[60] where they could be used as levers to prise open the doors of working-class suspicion. For, as Mrs Pankhurst was well aware, this suspicion could be easily roused by opposition and labour warnings that the most needy of working-class women would gain nothing by supporting the WSPU. Second, suffragists, particularly the Pankhursts, during the early years of the WSPU, were discovering that the mass of working-class women provided them with a good cause and a call to action, which the vote by itself was not. Even as a symbol of the sex war the vote appealed to few. And many active suffragists came to the women's suffrage cause from liberal humanitarianism, labour and social work. Initially the leadership of the WSPU made great play with this fact and with the importance of the vote as a way to solve a wide range of social problems.

The WSPU deliberately set out, through subsidy and organization, to connect votes for women with social reform and the working class. One measure of their initial success in achieving this object is shown in this extract from the *Daily News* in June 1908.[61]

The demonstration of Saturday week was both dignified and impressive. It proclaimed the determination of thousands of educated women, doctors, teachers, artists and nurses to assert their claim to citizenship. Yesterday's demonstration [by the

WSPU], to our thinking, was even more impressive, and
certainly not less dignified. The graduates and doctors and teachers
were conspicuous among the leaders, but they had behind them an
immense mass of working women, who understand from their
own experience how enormous a part legislation may play in
their daily lives.

As *The Times* said, 'If the demonstrations (attended by 250,000)
proved nothing else, it would prove incontestably that the suffragists
have acquired great skill in the art of popular agitation.'[62]

The ability of the WSPU to revive the flagging energies of the
suffrage agitation, by establishing working-class women as cause
and support, depended on the convergence of a number of related
influences. First, there was the growing awareness that a hundred
years of economic development and rising average real income still
left a third of the population living at a miserably low level of subsistence. Working-class women were at the bottom of all, and,
apparently, without the support of trade unions and the labour
movement. There was also a reluctant acceptance that arbitrary
charity was no guarantee that even the deserving would get some
easement during periods of high unemployment, rising food prices
and stagnant or declining real wages. The dead weight of poverty
had grown too large even for the Charity Organisation Society.
This fact struck middle- and upper-class women more, perhaps, than
it occurred to their men since charity had been a sphere in which
women had been free, and freely encouraged, to act throughout the
nineteenth century. It was a sphere in which women like Octavia
Hill, Josephine Butler and the workers of the COS had made considerable mark and exerted a real influence which accorded well
with their religious and social concept of their place in humanity
and society. But, just as industrialization denied them their role
as 'perfect wife' and set those who were unable to become 'perfect
ladies', as well as those who rejected the gentlewoman's oppressive
liberty, on the road to emancipation, it made their role as perfect
Christian wives and charitable ladies impossible to fulfil.[63] Their
charity achieved little. Furthermore, socialists of all kinds were
offering other more soul-restoring panaceas.

The result was that many charitable and welfare workers entered
the ranks of the suffragists, and then of the Suffragettes, believing
that the possession of the vote would release the women's vision, and

break through the monstrous barrier of poverty. Mrs Pethick Lawrence accounted for her prison sentence in 1909 by saying,[64]

> It is the logical outcome of all that I have thought hitherto, all
> that I have felt and done. . . . By this time the names of both
> [herself and Miss Neal, another social worker] were well-known
> in the London world of social amelioration. . . . Miss Neal and
> I started a cooperative workroom for girls. In our workroom no
> overtime was allowed: a minimum wage of 15s a week was
> secured to all girls over sixteen years of age. These and other
> social experiments succeeded, expanded, and gave rise to new
> developments, and sometimes we felt very satisfied with the result
> of our life of human fellowship and social service.
> But at other times we were appalled by the tide of human
> misery that swept past our door. And when we thought of the
> future of these children and girls who belonged to the family
> circle which we had built up round us, we were often dismayed.
> For in all our work we were continually coming up against a
> blank wall. What could we do against the artificially imposed
> helplessness of women as wage earner, as wife, as mother? How
> could we lift up our girls out of the morass of that moral, physical,
> and economic subjection arising from their condition of political
> and legal subjection?
> We were baffled, too, by our own political helplessness.

On the eve of the great Hyde Park Demonstration in 1908, *Votes for Women* declared,[65]

> It is clear that the governing forces in Society have utterly failed
> to cope successfully with the new conditions produced by the
> rapid concentration of wealth and power. It is doubtful whether
> these conditions are even understood. . . . Women ask for political
> enfranchisement that they may take their part in solving the
> problem of how to secure for humanity the fullest benefits from
> its wonderful resources.

This view was summarized by one of the heroines of the suffrage novel *Suffragette Sally*. 'We can work philanthropically', she said. 'We shall never work effectively till we have the lever of the vote.'[66]

Racial health and the WSPU

To attain its ends the WSPU was concerned to cut across the barriers of class, and hoped to base its movements on a revival of racial excellence. This was to be achieved through women. To be exact, through women and the family. For these were the custodians of racial purity. And, given the restoration of women to their rightful place as the equal of men in the world at large, and if women were respected as the moulders of the young, it was argued, they would weld the nation into a whole.

Like Moseley in the 1930s and the MRA in the 1950s, the leaders of the WSPU believed that solutions to the social problems, which gave them life, meant unifying the nation for the release of a stream of self-denying enthusiasm under an *élite* authoritarian control. 'The question, Votes for Women,' said Mrs Pankhurst, 'besides being a bread and butter question, was more than that—it was a question of women's honour and self respect, a question of virtue and *social purity*.'[67] Mrs Pethick Lawrence declared, 'It means the coming into the world of new and *noble race ideals*; it means the release into the world of a new soul—the soul of women hitherto held in subjection and captivity.'[68] She was echoed by Annie Kenney. 'So I vowed that I would never be afraid. I would work and give myself to the great women's movement until I saw a better country for the mothers of the race.'[69]

By 1912 the tone of *Votes for Women* grew increasingly hysterical as racialism became more than nationalism. It argued that Suffragettes, like Joan of Arc, were chosen by God, that women's suffrage was causally related to low infant mortality and racial health, and that when prostitution and the dual standard of morality were removed, and only then 'the new life of the race will have begun'.[70] But it was left to an Australian to make the most extravagant claim. It was that the all-round superiority of the Australian male was the result of the equality which existed between the sexes in Australia,[71]

> where we have learned from childhood to reverence all that is
> great and noble in the traditions and history of our race, [whereas
> now] we see English girls being sold into slavery more hopeless
> and more cruel than the ancient world ever knew. . . . We see a
> country that puts party before patriotism, a nation that is divided
> against itself, filled with bitterness and hate and not with high

ideas and hope. . . . We see the noblest women in the land treated with dull, unimaginative brutality by 'gentlemen' and hooligans alike. And we Australians, whose destiny is so closely bound up with that of the Motherland, wonder whether the might of England is passing away, whether like Imperial Rome, she has had her day.

Thus, and unfortunately for women and their cause, the WSPU was one of those politically naïve movements (like some earlier Radical, later Fascist, MRA and CND movements) which see the world through a lenseless tube—all attention is concentrated away from complexity and focused on a single point—in this instance, the vote. Instead of leading outwards to programmes of social reform, it led inwards towards nihilism. Perhaps inevitably so.

Furthermore, the WSPU's assumption that the class of women was homogeneous, and the consequent denial of differing class interests; its *élitist* and pseudo-revolutionary organization; its racialist and sexual overtones; its rejection of a platform containing anything more than the vote 'on the same terms as men'; and its subjection of all interests and social objectives to this end, meant that personality predominated and factionalism was rife.

As power in the WSPU became concentrated in 1904, 1907 and 1912, the claims of working-class women were forgotten. The movement, never part of the class war, lost itself in appeals to chastity and destruction. As the following assessment by one of the earliest members of the WSPU argues, the futility of 1913 was the consequence of the premise of 1903.[72]

The artificial method of awakening the spirit of rebellion has not succeeded. It has not strengthened the case for the granting of women's suffrage; it has not deceived the public. A certain numerical advance has been won by the united efforts of all Suffragists during the last eight years, but this dwindles into a disproportionately small result when compared with the effort put forth and by contrast with what might have been achieved had other lines of revolt been adopted. . . . The present attitude of the organised Suffragists of Great Britain, that of cautious concentration upon the voting disability alone, apart entirely from every other legal and social injustice, commits women to years of barren effort, in which neither the vote nor any other feminist advance can be won. This is not wisdom; it is a spurious imitation of wisdom. It has been thought that the right of women to use the parliamentary vote would be the sooner won if the feminist demand for sex equality were whittled down to a fictitious simplicity. But such action has cut off the suffrage movement and the Suffragist workers from their armoury and their inspiration. . . . Revolt upon artificial lines has left things as they were. The movement is still separated from the real life of the women of the nation; it is still a thing apart, detached; it is still, by a policy of short-sighted cowardice, closing up the avenues of its own re-birth, giving its best forces no outlet, maiming itself, restricting the area of its own influence and effort. . . . The worst result of this policy is that the majority of Suffragists have been left crudely ignorant and fearful of the very problems they must finally solve. . . . All these efforts have proved ineffectual because the original falsity of the position is understood (i.e. exclusive concentration on the vote). The movement now has no more interest than a puppet play, pathetic, pitiful, heroic, ridiculous, but a play only.

In this way many Suffragettes, some of whom were founder and important members of the WSPU, saw the end towards which the policies of the WSPU would take them and their movement. They withdrew. Among them Mrs Despard, Teresa Billington Creig, Sylvia Pankhurst and finally the Pethick Lawrences. The cotton unions, with their suffragist leaders, faded from the picture soon after their first painfully shy appearance. Labour hardened in its stand for universal suffrage, a stand which the working-class controlled Women's Co-operative Guild had urged on suffragists before 1911. And working-class women in the East End were organized in the Workers' Socialist Federation, which came to eschew Parliamentary action in favour of a policy which led it, in 1920, to change its name to Communist Party (British Section of the Third International).[73] Thus the militant movement disintegrated.

Conclusion

The discussion suggests that the growth of a class of working-class women did not result in a working-class women's initiative in the movement for the political emancipation of women at any time during the nineteenth and twentieth centuries. It shows, on the other hand, that there was a flow of middle-class women's suffrage influence towards working-class women to assist in the growth of trade unions, and to shape those women's unions, which already existed, into some kind of loose association giving mass support to the suffragists. It argues that the incident involving Annie Kenney and the question to Sir Edward Grey, when seen in its relationship with the earlier and later history of the suffrage movement, does not indicate any greater involvement, leadership or initiative by working-class women. (If anything, it marked the end of a phase of the constitutional suffragist movement after which the stage was dominated by the WSPU, which elevated the sex war and not the class struggle to pride of place.) Rather, it must be seen as the beginning of a more deliberate attempt to exploit the plight and numbers of working-class women to give point and weight to the more active phase of the movement, which was itself the result of middle-class frustration. As such it was a move away from the more patient yet 'democratic' efforts of Eva Gore-Booth and Esther Roper, and a reactionary move away from the interest of working-class women and the Women's Co-operative Guild in adult suffrage.

This militant phase was made possible by the growing realization of the magnitude of social problems, the stagnation of real wages and high unemployment, the failure of philanthropy and the end of women's role in it, the reluctance of trade unions and labour to act on behalf of the unorganized, and the autocracy and organization of the Pankhursts and the Pethick Lawrences. It is argued that in spite of this the real bases of the movement were slight. Its leaders, baulking at the adoption of a thorough-going socialist programme, increasingly concerned themselves with a belief in a nebulous, sex-linked, classless racism. In this process working-class women, as cause and support, were left behind unless they turned themselves into faithful Annie Kenneys. Only Sylvia Pankhurst followed the logic of the movement and set out to organize a working-class movement with a programme of social reform.

All the time the mass of working-class women, more perhaps than the working class as a whole, remained inert, exploited and apolitical. A mass which exerted the influence it did, not mainly because of its deliberate or conscious actions in support of this or that movement, but from the fact of its mere existence, which threw up causes and presented politicians with problems, as well as with the task of going through the motions of resolving them, if they wished to retain power.

Furthermore, before the problems of working-class women became political issues, exploited by the WSPU, the country had experienced 150 years of Radical agitation for universal suffrage; nearly 100 years of piecemeal concessions to the emancipation of women; an equally long period during which the advance of wealth, developments in technology and abundant domestic service had released increasing numbers of middle-class women to sample the affluence of the upper classes, thereby creating conditions in which some strove successfully to make life more meaningful through new forms of women's work; and there had been fifty years of persistent campaigning for an extension of the suffrage to women. Demographic changes, too, had affected the actions and beliefs of both men and women. New socialist and egalitarian philosophies were also at work. Consequently, as Asquith's biographer has recently written, 'There were only two effective obstacles to female enfranchisement before 1914. The first was the excess of militancy: and the second was the person of the Prime Minister.'[74] And both were mortal. Militancy was thus a tactical error probably more explicable by reference to middle-class attitudes to sex than in terms of an emergent class of working-class women.

Notes

INTRODUCTION

1 Recent works similarly concerned with some of the issues raised in
  these essays include: Harold Perkin, *The Origins of Modern English
  Society 1780–1880* (London, 1969); J. F. C. Harrison, *The Early
  Victorians, 1832–1851* (London, 1971); Geoffrey Best, *Mid-Victorian
  Britain, 1851–1875* (London, 1971); István Mészáros (ed.), *Aspects of
  History and Class Consciousness* (London, 1971).
2 John Foster, 'Nineteenth-Century Towns—a Class Dimension', in
  H. J. Dyos (ed.), *The Study of Urban History* (London, 1968).
3 Karl Marx, *Das Kapital* (Berlin, 1953), vol. 3, p. 421.
4 E. G. Wakefield, *England and America* (London, 1833), pp. 94–5.
5 John Stuart Mill, 'A letter to the Earl of Durham on reform in
  Parliament', LWR, xxxii (April 1839), pp. 475–508.
6 Foster, op. cit., p. 340.
7 Ibid., pp. 282, 291.
8 Perkin, op. cit., p. 26.
9 Ibid., p. 176.
10 F. M. L. Thompson, EHR, 2nd series, xxii, no. 3 (1969), p. 589.
11 Ralf Dahrendorf, *Class and Class Conflict in an Industrial Society*
  (London, 1959), p. 172. My italics. Also Ralf Dahrendorf, 'On the
  Origin of Social Inequality', in P. Laslett and W. G. Runciman
  (eds), *Philosophy, Politics and Society* (Oxford, 1967).
12 For a good introduction to the place of conflict in society see
  Anthony de Reuck and Julie Knight (eds), *Conflict in Society* (London,
  1966).
13 Thompson, op. cit.
14 R. S. Neale, 'Roebuck's constitution and the Durham proposals',
  HSANZ, vol. 14, no. 56 (April 1971).

CHAPTER ONE

1 R. S. Neale, 'The standard of living, 1780–1844: a regional and class
  study', EHR, xix (December 1966), pp. 590–606.
2 D. J. Rowe, 'The Peoples' Charter', PP, xxxvi (April 1967), pp. 73–86.
3 Joseph Hamburger, *Intellectuals in Politics: John Stuart Mill and the
  Philosophic Radicals* (New Haven, 1965).
4 Since the first draft of this article was written, Irving Kraus in the

169

SR has made similar observations for the benefit of sociologists (see 'Some perspectives on social stratification and social class', xv (July 1967), pp. 129–40).

5 An imperatively co-ordinated association will be any group of people in which authority is unequally distributed and in which those in dominant positions exercise legitimate authority. The state and industrial enterprises are examples of such associations.

6 Morris Ginsberg, *Sociology* (London, 1953), p. 40; Ralf Dahrendorf, *Class and Class Conflict in an Industrial Society* (Stanford, Cal., 1959), p. 180. Much of the general theoretical underpinning for this article is derived from a simplified version of Dahrendorf's brilliant exposition, particularly pp. 157–205.

7 David Lockwood, 'Sources of variation in working class images of society', SR, xiv (November 1966), pp. 249–67; John H. Goldthorpe and David Lockwood, 'Affluence and British class structure', SR, xi (July 1963), pp. 133–63; see also E. A. Nordlinger, *The Working Class Tories* (London, 1967).

8 One of the most perceptive comments on the subtleties of barriers at the end of the nineteenth century between the upper middle classes, the county families, and the aristocracy on the one hand and an aspiring member of the professional classes on the other is given in Leonard Woolf's autobiography. It places him in my middling class and is worth quoting at length :

I was glad when the tour of introductions ended. The children of Sir Leslie Stephen had, at the turn of the century, when their father died, broken away from the society into which they were born. That society consisted of the upper levels of the professional middle class and county families, interpenetrated to a certain extent by the aristocracy. But, although Vanessa, Virginia, and Adrian had broken away from it and from Kensington and Mayfair to live in Bloomsbury what seemed to their relations and old family friends a Bohemian life, there was no complete rupture; they still from time to time saw socially their Stephen and Duckworth relations and the old family friends. It was a social class and way of life into which hitherto I had only dipped from time to time as an outsider, when, for instance, I stayed as a young man with the Stracheys. I was an outsider to this class, because, although I and my father before me belonged to the professional middle class, we had only recently struggled up into it from the stratum of Jewish shopkeepers. We had no roots in it. The psychology of the different strata of English society is extremely important in its effects upon the individual (or was 50 years ago). The Stephens and the Stracheys, the Ritchies, Thackerays, and Duckworths had an intricate tangle of ancient roots and tendrils stretching far and wide through the upper middle classes, the county families, and the aristocracy. Socially they assumed things unconsciously which I could never assume either unconsciously or consciously. They lived in a peculiar atmosphere of influence, manners, respectability, and it was so natural to them that they were unaware of it as mammals are unaware of the air and fish of the water in which they live. Now that I was going to marry Virginia and went round to see her relations I began to see this stratum of society from the inside. I said in *Sowing* that I know that I am ambivalent to aristocratic societies, disliking and despising them and at the same time envying them their insolent urbanity. In a milder form there was the same ambivalence in my attitude to the society which I found in Dalingridge Place and St. George's Square. I disliked its respectability and assumptions while envying and fearing its assurance and manners. I should, perhaps, add that the class stratum or strata which I have been writing about in this paragraph are now practically extinct; they were almost destroyed by the 1914 war and were finally wiped away in the 1939 war.

(Leonard Woolf, *Beginning Again: an Autobiography of the Years 1911–1918* (London, 1964), pp. 74–5). Gissing was the writer who best expressed the predicament of the less successful members of the middling class after their brief moment of glory during the early nineteenth century.

9 I consider this concept self-explanatory. However, any reader interested in it and in the possibility of its connection with economic growth should start with David C. McClelland, *The Achieving Society* (Princeton, N.J., 1961). In my view McClelland has made out a *prima facie* case for a close causal relationship between high achievement motivation and high rates of economic growth.

10 Evidence for this generalization is in chapter 2 of this book.

11 Very little work has been done on the standard of living or the employment opportunities of the middling class during the early nineteenth century; nevertheless, a number of studies suggest that economic growth faltered and the real income of many social strata declined during the 1830s:

Growth rate of total national product per capita

1801–11—1831–41	1·5% p.a.
1811–21—1841–51	1·4% p.a.
1821–31—1851–61	0·9% p.a.

(Phyllis Deane and W. A. Cole, *British Economic Growth, 1688–1959, Trends and Structure* (Cambridge, 1962), p. 172)

Income per capita		Prices (1800=100)
1831	£25·90	69
1841	£23·99	76

(Phyllis Deane, 'Contemporary estimates of national income in the first half of the nineteenth century', EHR, viii (April 1956), p. 353)

Real wages in Bath (1838=100)

1833	114
1837	93
1839	102

(Neale, 'The standard of living, 1780–1844', appendix B, p. 604)

In giving evidence before Edwin Chadwick in 1834 the Assistant
Overseer of the Parish of St George in Southwark said, 'Indeed the
malady of Pauperism has not only got amongst respectable mechanics,
but we find even persons who may be considered of the middle class,
such as petty masters, small master bricklayers and other such persons,
who have never before been seen making application to parish officers,
now applying.' (*Report from His Majesty's Committee for Inquiring
into the Administration and Practical Operation of the Poor Laws,
Parliamentary Papers, 1834 (44), xxvii, p. 26.*)

12 John Wade (ed.), *The Extraordinary Black Book* . . . (London, 1832),
particularly pp. 452–590; Percy and Grace Ford (eds), *Luke Graves
Hansard, His Diary, 1814–1841: a Case Study in the Reform of
Patronage* (Oxford, 1962). At the level of local and parish politics see
*The Resolutions and Petitions of the Freeholders, Householders and
Inhabitants of the City of Bath 1817,* and *The Report of the Committee
appointed to examine into and control the Receipts and Expenditure
of the Parish of Walcot 1817,* both in the Bath Reference Library.

13 See the *Reports of the Charity Commissioners* printed between 1815
and 1839. There is an instructive account of the changing class origin
of university students in W. M. Mathew, 'The origins and occupations
of Glasgow students, 1740–1839', *PP*, xxxiii (April 1966), pp. 74–94,
particularly p. 80. For a case study of the son of a government official,
see chapter 4 of this book. For an account of the fortunes of the son
of a merchant in the Atlantic trade ruined by the revolt of the
colonies, see 'The letters of William Neate Chapman', with a preface
by Sir F. R. Chapman, holograph collection in the Mitchell Library,
Sydney, Location A1974.

14 See LWR, xxxiv (1840), p. 134.

15 In London, Francis Place. In Birmingham, George Edwards and even
Joseph Parkes—see G. J. Holyoake, *Life of Holyoake: Sixty Years of an
Agitator's Life* (London, 1906), pp. 26–32; Asa Briggs, 'Thomas
Attwood and the economic background of the Birmingham Political
Union', *CHJ*, ix (1948), p. 196; Mrs Grote, *The Personal Life of George
Grote* (London, 1873), p. 79; also the discussion on Parkes in
Hamburger, op. cit. In Leicester, John and William Biggs—see
A. Temple Patterson, *Radical Leicester* (Leicester, 1954), pp. 181–9. In
Bath, Thomas Falconer, George Cox and a score of others—see
R. S. Neale, 'Economic Conditions and Working Class Movements in
the City of Bath, 1800–1850', unpublished MA thesis, University of
Bristol (1963).

16 See note 8, and the bitter correspondence between George Cox, a
successful master hatter and the superintendent of a Baptist Sunday
School, and H. E. Carrington, editor of the *Bath Chronicle*, in the
Bath Journal, 10 June 1833, *Bath Chronicle,* 13 June 1833, and the
Bath and Cheltenham Gazette, 18 June 1833.

17 *England and America* (London, 1833), pp. 94–5.

18 The political question distinguishing the Philosophic Radicals most
clearly from other Radicals was the ballot, and that distinguishing

'ultra' Philosophic Radicals from the rest was their support for the
French Canadians even when the latter became rebels.

19 See Mill to Carlyle, 22 October 1832, to John Nicol, 10 July 1833, to
Gustav D'Eichthal, 29 November 1834, to Aristide Guilbert, 19 March
1835, in *The Earlier Letters, 1812–1848*, ed. F. E. Mineka, vol. 12 of
The Collected Works of John Stuart Mill, ed. J. M. Robson (London,
1963). For the ineffectiveness of Grote as leader right from the start
see Mill to D'Eichthal, 29 November 1834, and to Carlyle, 22
December 1833—'Grote has gradually sunk into a state always too
congenial to him, of thinking that no good is to be done and who
therefore will certainly never do any.' See also Mrs M. G. Fawcett,
Life of Sir William Molesworth (London, 1901), p. 122. Nevertheless,
see H. S. Chapman to H. Chapman, 4 March 1847: 'Roebuck set up
to lead a party—he might have led a small party of Radicals, but—I
doubt if any of the radical party of 1835, when the party was strong
would have acted with him. The Roebuck Pamphlets show his arrogant
assumption of superiority, and it was by the early numbers of it that
he lost some personal friends; Grote, Molesworth, the Romillies.'
(Chapman Holograph Letters, MSS. papers 53, Chapman IIb, Alexander
Turnbull Library, Wellington.)

20 Morse Peckham has recently suggested that most outstanding literary
Victorians were in fact anti-Victorian; see 'Can "Victorian" have a
Useful Meaning?' in VS, x (March 1967), pp. 273–7. In many ways
the Philosophic Radicals were also politically anti-Victorian although
their ideas did much to shape Victorian England.

21 Mill to Albany Fonblanque, 30 January 1838, in *The Earlier Letters;*
J. S. Mill, *Autobiography*, Signet ed. (New York, 1964), pp. 89–93;
H. S. Chapman, letters in the *Western Vindicator* dated 7 February
to 2 March 1835, in Chapman Papers, Scrap Book M.G. 24 B31, Public
Archives of Canada. See also *Pamphlets for the People*, various authors,
June 1835 to February 1836; and Hamburger, op. cit.

22 At one stage they also included Charles Austin, a barrister earning
£40,000 a year.

23 See Mrs Grote, *Life of Grote*; Neale, 'The standard of living,
1780–1844'; 'The Diary of Fanny Chapman', in the RC. In 1832
Charles Buller was returned unopposed for his old constituency of
Liskeard.

24 Mill to D'Eichthal, 7 November 1829 and 9 February 1830, in *The
Earlier Letters*, especially p. 49.

25 C. D. Collet, *History of the Taxes on Knowledge: Their Origin and
Repeal* (London, 1933), p. 25.

26 J. A. Roebuck, *Pamphlets for the People*, no. 22.

27 See chapter 2 of this book; also Conrad Gill, *Manor and Borough to
1865*, vol. 1 in *The History of Birmingham* (London, 1952), pp. 200–13;
and Asa Briggs, 'Thomas Attwood and the economic background of
the Birmingham Political Union', op. cit., pp. 199–200, for a similar
view of Birmingham. The following letter shows something of the

privatized and non-deferential characteristics of highly skilled and scarce artisans:

Thomas Rodda to Guest Lewis and Co.

William & Mary Mine,
Tavistock, Devon, April 23rd,
1837

In answer to your letter that I received from you on the 21st instant, I cannot think of agreeing with you for that wages which you have offered me 28/– per week, and as you have added the Blast pumps to the pit work, which I have no doubt but what the Blast pumps will require a great deal more tendance than the water lifts in the mine. You says you are not in the habit of allowing house rent and coals which i understand that House rent is very high. I should be very happy to engage in your service if the money you have offered would be sufficient to maintain my famely. i see it will not answer to remove them before i see the work. If you will alow me half of my expenses of coming to Dowlais Iron Works, which will be about £3, I will come and see you before I make any agreement, which I have no doubt but what I should agree with you for the work and give you every satisfaction that you require from me.

(*Iron in the Making: Dowlais Iron Company Letters, 1782–1860* (Cardiff, 1960), p. 26.) For an indication of the extent of mobility between the upper and lower social strata in the hosiery industry, see Charlotte Erickson, *British Industrialists: Steel and Hosiery, 1850–1950* (Cambridge, 1959), pp. 94–9.

28 The importance of education in this connection is nowhere more clearly emphasized than in the *Report of the Royal Commission on Hand Loom Weavers* (*Parliamentary Papers*, 1841 (296), 273) and the *Reports of Assistant Commissioners* (*Parliamentary Papers*, 1839 (159), 511 and 1840 (217), xxiv, 1; (220), xxiv, 373). See particularly the report on the West Riding of Yorkshire; also Roebuck's election address for 1832. A twentieth-century version of what the Philosophic Radicals had to say about the social function of education is in H. G. Johnson, 'An economic approach to social questions.' *Economica*, xxxv (February 1968), particularly pp. 17–21.

29 R. Eadon Leader, *Autobiography of Rt. Hon. J. A. Roebuck* (London, 1897), p. 325. Compare Lovett's very similar view in *Life and Struggles of William Lovett* (London, 1967), p. 78.

30 This print is reproduced in Gill, op. cit., p. 210.

31 Karl Marx and Friedrich Engels, *Selected Works in Two Volumes* (London, 1950); see vol. 1, 'The Eighteenth Brumaire of Louis Bonaparte,' pp. 249–50.

32 Published weekly in the *Bath Chronicle*.

33 T. A. Webster, *Encyclopaedia of Domestic Economy* (London, 1844), pp. 330–1. An enlightening discussion on relationships between these orders is in Brougham's review of Isaac Tomkins, *Thoughts upon the*

Aristocracy of England, in the *Edinburgh Review*, cxxiii (April 1835), pp. 64–70.

34 Some historians consider that model-building has no value; see W. A. Speck, 'Social status in late Stuart England', *PP*, xxxiv (July 1966), pp. 127–9. Yet the fact remains, unless our minds are blanks, that each of us *does* have a set of preconceptions which is carried around with, and mixed up in, whatever happens to be our favourite stereotype. For example, those who believe that history can best be treated by having regard to the uniqueness of each person either as an individual capable of a rational free choice or as the psychological product of a unique set of circumstances, are also model-building. In their models every individual is in a stratum or class of his own and relationships between strata and classes are unique to each group of strata or classes concerned. The corollary of such a model is that history is biography and that there can be no history until all biographies are written. One supreme value in model-building is that it serves to make explicit the essence of the conceptual apparatus used, and of the assumptions which are always made.

35 For examples of contemporary uses of this term see Asa Briggs, 'The Language of "Class" in Early Nineteenth Century England', in *Essays in Labour History*, ed. Asa Briggs and John Saville (London, 1960), pp. 40–73.

36 For a discussion of the United Nations and San Gimignano models of social stratification and structure see Lawrence Stone, 'Social mobility in England, 1500–1700', *PP*, xxxiii (April 1966), pp. 16–55.

37 The role of the colonies in drawing off some of the pressure from the petit bourgeois, the professionals and impecunious younger sons is suggested by the five hundred entries in the *Australian Dictionary of Biography*, vol. 1, 1788–1850. See the review of the volume by A. W. Martin in HSANZ, vol. 12 (April 1967), pp. 584–6.

38 See Asa Briggs, 'Thomas Attwood and the economic background of the Birmingham Political Union', op. cit.; Gill, op. cit.; *The Bristol Riots, Their Causes, Progress and Consequences*, by A Citizen (London, 1833), pp. 1–56; the *Bath and Cheltenham Gazette*, 8 November 1831; the *Bath Chronicle*, 17 November 1831; and Neale MA thesis, op. cit., pp. 213–16. There is no evidence of artisan disillusionment with the results of the Reform Bill in Bath.

39 *Bath Elections: a Collection of Newspaper Cuttings, Pamphlets and Posters Relating to the 1832 Election*, collected by Thomas Falconer, in the Bath Reference Library, p. 12. See also *The Times*, 20 September 1832; the *Bath and Cheltenham Gazette*, 10 July and 25 September 1832; the *Examiner*, 29 September 1832; the *Bath Chronicle*, 20, 27 September 1832.

40 See Lovett, op. cit., pp. 91–5, 136, and Eadon Leader, op. cit., p. 15. For the beginning of Roebuck's association with the LWMA in February 1837 see Thomas Falconer to Alderman Crisp, 9 February 1837, holograph letter AL637, Bath Reference Library.

41 Asa Briggs (ed.), *Chartist Studies* (London, 1959), pp. 42–3, 65,

100–3; A. R. Schoyen, *The Chartist Challenge; a Portrait of G. J. Harney* (London, 1958), pp. 14–21; E. P. Thompson, *The Making of the English Working Class* (London, 1963); Neale, MA thesis, op. cit., pp. 275–6.

42 The *Bath Chronicle*, 23 March 1837.

43 See Roebuck's letter to the secretary of the Bath Working Men's Association, quoted in Eadon Leader, op. cit., p. 126; also the *Bath and Cheltenham Gazette*, 17 October 1837. For Napier's view, see his letters to Thomas Bolwell, June to September 1838, quoted in H. A. L. Bruce (ed.), *Life of General Sir William Napier*, 2 vols (London, 1864), vol. 1, pp. 475–522.

44 See Neale MA thesis, op. cit., pp. 307–35.

45 *Democracy or Despotism*, broadsheet advertising meeting called by LWMA in April 1838, and newspaper cuttings in Chapman Papers, Scrapbook M.G. 24, B31.

46 See Lovett, op. cit., pp. 84–91; also E. B. O'Callaghan to Chapman, Falconer and others in the Chapman Papers, Correspondence M.G. 24, B31.

47 Since I first wrote this article, J. R. Vincent in *Pollbooks: How Victorians Voted* (London, 1967), has advanced a theory of political conflict in the early nineteenth century with a starting point similar to my own. What I call a middling class he refers to as an urban 'free peasantry'. But political conflict in his view is derived directly from the opposition between those with large and those with small property. In my model, as in Dahrendorf, whom we both claim to follow, conflict is about authority. Furthermore, in my model social classes as conflict groups are not necessarily homogeneous when looked at as social strata (in Vincent they have to be) and there is explicit recognition that working class A was also a political class in areas where a middling class already existed.

CHAPTER TWO

1 *German Ideology* (London, 1947), p. 28.

2 E. P. Thompson, *The Making of the English Working Class* (London, 1963); Asa Briggs (ed.), *Chartist Studies* (London, 1959), particularly chapters 1 and 9; G. D. H. Cole, *Chartist Portraits* (London, 1965), particularly the introductory study and Asa Briggs's introduction; Neil J. Smelser, *Social Change in the Industrial Revolution* (London, 1959); J. A. and O. Banks, *Feminism and Family Planning in Victorian England* (Liverpool, 1964); Bridget Hill, 'The emancipation of women and the women's movement', *MQ*, January 1965.

3 R. B. Pugh, 'Chartism in Somerset and Wiltshire' in Asa Briggs, op. cit., pp. 174–219.

4 R. Warner, *History of Bath* (Bath, 1801), p. 344; *Bath Guide* (1812), p. 114.

5 G. D. H. Cole and R. Postgate, *The Common People* (London, 1946), p. 32.

6 Ibid., p. 286.
7 G. D. H. Cole, *British Working Class Politics 1832–1914* (London, 1941), pp. 14–15, 256. J. A. Roebuck is not included in the list of Radicals elected in 1832 nor is he listed in the index, whereas W. P. Roberts, accused locally of being a Tory agent, gets an honourable mention on p. 21.
8 A. R. Schoyen, *The Chartist Challenge: a Portrait of G. J. Harney* (London, 1958), pp. 109–60.
9 R. B. Pugh, op. cit., pp. 174–5.
10 However, Pugh also recognizes the importance of discontent among rural populations and in domestic industries.
11 R. S. Neale, 'The standard of living, 1780–1844: a regional and class study', *EHR*, xix (December 1966), pp. 590–606; R. S. Neale, 'Economic Conditions and Working Class Movements in the City of Bath, 1800–1850', unpublished MA thesis, University of Bristol (1963), chapters 3, 4 and 5; *Bath Chamberlain's Accounts*, 1700–1835.
12 R. S. Neale, 'Economic Conditions and Working Class Movements in the City of Bath, 1800–1850', op. cit., pp. 2–4.
13 R. S. Neale, 'The industries of the city of Bath in the first half of the nineteenth century', *Proceedings of the Somersetshire Archaeological and Natural History Society*, cviii (1964), pp. 132–44.
14 Overseer's copy of the list forwarded to the central government filed in St James Parish Records, Bath Reference Library.
15 R. S. Neale, 'An equitable trust in the building industry 1794', *Business History*, July 1965; *Bath Chamberlain's Accounts*, 1700–1835. I hope soon to publish an essay on the economics of building in Bath from 1700 to 1835.
16 *Bath and Cheltenham Gazette*, 18 September 1832.
17 J. A. Roebuck (ed.), *Pamphlets for the People*, no. 7.
18 Ibid., no. 22.
19 R. S. Neale, 'Economic Conditions and Working Class Movements in the City of Bath, 1800–1850', op. cit., chapters 8 and 9.
20 Charles Hibbert, *A View of Bath, Historical, Political, Chronological* (Bath, 1813). In 1813 Allen with the co-operation of the *Bath and Cheltenham Gazette*, a perfumer and a carpenter displayed a petition demanding: (1) representation co-extensive with direct taxation; (2) equal voting districts; (3) annual Parliaments. *Bath and Cheltenham Gazette*, 24 February 1813. Allen was one of the wealthiest property-owners in the city.
21 *Memoirs of Henry Hunt* (London, 1820), vol. 3, pp. 327–420; E. P. Thompson, op. cit., pp. 631–7; *The Resolutions and Petitions of the Freeholders, Householders and Inhabitants of the City of Bath and its Vicinity*, 6 January 1817, Bath Reference Library.
22 *Bath and Cheltenham Gazette*, 18 October 1831.
23 *Bath Elections: a Collection of Newspaper Cuttings, Pamphlets and Posters Relating to the 1832 Election*, collected by Thomas Falconer, in the Bath Reference Library, p. 10.
24 The trades and occupations of the voters are taken from the 1829

Directory. The category 'artisans' includes all men designated carpenter, mason, etc. The category 'tradesmen' includes those designated baker, grocer, etc. Men with the title Esquire or Mister without any calling attached to their names are included in the category 'middle stratum' as are men in the professions, the forces and the Church. These categories are quite arbitrary. Any artisan or tradesman so designated in a directory may well have been a man in a small way of business working on his own account. Moreover, he might have been an employer of labour on a scale sufficient to differentiate him from those who worked for wages. Unfortunately, it is difficult if not impossible to attempt to sub-divide occupation categories according to any measure of the distribution of capital ownership. Nevertheless, it is reasonably certain that any artisan not credited with the title mister had not prospered sufficiently to merit inclusion in the middle stratum. The fact that 46 out of the total of 125 who voted for Roebuck were not recorded in the *Directory* suggests that a good many of his supporters were no more than journeymen artisans or shop assistants. See the discussion in chapter 3.

25 *Bath and Cheltenham Gazette*, 18 October 1831.
26 Ibid., 29 June 1841.
27 *Diary of Fanny Chapman, 1837–1841*, RC.
28 Thomas Falconer to Alderman Crisp, holograph letter, March 1837, AL636, Bath Reference Library. My italics.
29 R. E. Leader (ed.), *Autobiography of the Rt. Hon. J. A. Roebuck* (London, 1897), p. 126; H. A. Bruce, *Life of General Sir William Napier* (London, 1864), vol. 1, p. 475; *Bath and Cheltenham Gazette*, 12 June 1838.
30 *Bath and Cheltenham Gazette*, 19 December 1837.
31 Ibid.
32 *Bath Chronicle*, 21 September 1838.
33 *Western Vindicator*, 6 April 1839; *Bath and Cheltenham Gazette*, 7 and 14 May 1839; *Bath Chronicle*, 21 and 28 February, 1839, 2 May 1839.
34 *Western Vindicator*, 9 March 1839.
35 The forces of order deployed to deal with any revolutionary outbreak included : 200 pensioners, 600 special constables, 130 police armed with cutlasses, six troops of the North Somerset Yeomanry and two troops of Hussars. The Chartist procession mustered about 200 with about 3,000 at the place of assembly where they met under banners displaying the slogan, 'Peace, Law and Order'.
36 *Western Vindicator*, 24 and 31 August 1839.
37 J. A. Roebuck to Alderman Crisp, May 1839, holograph letter, AL629, Bath Reference Library.
38 R. S. Neale, 'Economic Conditions and Working Class Movements in the City of Bath, 1800-1850', op. cit., pp. 299–306.
39 *Bath and Cheltenham Gazette*, 8 June 1841. See also J. A. Roebuck

to Alderman Crisp, May 1839: 'In the meantime every effort
ought to be made to unite parties . . . act as if an election were
pending. . . . Let a good committee be formed—ask all liberal
parties to join it—do not exclude anybody. . . . There is no
reason to doubt of success. Everybody here desires me to succeed
who wishes the new ministry to continue, *working men being
wanted in the Commons.*' Note Roebuck's identification of himself
as a working man (my italics).

40 *Bath and Cheltenham Gazette,* 21 December 1841; *Bath Chronicle,*
23 December 1841.

41 Ibid.

42 Joseph Sturge, a Birmingham Quaker, and Edward Miall, editor of
the Radical *Nonconformist,* initiated a move within the more
democratic section of the Anti-Corn Law League and declared
for manhood suffrage. In April 1842, Chartist and Repealer
representatives met together in the hope of merging the two
movements. John Bright, Lovett, Vincent and O'Brien gave their
support. The delegates reached agreement on the basis of the six
points and decided to call a convention in September. O'Connor
opposed this move. The *Northern Star* castigated the 'New Movers'
as 'pedlaring', 'prostitute' and 'pussy cat' Chartists.

43 R. S. Neale, 'Economic Conditions and Working Class Movements
in the City of Bath, 1800–1850', op. cit., chapters 1, 2 and 5.

44 *Bath Chronicle,* 8 July 1847.

45 Ibid., 22 July 1847.

46 Ibid., 5 August 1847, 16 November 1848 and September to
November 1850.

47 *Pamphlets for the People,* no. 23.

CHAPTER THREE

1 Cambridge, 1967.

2 Ibid., p. 7.

3 Ibid., p. 25.

4 Ibid., p. 6. My italics.

5 Ibid., pp. 24–5. My italics.

6 Ibid., p. 38.

7 P. V. Turner, *One Hundred Years of Charity* (Bath, 1914).

8 Mark Abrams, *The Condition of the British People 1911–1945*
(London, 1945), p. 110.

9 E. J. Hobsbawm and George Rudé, *Captain Swing* (London, 1969),
and my review under the title, 'Where were the gentlemen in green
gigs?', THR, October 1969.

10 For a good discussion of some of the sources and consequences of
conflict see Anthony de Reuck and Julie Knight (eds), *Conflict in
Society* (London, 1966).

11 A. Aspinall, *The Early English Trade Unions* (London, 1949).

12 See notes to previous chapter, p. 177, nn. 12, 13.

13 *Bath Chronicle*, 4 April 1845.
14 See also John Foster, 'Nineteenth-Century Towns—a Class Dimension', in H. J. Dyos (ed.), *The Study of Urban History* (London, 1968).

CHAPTER FOUR

1 P. 175, n. 34.
2 Ernest Scott, 'A history of the Victorian ballot', *VHM*, November 1920 and May 1921.
3 The details of Chapman's private life are taken from letters and papers in the possession of Ann and Wolf Rosenberg of Christchurch, New Zealand. Ann Rosenberg is the great-grand-daughter of H. S. Chapman. It would clutter the pages unnecessarily to give specific references to each fact of Chapman's life. References to this collection are indicated by RC (Rosenberg Collection). All existing accounts of Chapman's life are inaccurate as well as insufficiently detailed to be of any use. For example: Scott, op. cit., claims that Chapman practised at the Canadian Bar; Duffy that he had held office in Canada (Sir Charles Gavan Duffy, *My Life in Two Hemispheres* (London, 1898)); the *Argus*, 29 December 1880, said he went to Canada in 1832 and practised at the Bar; and Mennell's *Dictionary of Australian Biography* described him as a merchant in Canada. None of this is true.
4 Scott, op. cit., p. 53; a similar view is in Geoffrey Serle, *The Golden Age; a History of the Colony of Victoria 1850–1861* (Melbourne, 1963), pp. 209, 255.
5 T. A. Webster, *Encyclopædia of Domestic Economy* (London, 1844), pp. 330–1.
6 H. S. Chapman to Fanny Chapman, September 1842, RC.
7 The only extant copies are as follows: 28 May 1833, 24 March 1834 in Library of Congress, Washington DC; 11 October 1833 in New York State Library, Albany, NY; and 8 May, 28–31 July, 14–15 August, 9, 17, 19, 20, 22, 23, 29, 30 September, 1, 2, 3, 22, 29 October 1834 in McGill University Library, Montreal, Canada.
8 The ninety-two resolutions which constituted the basis of demands for an Elective Legislative Council. Chapman was in agreement with them, see *What is the Result of the Election?* reprinted from the *Daily Advertiser* (Montreal, 1834).
9 Appointed governor in 1830.
10 F. R. Chapman, 'Notes on H. S. Chapman', quoting from the last issue of the *Daily Advertiser*, December 1834, RC.
11 *Daily Advertiser*, 14 August 1834.
12 Ibid., 29 October 1834.
13 H. S. Chapman, *What is the Result of the Election?*, op. cit.
14 Helen Taft Manning, *The Revolt of French Canada, 1800–1835* (London, 1962), pp. 363–5.
15 *Vindicator*, letter dated London, 29 May 1835.
16 Ibid., letter dated London, 5 June 1835.

17 *Montreal Gazette* and *Quebec Gazette* throughout August 1838, and
   Morning Herald, November 1843.
18 Helen Taft Manning, op. cit., p. 368.
19 Letter, E. O'Callaghan to H. S. Chapman, 3 October 1838,
   Chapman Papers, Correspondence, M.G.24.B31, Public Archives of
   Canada.
20 Chapman and Roebuck were both members of a committee which
   presented some three hundred petitions to the House of Commons
   requesting the abolition of the Newspaper Stamp. C. D. Collet,
   History of the Taxes on Knowledge (London, 1933), p. 25. Chapman
   also acted in a sub-editorial capacity under J. S. Mill for the *London
   Review*. J. S. Mill to H. S. Chapman, November 1835 and February
   1836, RC.
21 *Pamphlets for the People*, nos 5, 7, 13, 15, 22, 23.
22 Ibid., no. 22.
23 The system was such that the revising barrister had considerable
   powers, and elections could be won or lost in the preliminary clashes
   over application to be placed on the electoral roll.
24 *Pamphlets for the People*, no. 22.
25 Ibid.
26 The main differences were (1) the Radical Charter contented itself
   with an occupier suffrage and (2) omitted mention of payment of
   members. Instead it asked for a reform of registration and the abolition
   of the Newspaper Stamp. Roebuck, however, was personally committed
   to universal suffrage—*Pamphlets for the People*, no. 7, 'Of what use
   is the House of Lords'. He also helped to draft the Charter.
27 *Lord Beaconsfield's Correspondence with his Sister, 1832–52* (London,
   1886), pp. 67–76; S. Maccoby, *English Radicalism 1832–52* (London,
   1935); *Hansard*, xxxix 81, which shows the vote on Molesworth's
   motion to amend the address defeated 509 : 20; F. E. Mineka (ed.),
   Collected Works of John Stuart Mill (London, 1963), xii, letter 213.
   Also, chapter 2 of this book : 'Class and ideology in a provincial city :
   Bath 1800–50'.
28 See for example, *Collected Works of John Stuart Mill*, op. cit., xiii,
   pp. 396–7, on Lord Durham. Also Charles Buller, MP for Liskeard,
   who in 1838 left for Canada as Durham's chief secretary, became
   secretary of the Board of Control in 1841 and Judge Advocate
   General in 1846. As early as 1836 Buller is reputed to have
   said to Grote, 'I can see what we are coming to; in no very
   long time from this you and I shall be left to tell Molesworth'.
   See article in DNB.
29 The ballot division of 15 February 1838 showed a majority of 315
   noes to 198 ayes. Grote, the great mover of ballot motions, had lost
   popular support. From being top of the poll in 1832 he had fallen to
   fourth place with a Tory only six votes behind in 1837. Article in
   DNB. Chapman's own evaluation of the Whig record, as early as
   1835, was, 'They have betrayed the People; they desire not Reform;
   their sole object is to hold power against a rival section of the

Aristocracy. . . . The People are not to Blame.' *Pamphlets for the People*, no. 23.

30 Chapman's pamphlet *Will Cheap Bread Produce Low Wages?* sold over a quarter of a million copies and earned him £52 10s. for fifteen hours' work. H. S. Chapman to H. Chapman, 5 September 1846. Also chapter 6 of this book, ' "Middle-class" morality and the systematic colonizers'.

31 E. O'Callaghan to H. S. Chapman and others, December 1837 to November 1838, Chapman Papers, Correspondence M.G.24.B31, Public Archives of Canada; Sir F. R. Chapman, manuscript on H. S. Chapman, RC.

32 Chapman's annual net income from all sources was : 1835–9, £266; 1840–2, £359.

33 H. S. Chapman to Fanny Chapman, September 1842, RC; S. Revans to H. S. Chapman, 26 May 1841, RC.

34 H. S. Chapman, 'Letter to Lord Stanley on the Administration of Justice in New Zealand', 1842, reprinted in *New Zealand Portfolio* (London, 1843).

35 H. S. Chapman to H. Chapman, 24 March 1844, RC.

36 H. S. Chapman to H. Chapman, 24 August 1844, 17 January 1845, 25 November 1845, 16 December 1846, 3 February 1847, RC.

37 H. S. Chapman to H. Chapman, 4 June 1844, RC; Queen *v.* Symonds in *Annual Blue Book on New Zealand*, 1847; J. S. Marais, *Colonization of New Zealand* (London, 1927), pp. 275–84; Guy Lennard, *Sir William Martin* (Christchurch, 1961), pp. 41–6.

38 This appointment was accepted for Chapman in England by his father and friends. The first Chapman knew about it was via a letter of instruction from Government House in Wellington telling him to proceed to take up his appointment as soon as possible. (The previous colonial secretary had died and the new constitution was in operation.) Chapman, regarding the Colonial Service as one, carried out these instructions. Later he attempted to defend his attitude on the government's policy of transportation by reference to the manner of his appointment which, he said, gave him no choice.

39 H. S. Chapman to H. Chapman, 4 September 1852 : 'If transportation is not very shortly to be discontinued, I hope and believe my letters by the Chatham will have a very considerable effect on the determination of the ministry. If Gladstone is in I am very certain it will, and I think I may say the same of Lord Derby.' (In the event Lord Aberdeen formed a coalition of Whigs and Peelites, and Gladstone became Chancellor of the Exchequer in 1853.)

40 See correspondence between the bishop of Tasmania and others in MSS. papers 53, Chapman 1, Alexander Turnbull Library, Wellington.

41 H. S. Chapman to H. Chapman, 4 September 1852, RC.

42 MSS. papers 53, Chapman 45, Alexander Turnbull Library, Wellington; W. A. Townsley, *The Struggle for Self Government in Tasmania 1842–1856* (Hobart, 1951), pp. 108–21.

43 H. S. Chapman, *Journal*, 13 and 27 December 1852; notes by

F. R. Chapman on discussions with his father, H. S. Chapman; also
H. S. Chapman to Fanny Chapman, 29 January 1855, RC.

44 H. S. Chapman to Kate Chapman, 26 August and 29 November 1853.

45 *State Trials 1855, Queen* v. *Hayes, Queen* v. *Joseph*, Library of
Supreme Court of Victoria; Sir Arthur Dean, *A Multitude of
Counsellors* (Melbourne, 1968), pp. 33–40.

46 'To the electors of South Bourke, Evelyn and Mornington'. Election
address and newspaper cuttings, MSS. papers 53, Chapman 13,
Alexander Turnbull Library, Wellington.

47 H. S. Chapman, 'Remarks on the alienation of lands in New Zealand
and other colonies and on the sufficient price', RC.

48 Scott, op. cit.

49 *Victoria, Votes and Proceedings of the Legislative Council*, 1855–6,
i, pp. 29–31, 64, 70; ii, pp. 575–82.

50 *Argus*, 20 December 1855.

51 Ibid., 14 March 1856. Report of the Third Reading. (My italics.)

52 Ibid., 21 December 1855; also Thomas McCombie, *History of the
Colony of Victoria* (Melbourne, 1858), p. 295.

53 Sir F. R. Chapman, MSS. on the ballot, RC.

54 Vincent Pyke, 'The true history of the Australian ballot', *Otago
Witness*, 5 January 1893. See also letter by Sir F. R. Chapman in
Otago Daily Times, 18 January 1892.

55 Newspaper cutting, 25 February (no year), signed Zepho. In my
possession.

56 H. S. Chapman, *What is the Result of the Election?*, op. cit.; H. S.
Chapman, 'Preliminary reforms', *Pamphlets for the People*, no. 22,
1835; H. S. Chapman to H. Chapman, 4 September 1852; *Journal and
Observations*, 14 February 1853, RC; H. S. Chapman, *Parliamentary
Government; or Responsible Ministries for the Australian Colonies*
(Hobart, 1854).

57 'To the electors of St Kilda and Prahran', electoral address, 11 July
1856.

58 Private communication from R. W. Mason, Senior Finance Officer,
Commonwealth Treasury. 'This legislation was far ahead of anything
in the rest of Australasia and the other British possessions with
responsible government such as Canada, and much more precise and
definite than anything in the United Kingdom.' Chapman revised and
reintroduced the Audit Act of 1857 in 1859.

59 J. S. Mill to H. S. Chapman, 8 July 1858, RC. The full text of this
letter is also in R. S. Neale, 'John Stuart Mill on Australia : a note',
HSANZ, 13, no. 50, April 1968, pp. 239–45.

CHAPTER FIVE

1 A. C. V. Melbourne, *Early Constitutional Development in Australia*
(Brisbane, 1963), p. 6.

2 For full discussion on the right of colonial governors to legislate see

E. Campbell, 'Prerogative Rule in New South Wales 1788-1823', *JRAHS*, l, part 3, 1964, pp. 161-90. See also C. M. H. Clark, *Select Documents in Australian History* (Sydney, 1966), pp. 314-18.

3 A. C. V. Melbourne, op. cit., pp. 104-6. For details of the first executive council in NSW see *HRA*, i, 12, pp. 101-2, 108-10.

4 *HRA*, i, 14, p. 366.

5 H. S. Chapman to Henry Chapman, 25 April 1852, RC. :
When some matter of considerable importance is to be discussed the Executive Council is summoned. It consists of Governor, the commander of the forces, the Chief Police Magistrate, and myself. But such measures are previously fully and carefully discussed by the Governor and myself beforehand and I believe very little discussion ever takes place in the Executive Council. A conversation of the Governor with me on one occasion will show this. . . . he said, 'by the by I want to talk to you about such a subject (one respecting which the Council stood summoned). You will understand that you and I constitute "the Government", the Council will seldom interfere, hence we ought fully to discuss the subject before we go into Council. This will of course reduce the Council to a form.'

6 Bourke faced considerable opposition from certain members of his council, notably Alexander Macleay the colonial secretary and Campbell Riddell the treasurer, and frustrated by the continual and sometimes open attacks on his authority and person Bourke suspended Riddell after he had been elected chairman of the Quarter Sessions in opposition to the governor's wishes. The secretary of state diplomatically ordered Bourke to reinstate Riddell in the council; Bourke reluctantly did so but made it quite clear that he resigned his governorship over the incident. As Riddell's biographer in the ADB writes, '. . . Bourke the great man went while Riddell the little man stayed'. See also, Sir Charles Jeffries, *The Colonial Office* (London, 1956), pp. 106-8.

7 A. C. V. Melbourne, op. cit., p. 281.

8 For members of the NSW Council see T. Richards, *An Epitome of the Official History of New South Wales* (Government Printer, 1883), pp. 712-5. For Victoria, E. Sweetman, *Constitutional Development of Victoria 1851-6* (Melbourne, n.d.), pp. 71-84. For Van Diemen's Land, see 'Minutes of the Executive Council' (EC4) and 'Van Diemen's Land Statistics' (CSO 50). For South Australia, membership of the council compiled from the annual statistical year books (S.A. Archives Department, Accession 54). For Western Australia, L. P. Hawley (comp.), *The Western Australian Parliamentary Handbook* (Government Printer, 12th ed., 1968), pp. 54-5, 83-4.

9 L. P. Hawley, op. cit., p. 83. G. C. Morphett, *Sir James Hurtle Fisher* (Adelaide, 1955) (limited edition), pp. 17-18.

10 Quoted, P. J. Boyce, 'The Role of the Governor in the Crown Colony of Western Australia 1829-1890', MA thesis, University of Western Australia (1961), p. 15.

11 W. Greswell, 'Colonial governors', *National Review*, no. 6, 1885–6, pp. 671–8.
12 A. G. L. Shaw, 'Some early officials of Van Diemen's Land', *THR*, xiv, no. 4, April 1967, pp. 129–41.
13 J. J. Auchmuty, 'The background to the early Australian governors', *HSANZ*, vol. 6, no. 23, November 1954, pp. 301–14.
14 P. J. Boyce, op. cit., pp. 46–69.
15 Including Major Johnston and the two lieutenant governors who administered New South Wales after Governor Bligh had been deposed.
16 For example, W. H. Hamilton, later to become colonial secretary in Van Diemen's Land, first joined the navy in Britain in 1808 where he remained until 1820 when he was placed on half pay. For three years before coming to Australia he was a partner in a mercantile house at Bombay; his occupational category in his country of origin is taken as 'merchant'.
17 The inclusion of ten illegitimate children recorded for three subjects increases the average number of children born from 4·51 to 4·64.
18 For example, of those who went to NSW only Macquarie and Phillip in addition to Bourke had any connection with the land but in neither case was it a principal occupation or a main source of income. Macquarie's father had merely farmed a Hebridean croft and he only acquired his own landed estate in 1802 with the proceeds from a rich marriage and a successful military career in India. It is true that Phillip had spent some years on his Hampshire estates before leaving for Australia, but they were probably bought with money provided by his wife from whom he separated after six years. The fact is that before leaving for Australia, Phillip had spent most of his life at sea. Consequently neither Macquarie nor Phillip is classified as a land-owner. Other commentators who may choose to regard both as suitable for classification as landowners should be able to adjust our calculations accordingly.
19 Lawrence Stone, 'Social mobility in England, 1500–1700', *PP*, xxxiii, April 1966.
20 Sigismund Peller, 'Births and Deaths Among Europe's Ruling Families Since 1500', in D. V. Glass and D. E. C. Eversley (eds), *Population in History* (London, 1965), pp. 87–100.
21 T. H. Hollingsworth, 'A Demographic Study of the British Ducal Families', in D. V. Glass and D. E. C. Eversley, op. cit., pp. 354–78.
22 E. A. Wrigley, 'Family limitation in pre-industrial England', *EHR*, 2nd series, xix, no. 1, April 1966.
23 N. L. Tranter, 'Population and social structure in a Bedfordshire parish : the Cardington listing of inhabitants, 1782', *PS*, xxi, 1967, pp. 261–82.
24 Ibid.
25 Wrigley, op. cit.
26 Hollingsworth, op. cit.
27 *The Registrar General's Statistical Review of England and Wales for the Year 1958* (HMSO, 1960), part 3, table xxiv.

N

28 Mortality among children in ducal families for the cohort born 1780–1829 was 18 per cent for males and 9 per cent for females. The 1834–54 life table shows 26 per cent dying under five. A specific example is Gawler's family; he had twelve children but only five survived childhood.

29 *The Registrar General's Statistical Review of England and Wales for the Year 1958*, op. cit., part 3, table xxiv.

30 Ronald Wraith and Edgar Simpkins, *Corruption in Developing Countries* (London, 1963), pp. 55–177; John Wade (ed.), *The Extraordinary Black Book* (London, 1832).

31 For the concept of 'n' achievement see David C. McClelland, *The Achieving Society* (Princeton, 1961).

CHAPTER SIX

1 The terms 'middle class' and 'middle classes' are written thus to indicate my scepticism about the value of the conventional terminology even though I use it so as not to complicate the discussion unduly.

2 Peter T. Cominos, 'Late-Victorian sexual respectability and the social system', *International Review of Social History*, viii, 1963, pp. 18–48, 216–50; Steven Marcus, *The Other Victorians* (London, 1966).

3 Cominos, op. cit., p. 18.

4 Ibid., p. 28.

5 Ibid., pp. 216, 218, 223.

6 Marcus, op. cit., Corgi ed., p. 150, n. 20.

7 Ibid., pp. 136, 149.

8 Thus an imagery of scarcity was associated with normal sexuality and one of plenty with abnormal sexuality. The body, Marcus says, 'is regarded as a productive system with only a limited amount of material at its disposal. And the model on which the notion of semen is formed is clearly that of money. . . . Furthermore, the economy envisaged in this idea is based on scarcity and has as its aim the accumulation of its own product. And the fantasy of pornography, as we shall have ample opportunity to observe, is this idea's complement, for the world of pornography is a world of plenty'; op. cit., p. 22. Also :

> Semen becomes a metaphor for all the fluids of the body, including that original one by which we were nourished. This is demonstrated most clearly in that image which I take to be the final, or most inclusive form of this particular notion : a man and woman, reversed upon each other, sucking away, 'spending', and swallowing each other's juices. This fantasy may be an immemorial one, but it is also peculiarly apposite to the eighteenth and nineteenth centuries. It imagines nothing less than a perfect, self-enclosed economic and productive system. Intake and output are beautifully balanced; production is plentiful, but nothing

is lost, wasted or spent, since the product is consumed only
to produce more of the raw material by which the system is
sustained. The primitive dream of capitalism is fulfilled in the
primitive dream of the body.

Marcus, op. cit., p. 246.

9 Havelock Ellis, *Studies in the Psychology of Sex* (New York, 1936),
vol. 2, pp. 189–255.
10 William Godwin, *Of Population* (London, 1820), pp. 532–3;
Alexander Walker, *Woman* (London, 1839), p. 96; and
Intermarriage (London, 1841), 2nd ed., p. 77 and whole of part II
(there were three editions of *Woman* and four of *Intermarriage*,
the last in 1897); Carlisle to Place, 8 August 1822, BM Place
Collection, lxviii, 89.
11 J. S. Mill, *The Subjection of Women* (London, 1870), 3rd ed.,
pp. 123–5.
12 Ellis, op. cit., pp. 211-27.
13 Peter Fryer, *The Birth Controllers* (London, 1965), p. 111. See also
F. H. Amphlett Micklewright, 'The rise and decline of English
neo-Malthusianism', PS, xv, July 1961, pp. 32–51.
14 E. A. Wrigley, 'Family limitation in pre-industrial England', EHR,
xix, no. 1, 1966, pp. 82–109; Richard T. Vann, 'History and
demography', *History and Theory*, Beiheft 9, 1969, pp. 71-4.
15 T. H. C. Stevenson, 'The fertility of various social classes in
England and Wales from the middle of the nineteenth century to
1911', *Journal of the Royal Statistical Society*, lxxxiii, 1920,
pp. 401–44.
16 T. L. Nichols, *Human Physiology, the Basis of Sanitary and Social
Science* (London, 1872), p. 300 (my italics).
17 H. J. Habakkuk and P. Deane, 'The take-off in Britain', in W. W.
Rostow (ed.), *The Economics of Take-off into Sustained Growth*
(London, 1963); S. Pollard, 'Investment, consumption and the
Industrial Revolution', EHR, 2nd series, xi, no. 2, December 1958,
pp. 215–26; A. Maddison, *Economic Growth in the West*,
Twentieth Century Fund (New York, 1964), pp. 239-40; London
and Cambridge Economic Service, *The British Economy: Key
Statistics 1900–1964* (London, n.d.), pp. 4, 215–26; P. Deane and
W. A. Cole, *British Economic Growth 1688–1959* (Cambridge, 1962),
pp. 259–77.
18 T. S. Ashton, *The Industrial Revolution, 1760–1830* (Oxford, 1948).
19 Total investment in housing in Bath in 1800 was in the region
of £2 million. Investment in fixed capital in the British cotton
industry in 1795 was also of this order; see Stanley D. Chapman,
'Fixed capital formation in the British cotton industry, 1770–1815',
EHR, xxiii, August 1970, pp. 235-66.
20 See, for example, R. M. Hartwell, 'The causes of the Industrial
Revolution: an essay in methodology', EHR, 2nd series, vol. xviii,
no. 1, 1965; M. W. Flinn, *Origins of the Industrial Revolution*

188 Notes to pp. 128-31

(London, 1966); David S. Landes, *The Unbound Prometheus, Technological Change and Industrial Development in Western Europe from 1750 to the Present* (Cambridge, 1969).

21 E. H. Phelps Brown and S. J. Handfield Jones, 'The climacteric of the 1890s', *Oxford Economic Papers*, iv, 1952, p. 305; D. H. Aldcroft, 'The entrepreneur and the British economy, 1870–1914', *EHR*, xvii, no. 1, August 1964, pp. 113-34; David S. Landes, ibid., especially pp. 231–358; A. L. Levine, *Industrial Retardation in Britain 1880–1914* (London, 1967). For a contemporary view of the problem see L. G. Chiozza Money, *Things That Matter* (London, 1912). The rate of investment did improve at the turn of the nineteenth/twentieth centuries but this was also the gestation period for the writings of Havelock Ellis and Marie Stopes. Finally, see Charles Wilson, 'Economy and Society in late Victorian Britain', *EHR*, 2nd series, xviii, no. 1, August 1965, for a critique of the above view but also for emphasis on late Victorian interest in consumption.

22 Adam Smith, *An Inquiry into the Nature and Causes of the Wealth of Nations*, Everyman ed. (London, 1947), vol. 1, pp. 1–2; T. R. Malthus, *An Essay on the Principle of Population as it Affects the Future Improvement of Society* (London, 1798), pp. 2–3; David Ricardo, *The Principles of Political Economy and Taxation*, Everyman ed. (London, 1955), p. 1 and the Introduction v–xv; J. S. Mill, *Principles of Political Economy with Some of Their Applications to Social Philosophy*, Peoples ed. (London, 1880), p. 1; also J. S. Mill to Gustav D'Eichthal, 8 October 1829, in F. E. Mineka (ed.), *Collected Works of John Stuart Mill* (London, 1963), pp. 36-7.

23 It was not until Adam Smith formulated and published his theory of capital in 1776 that political economy took cognizance of the importance of capital. This poses a difficulty for Cominos's argument which asserts that the norm of gentlemanly continence commenced in 1765, i.e. some eleven years *before* political economy began to recognize the importance of capital. See 'Adam Smith and the Classical Theory of Profit' in R. L. Meek, *Economics, Ideology and Other Essays* (London, 1967), pp. 18–33.

24 R. L. Meek, 'The Decline of Ricardian Economics in England', loc. cit., pp. 51–74; Mark Blaug, *Ricardian Economics* (Yale, 1958), p. 3 : 'By the test of doctrinal assent, almost every economist in the period came under the sway of the Ricardian tradition. In this sense, the theories of Ricardo did exert an overwhelming influence on British economic thought throughout the period from Waterloo to the Franco-Prussian War.'

25 David Ricardo, op. cit., p. 72.

26 Ricardo to Trower in P. Sraffa (ed.), *Works and Correspondence of David Ricardo*, vol. 6, p. 103.

27 James Mill, *Elements of Political Economy*, 3rd ed. (London, 1844), p. 211. See also Meek, op. cit.

28 A. K. Cairncross, 'The Victorians and investment', *Economic History*, iii, 1934–7, p. 280.
29 Quoted in Cairncross, op. cit.
30 Ibid., p. 281, n. 1.
31 Malthus, op. cit., p. 11.
32 Ibid., pp. 64–5. Malthus's work was in high demand in the first quarter of the nineteenth century. There were six editions between 1798 and 1822.
33 See for example: H. H. Dodgson to H.S.C., 30 May 1847; H.S.C. to H.C., 7 November 1843; RC. Letters of D. Cochran and G. Beaven relating to their voyage to New Zealand, M 1293, Alexander Turnbull Library, Wellington; I. T. Tylee, Diary 1848–9, M 1503, Hocken Library, Dunedin, New Zealand; J. L. Bailey, Diary 1850, q MS. 1850P, Alexander Turnbull Library, Wellington.
34 The best examples of the importance of status and achievement as motivations outweighing concern for profit or capital accumulation that I have been able to discover are the two quoted here. The author of the first is one of the leading economists of the 1840s, Professor Babbage, quoting the outstanding engineer of his generation, I. K. Brunel. The second is from W. R. Chambers.

'I would advise you to dissuade your friend from making an engineer of his son, as I always do very strongly everybody', said Brunel, 'However, if people *will* be engineers . . . they had better get into a respectable connection. . . . I should recommend Mr. Mantell to seek something in London rather than in Leeds— particularly if he has any anxiety about the gentlemanly habits of his son.'

'This part of the question', added Babbage, 'is in my opinion of great importance. I have always from the beginning impressed upon my own son the principle that an engineer is not *necessarily* by *profession* a *gentleman* as a soldier or a parson is and that consequently he must be more careful by his conduct to place himself amongst that class.'

Source: Babbage to G. Mantell, 14 December 1843, Mantell Papers 83–4, Alexander Turnbull Library, Wellington.

'Whether influenced by my father's harangues about independence, or by my own natural instincts', he wrote, 'I had formed the resolution to be my own master, and concluded that the sooner I was so the better'. . . . He resolved, therefore, 'to fight my way, inch by inch, entirely on my own account.'

Source: W. R. Chambers, *Memoirs of Robert Chambers with Autobiographical Reminiscences of William Chambers* (Edinburgh and London, 1873), p. 143. See below for H. S. Chapman's view about commerce being disgusting. Richard Faber, *Proper Stations, Class in Victorian Fiction* (London, 1971), has many examples of fictional characters motivated by achievement and status rather than profit. For a discussion of the importance of achievement motivation, see David C. McClelland, *The Achieving Society* (Princeton, 1961) and *Motivating Economic Achievement* (New York, 1969).

35 E. G. Wakefield, *England and America* (London, 1833), p. 103.

36 Ibid., p. 104.

37 Ibid., p. 134. Alexander Walker was also explicit about the connection between celibacy, immorality and civil war; see *Woman*, pp. 98–9. Mill, too, argued that Radicalism was the product of 'low profits and an overcrowded field of employment', LWR, xxxii, April 1837, pp. 475–508.

38 E. G. Wakefield, 'The Art of Colonization' in A *Letter to Sydney*, Everyman ed. (London, 1929), p. 252.

39 *Reports of Royal Commission and Assistant Commissioners on the Conditions of the Handloom Weavers, 1839–1841*, part iii, p. 545.

40 H. S. Chapman to Henry Chapman, 16 December 1846, RC. Chapman did not share all the beliefs of respectable sexual ideology; he permitted his adolescent daughter to swim with her brothers and described in some detail, in a letter to his aunts, the birth of one of his sons.

41 The evidence for this belief is scattered throughout the journals and diaries of numerous unimportant people. I collect together here a sample of those I have used. H.S.C. to Fanny Chapman, September 1842; H. H. Dodgson to H.S.C., 30 May 1847; H.S.C. to H.C., 30 May 1847; H.S.C. to H.C., 7 November 1843; diaries of Fanny Chapman; all in the RC. Letters D. Cochran and G. Beaven relating to their voyage to New Zealand M 1293; J. L. Bailey, Diary 1850, q MS. 1850P; Edward Ashworth, Journals 1841–5, MS. 126/174; P. B. Fox, 'The Unsuccessful Colonist', MS. 1878; all in Alexander Turnbull Library, Wellington. I. T. Tylee, Diary 1848–9, M 1503, Hocken Library, Dunedin.

42 NZJ, 30 October 1841; also LWR, xxxiv, 1840, pp. 132–87.

43 9 July 1842.

44 Ibid., 1 October 1841; also *The Great Metropolis* (London, 1837), vol. 2 (no author).

45 D. Cochran to G. Beaven, 12 February 1853, M 1293, Alexander Turnbull Library. See also NZJ, 9 July 1842; Elizabeth Gaskell, *Mary Barton* and *Wives and Daughters*, for the same kind of therapeutic value attributed to colonization.

46 D. Cochran to G. Beaven, 27 February 1853.

47 Subjects who prefer long odds are ranked low in 'n' achievement in McClelland, see D. C. McClelland, *Motivating Economic Achievement* (New York, 1969), pp. 15–19.

48 E. G. Wakefield, op. cit., Everyman ed. (London, 1929), pp. 112–13.

49 E. G. Wakefield (ed.), *The Wealth of Nations* (London, 1835), vol. 1, pp. 237–9, 251–2.

50 H. S. Chapman, 'Remarks on the Alienation of Land', RC.

51 H. S. Chapman to Henry Chapman, 19 August 1847, and Sir F. R.

Chapman's MS. on H. S. Chapman in the RC.

52 Charles Buller, speech on systematic colonization, House of Commons, 6 April 1843, reported in NZJ, April 1843, and reprinted as a pamphlet by John Murray, London, 1843, and as an appendix to E. G. Wakefield, A View of the Art of Colonization. All quotations are from the pamphlet version published by John Murray.

53 For evidence of the origin of Buller's argument and of the continuation of it in the work of J. S. Mill, see the following: E. G. Wakefield (ed.), The Wealth of Nations (London, 1835), vol. 1, pp. 239, 251, 252; H. S. Chapman, 'Remarks on the Alienation of Land', in the RC; the Spectator quoted in the NZJ, 25 December 1841; NZJ, 8 January 1842. It was not until the 1865 and 1871 editions of his Principles that J. S. Mill thought colonization no longer an urgent necessity. Even then he wrote that the arguments of the colonizers remained 'true in principle'. See J. S. Mill, Principles of Political Economy in Collected Works, ed. F. E. Mineka, vol. 2, p. 378, vol. 3, p. 967. See also J. S. Mill to H. S. Chapman in Hugh Elliott (ed.), Letters of J. S. Mill, vol. 2, pp. 237-8. For a recent discussion on the place of Wakefield in political economy see: E. R. Kittrell, 'The development of the theory of colonization', SEJ, xl, no. 3, January 1965; Donald Winch, 'The classical debate on colonization comment', and E. R. Kittrell, 'Reply', SEJ, xxxii, no. 3, January 1966.

CHAPTER SEVEN

1 R. M. Hartwell, 'The rising standard of living in England 1800-1850', EHR, April 1961, p. 416.

2 E. H. Phelps Brown, The Growth of British Industrial Relations (London, 1959), pp. 69-70.

3 H. A. Turner, Trade Union Growth Structure and Policy (London, 1962), p. 185. The formulation of the rest of the paragraph suggests that the campaign by the cotton unions was initiated after the induction of Annie Kenney into the suffrage movement.

4 See Elie Halévy, A History of the British People in 1905-1915 (London, 1949-52), pp. 478-9, for a non-Marxist view of how Marxists 'explained' the feminist movement, and W. W. Rostow, The Stage of Economic Growth (Cambridge, 1960), pp. 145-9, for a statement about the nature of Marxist determinism. See, however, the same reference, pp. 39, 163, and the same writer's The Economics of Take-off into Sustained Growth (London, 1963), p. 313, and British Economy of the Nineteenth Century (Oxford, 1948), p. 109, for indication of belief in economic determinism.

5 H. G. Wells, The New Machiavelli (London, 1911), book 3, chapter iv.

6 See for example Brougham Villiers (ed.), The Case for Women's Suffrage (London, 1907); Ethel Snowden, The Feminist Movement (London, 1913); Mrs St Clair Stobart, 'Sex and suffrage' in Fortnightly Review, January-June 1907; Christabel Pankhurst, Unshackled

(London, 1959); Roger Fulford, Votes for Women (London, 1957).
See also the way the pages of the newspaper Votes for Women
reflect middle- and upper-class aspirations for themselves and for
others. For the Suffragettes' own view of their movement see
E. Sylvia Pankhurst's contributions on the history of the movement.

7　Halévy, op. cit., p. 482.

8　G. D. H. Cole and R. Postgate, The Common People (London, 1946),
p. 477.

9　Bridget Hill, 'The emancipation of women and the women's movement', MQ, January 1956, pp. 41, 44.

10　See J. A. and O. Banks, Feminism and Family Planning in Victorian
England (Liverpool, 1964), chapter 1, for an attempt to clarify some
of the terminology.

11　Bath and Cheltenham Gazette, 2 October 1838.

12　Edward Thompson, The Making of the English Working Class
(London, 1963), pp. 415–17; Roger Fulford, op. cit., pp. 38–9; Bridget
Hill, op. cit., p. 52.

13　William Cobbett, 'Plan of Parliamentary reform, addressed to the
young men of England', Political Register, 30 October 1830; 'The
Resolutions and Petitions of the Inhabitants of the City of Bath',
drawn up by Henry Hunt, 6 January 1817. For Hunt's own evaluation
of this petition see his Memoirs, vol. 3, pp. 327–420, also chapter 2
of this book. Hunt appears to have shifted his position by 1832 when
he presented a petition calling for an extension of the franchise to
unmarried women. Fulford, op. cit., pp. 33–5.

14　John Stuart Mill, Autobiography (New York, 1964), pp. 88–9; Elie
Halévy, The Growth of Philosophic Radicalism (London, 1952), pp.
422–3; G. M. Young, Victorian England—Portrait of an Age (London,
1953), p. 9; J. A. Roebuck in Pamphlets for the People, no. 22, argued
for 'An extension of the suffrage to all occupants'.

15　Edward Thompson, op. cit., p. 417.

16　George Holyoake writing in the Free Press in 1847, quoted in his
autobiography, Life of Holyoake, Sixty Years of an Agitator's Life
(London, 1892), pp. 222–3.

17　See for example the 'Jackson' or Clitheroe case of March 1891
discussed by E. Sylvia Pankhurst in VFW, 10 September 1908,
November 1907; also 'The wage of the married woman' and a letter
signed 'social worker' on the position of the deserted wife in applying
for poor relief, VFW, January 1908.

18　Annie Kenney, 'To the women of Germany' in VFW, October 1907.

19　E. Sylvia Pankhurst, 'History of the Suffrage Movement', Votes for
Women 1907 to 1908; Christabel Pankhurst, op. cit., pp. 15–39;
Brougham Villiers (ed.), op. cit., pp. 22–41; Roger Fulford, op. cit.,
pp. 19–118.

20　Charles Booth, Labour and Life of the People of London (London,
1891), vol. 2, chapter vi. Figures of wages given by Booth confirm
the impression that a wage of 18s. to 20s. per week was outside the
reach of the mass of working women in the 1880s. Booth's level of

subsistence was 21s. per week for a family of five. Also S. Pollard, *History of Labour in Sheffield* (Liverpool, 1959), p. 211, and *Board of Trade Enquiry*, 1906, vol. 2, p. 525.

21 B. Seebohm Rowntree, *Poverty, a Study of Town Life* (London, 1901), pp. 152–5.

22 Oscar Lewis, *The Children of Sanchez* (London, 1962), pp. xi–xxii; *Beyond all Pity, the Diary of Carolina Maria de Jesus* (London, 1964); Margery Spring Rice, *Working Class Wives* (Harmondsworth, 1939).

23 Millie Toole, *Mrs Bessie Braddock, MP* (London, 1957), evokes a vital picture of Mrs Braddock's mother 'Ma Bamber' in Liverpool in the early twentieth century, and Jack London's *The People of the Abyss* (New York, 1903) gives a journalist's semi-anthropological survey of London at about the same time.

24 See for example S. Pollard, *History of Labour in Sheffield*, op. cit., p. 250, and W. H. Warburton, *History of Trade Union Organisation in the Potteries* (London, 1931), p. 199.

25 E. Pethick Lawrence, VFW, 30 July 1908.

26 Charles Booth, op. cit., vol. 1, p. 154.

27 The evidence of hostility and indifference to women by trade unions is extensive. See numerous references in H. A. Clegg, A. Fox and A. F. Thompson, *History of British Trade Unions from 1889* (Oxford, 1964); A. E. Musson, *The Typographical Association* (London, 1954) pp. 101–3, 235, 237, 287; B. C. Roberts, *The Trade Union Congress* (London, 1958), pp. 215–17; Cuthbert, *The Lace Makers' Society* (Nottingham, 1960), pp. 63–4; H. Pelling, *A History of British Trade Unionism* (London, 1963), p. 86; S. Pollard, op. cit., p. 271, n. 5; Barbara Drake, *Women in Trade Unions* (London, 1921), chapter ii.

28 Annie Kenney, op. cit., p. 31; H. A. Turner, op. cit., pp. 293–4; N. Barou, *British Trade Unions* (London, 1947), appendix viii; Barbara Drake, op. cit., appendix, table ii.

29 See the article in the *Dictionary of National Biography*; Barbara Drake, op. cit., chapter ii; Roberts, op. cit., p. 85.

30 Roberts, op. cit., pp. 215–17.

31 Eva Gore-Booth, 'The Women's Suffrage Movement Among Trade Unionists', in Brougham Villiers (ed.), op. cit.

32 Ibid., pp. 50–1.

33 Annie Kenney, op. cit., pp. vi, 24, 27.

34 E. Sylvia Pankhurst, VFW, 15 October 1908.

35 Annie Kenney, op. cit., p. 31. See also a short biography of Nell Kenney who developed in the same way, VFW, 7 May 1907.

36 Annie Kenney, op. cit., pp. 31–2.

37 Ibid., p. 34 (my italics).

38 Christabel Pankhurst, op. cit., p. 50.

39 Ibid. Also E. Sylvia Pankhurst, *The Suffragette* (New York, 1911), p. 26.

40 VFW, October 1907. Mrs Pankhurst's version was different again, see Emmeline Pankhurst, *My Own Story* (London, 1914), pp. 46–7.

41 VFW, October 1907, p. 4. Annie Kenney made no mention of the written question in her *Memories of a Militant* written in 1924.
42 VFW, October 1907, p. 3.
43 VFW, 1 October 1908; also E. Sylvia Pankhurst, *The Suffragette*, op. cit., p. 27; Emmeline Pankhurst, op. cit., p. 47 (my italics).
44 See for example 'What women want', VFW, 2 July 1908; 'Elements of the women suffrage demand', VFW, 26 February 1909; Emmeline Pankhurst, op. cit., p. 59; E. Sylvia Pankhurst, *The Suffrage Movement*, op. cit., p. 517.
45 Annie Kenney, op. cit., p. 34.
46 E. Sylvia Pankhurst, *The Suffrage Movement*, op. cit., pp. 215–18, 265, 517.
47 H. Pelling, *The British Communist Party* (London, 1958), pp. 6–7.
48 E. Sylvia Pankhurst, *The Suffrage Movement*, op. cit., p. 517.
49 Ibid., p. 189.
50 Ibid., p. 186.
51 Annie Kenney, op. cit., pp. 306, 10–11.
52 In 1907 the party dropped female suffrage in favour of universal suffrage.
53 R. Postgate, *The Life of George Lansbury* (London, 1951), pp. 118–33.
54 Margaret Cole, *The Story of Fabian Socialism* (London, 1961), pp. 126–9.
55 Carr-Saunders, Sargant Florence, Robert Peers, *Consumer's Co-operation in Great Britain* (London, 1938), pp. 238–9. J. Bailey, *British Co-operative Movement* (London, 1955), p. 124. However, Miss Llewelyn Davies, of middle-class origin, was general secretary from 1889–1920.
56 Rosalind Nash, 'Co-operation and Citizen', in Brougham Villiers (ed.), op. cit., p. 70. Membership in 1893 was 6,000, see Carr-Saunders *et al.*, op. cit. Neither Roger Fulford nor Christabel Pankhurst mention this working-class organization in their accounts of the suffrage movement.
57 Rosalind Nash, op. cit., p. 72.
58 Ibid., p. 75.
59 See for example the editorial from *The Times* quoted in VFW, 25 June 1908.
60 The 'typical' leading speaker at the Hyde Park Rally in June 1908 was likely to be unmarried, twenty to twenty-three years old, of middle- or upper-class origin, educated beyond the age of thirteen and employed in one of the lower professions like teaching. VFW, 7 May 1908.
61 Quoted in VFW, 25 June 1908.
62 Ibid.
63 For a discussion of the shift from 'perfect wife' to 'perfect lady' see J. A. and O. Banks, op. cit.
64 E. Pethick Lawrence, 'Why I am in prison', in VFW, 12 March 1909.
65 VFW, 11 June 1908.
66 G. Colmore, *Suffragette Sally* (London, 1911), p. 164.

67 VFW, April 1908. (My italics.)
68 Ibid., January 1908.
69 Ibid., October 1907.
70 VFW, 20 September 1913, 13 and 6 September 1912; also Mrs Swinney, *Racial Problems*, no. 7 (The League of Isis); Lady Sybil Smith, *Women and Evolution* (Women's Freedom League).
71 Gertrude Lucie Burke, 'Sons of women voters, to rebel women from a more fortunate sister', VFW, 9 August 1912.
72 Teresa Billington Creig, 'Militant methods: an alternative policy', *Fortnightly Review*, lxxxxiv, July-December 1913, pp. 1096–9.
73 Pelling, op. cit., p. 7.
74 Roy Jenkins, *Asquith* (London, 1964), p. 248.

Index

achievement motivation, 16, 21, 31, 33, 78, 111, 117, 142, 171 n. 9, 189 n. 34
Allen, John, delegate to 1817 Spa Fields meeting, 48, 49
Anti-Corn Law League, 57, 86, 179 n. 42
aristocracy, 15, 19, 30, 42, 53, 64, 80, 112
Ashley, Lord, 58–9; support for, 69–70
association, imperatively co-ordinated, 8, 19, 63, 67, 170 n. 5
Association of Working Men to Procure a Cheap and Honest Press, 17, 37
Australia, 1, 4, 12, 13, 88, 97–120 passim, 164; South, 100–20 passim; Western, 101–20 passim; see also New South Wales; Van Diemen's Land; Victoria
authority, 13; authority structure and authority/subjection relationships, 8–9, 19–24, 26, 32, 34, 63–7, 143

ballot: annual vote on, 85–6, 181 n. 29; Australian, 75; and Canada, 79; and H. S. Chapman, 75–96; in Chapman's Charter, 26, 47, 84; in the Charter, 53; in Hunt's petition, 48–9; key to political progress, 79, 85; and J. S. Mill, 95; in Roebuck's programme, 46, 51–2; symbol of protest against authority, 13; in Victoria, 75, 91–6; see also Charter
Banbury, 57
Bartlett, George, Chartist, 57
Bath, 5, 10, 12, 25, 36, 41–61 passim; Charter introduced, 54; Chartists in, 37; class structure, 41–6 passim, 60; changing class structure, 58–9; Independent Association in, 36, 50; Political Union in, 36; shoemakers, 68–70; voting, 51–3, 69–74; Working Men's Association in, 54
Bentham, Jeremy, 84, 126

Birmingham, 5, 12, 172 n. 15, 173 n. 27; gathering of the unions in, 28; Political Union in, 36–7
Black, J. R. Dr, 26, 34–7
Blackburn, 155
Bolwell, Thomas, Chartist, 55, 57
Boyce, P. J., 102
Bristol, 12, 152; 1812 election in, 48; National Union of Working Women in, 151; 1817 petition from, 49; Political Union in, 36–7; riots, 38
Broadhurst, Henry, trade union leader, 152
Brougham, Lord, 25, 86
Buller, Charles, 25, 87; on colonization, 136–41
Burdett, Sir Francis, 35, 49

Cairncross, A. K., 131
Cambridgeshire, 65, 66
Canada, 12, 33, 35, 40, 54; conflict, 80; Radicals, 26; rebellion, 79–83
capital: accumulation, 127–31; distribution at death, significance of, 65–7; glut, 133, 137–41
Chapman, H. S., 6, 12, 25, 34–6, 47, 54, 60, 75–96, 134–37
Charter, 12, 17, 18, 33–40, 54–61 passim
Chartism, 41–61 passim; and Radicals, 54–61; and women's movements, 146–7
class: classification of classes and categories, 3–6, 15–16, 29–32, 41–2, 62–7, 102, 105; consciousness, 1, 3; deferential, 20; homogeneity, 64–74 passim; intermediate classes, 5; middle, 6, 15, 30–2; middle-class morality, 121–42 passim; middling, 3, 30–40 passim, 78, 79, 82, 96, 97; J. S. Mill and, 6; political definition, 7–8, 19–20; privatized, 20; prole-tarian, 17, 20, 38–40, 70, 75; radical, 17; 'uneasy class', 6, 23, 133; women as, 13, 143, 148–51; working, 15,

30–40 *passim*, 41, 75; *see also* conflict; models
colonization: alternative to continence, 135; and Canada, 80; and middle-class morality, 121–42; and social mobility, 97–120 *passim*; systematic, 12, 86, 133–42 *passim*
Cominos, Peter, 13, 121–4
Communist Party, British, 157, 166
conflict: class conflict, 7; causes, 62–4, 67–9; conflict groups, identification of, 8, 74; definition, 19, 20; intensity, 9, 21; in a patriarchal society, 143; *see also* class; models
contraception, 121, 126; age of marriage and family size, 111–14
Cox, George, Radical, 47
Crisp, James, Radical and Chartist, 43, 47, 48, 54

Dahrendorf, Ralf: concept of quasi-group, 19; conflict model, 1, 7, 63–4; definition of social class, 8, 19
determinism: economic, 122–3, 191 n. 4; monistic explanation, 41; wrongly attributed to Marxists, 145
Devizes, 55
Dilke, Sir Charles, 152
Durham, Lord, 12, 35, 86; ordinance 26, 86; report 12, 26

Edinburgh, 152
education, 22, 52, 77, 91; and social mobility, 114–16; Roebuck's opposition to sectarian, 70; secular, 47
élites, Australian, 4, 12, 97, 101, 110–20; colonial, 11
Ellis, Havelock, 125
embourgeoisement, 34
empire, 12, 60, 141; and position of women, 165
Eureka, 90–1
executive councillors, analysis of, 102–20
executive councils in Australia, 98–105; function, 98–100
Exeter, 5

Falconer, Thomas, Philosophic Radical, 26, 35, 47, 50
field of production, 133–41; *see also* colonization
Foster, John, 7

Godwin, William, 125
governors, in Australia, 97–120; Bligh, 118; Bourke, 100, 101; Brisbane, 101, 118; Darling, 99, 100; Deas-Thomson, 116; Denison, 89, 99; FitzRoy, 88, 99, 118; Gipps, 99,

116; Grey, George, 88, 116; Hotham, 99; La Trobe, 99; Macquarie, 118; Phillip, 98, 118, 185 n. 18; Stephens, 118
Greeves, Dr, 92
Grey, Sir Edward, 145, 146, 147

Hamburger, Joseph, 18
Hetherington, Henry, 34
Hobhouse, W. H., 50
Holyoake, George, Radical, 147
House of Lords, 47, 79, 85
Hume, Joseph, 50
Hunt, Henry, 48–9

ideal types, 4, 141
ideology, 14, 16, 24–5, 34–5, 37, 41–61 *passim*, 74, 76, 82, 94, 146; economic component in, 127–42 *passim*; middle-class, 121–42 *passim*; sexual, 121–7 *passim*, 190 n. 40
industrialization: in Bath, 45–6; in Britain, 22, 40; and capital accumulation, 127–31; and social mobility, 21–4

Kenney, Annie, 13, 144, 146, 148; and Sir Edward Grey, 154–9 *passim*, 161, 167
Kennington, 76
Kerr, W., town clerk, Melbourne, 93

Lancashire and Cheshire Women Textile and Other Workers Representation Committee, Manifesto 1904, 153–4
Lansbury, George, 159
Leicester, 5, 172 n. 15
London, 12, 36–8, 40, 50, 149–52; East End and East London Federation, 157
London Political Union, 36, 50, 54
London Working Men's Association, 17–18, 35–40 *passim*

MacArthur, Mary, 152
Malthus, Rev. T., 128, 131–2, 147; neo-Malthusians, 127, 133, 135
Manchester, 152; Women's Suffrage Committee, 148
Manning, Helen Taft, 82
Marcus, Steven, 13, 121–4
Markov chain analysis, 33
Martin, Chief Justice, New Zealand, 88
Marx, Karl, 5, 8, 28, 124; Marxist socialists, 24; Marxist views on women's movements, 145–6; *see also* class; conflict; ideology; models
Maynooth grant, 70